HEIDEGGER AND THE ESSENCE OF MAN

SUNY Series in
Contemporary Continental Philosophy

Dennis J. Schmidt, Editor

HEIDEGGER AND THE ESSENCE OF MAN

Michel Haar

Translated by
William McNeill

STATE UNIVERSITY OF NEW YORK PRESS

Production by Ruth Fisher
Marketing by Lynne Lekakis

Published by
State University of New York Press, Albany

© 1993   State University of New York

For information, address State University of New York Press,
State University Plaza, Albany, NY 12246

Library of Congress Cataloging-in-Publication Data

Haar, Michel.
    [Heidegger et l'essence de l'homme. English]
    Heidegger and the essence of man / Michel Haar : translated by
William McNeill.
        p.   cm. — (SUNY series in contemporary continental
philosophy)
    Translation of: Heidegger et l'essence de l'homme.
    Includes bibliographical references and index.
    ISBN 0–7914–1555–4 (CH : alk. paper). — ISBN 0–7914–1556–2 (PB :
alk. paper)
    1. Heidegger, Martin, 1889–1976—Contributions in philosophical
theology. 2. Philosophical anthropology—History—20th century.
I. Title. II. Series.
B3279.H49H2313   1993
128'.092—dc20   93–18085
                                                                      CIP

10 9 8 7 6 5 4 3 2

CONTENTS

- 1927: "The origins which are relevant for traditional anthropology...indicate that over and above the attempt to determine the essence of 'man' as an entity, the question of his being has remained forgotten..." (SZ, p. 49)

- 1929: "More original than man is the finitude of *Dasein* in him." (KPM, p. 222)

- 1929–30: "What is man? A transition, a direction, a storm sweeping over our planet, a recurrence or a vexation for the gods? We do not know." (GA 29/30, p. 10)

- 1936–38: "The question of who man is has now opened up like a track running through an unprotected realm, as it were, thus letting the storm of being come over it." (GA 65, p. 300)

- 1944: "Being itself could not be experienced without a more original experience of the essence of man and vice versa." (GA 55, p. 293)

- 1946: "The descent, particularly where man has strayed into subjectivity, is more arduous and more dangerous than the ascent. The descent leads to the poverty of the ek-sistence of *homo humanus*. In ek-sistence the region of *homo animalis*, of metaphysics, is abandoned." (*Letter on Humanism*, in Wm, pp. 348–349)

- 1954: "We are only ourselves, and are only those who we are, in our pointing towards what withdraws. This pointing is our essence. We are, insofar as we show in the direction of what withdraws. As the one who shows in this direction, man *is* the one who shows." (VA, p. 129)

- 1954: "The mortals are human beings." (VA, p. 171)

- 1959: "Man is man as the one who speaks." (US, p. 11)

A NOTE ON THREE CAPITALS:
BEING, HISTORY, EARTH

Being and being

We shall adopt the convention of writing *Being* with a capital when referring to *entities as a whole,* or to the *being of entities,* or to the *beingness of entities*; that is, to Being traditionally conceived as the primary, essential or fundamental entity, such as the Idea, Substance, Subject, or Will. The capital letter therefore refers to these grand metaphysical names of the History of Being in its successive epochs.

We shall write *being* with a small letter to indicate being in the active sense of the unfolding of that which is in the horizon of time. Being must be understood as a *verb* and not as a substantive or abstract concept. Though inseparable from entities, it nonetheless differs from every entity.

In German, the nonsubstantive character of being cannot be written so easily. Here, at last, we find an inferiority of German! Heidegger has written *Seyn* or *Sein* to try to avoid positing being—due to a simple effect of grammar—as subject, hypostatized and separated, in particular from man whose essence is to be open to being through being itself.

There remains an ambiguity as regards the relation between Being in the metaphysical sense and being in the phenomenological sense, at least in certain formulations such as "The History of Being is being itself and this alone" (*Nietzsche II*, p. 489). The possibility of the forgetting of being is what is at play in the difference between Being and being.

History and history

History (*Geschichte*) as the sequence of *epochs* in which being gives itself and suspends itself (*épochè* means "suspension") is to be distinguished from historical inquiry (*Historie*). The adjective *historial* refers to the History of Being.

Earth and earth

As every earth is particular—the earth of a people, the earth of a work of art—this seems to call for a lowercase letter. However, we shall make use of the capital letter to underline the nonfactual, nongeographical, nonplanetary character of the Earth as a *site of rootedness* that, in the face of our epoch and world, is capable of unfolding a nonhistorial possibility. Earth written with a lowercase letter simply designates the earth as planet.

TRANSLATOR'S NOTE

Reference to English translations, where available, has been made in the footnotes, except in the case of *Being and Time* and the translations published by Indiana University Press, all of which include the original German pagination. However, translations have been substantially modified in many cases. Standard translations of key Heideggerian terms have for the most part been retained, with the following exceptions: *vorhanden* will usually be translated as "subsistent" or "present at hand"; *Stimmung* will be rendered as "attunement" or "disposition"; and *das Man* as "the 'One'." The word *Technology*, when capitalized, translates the German *die Technik*, and is used by Heidegger to designate the *essence* of the technologically organized world, rather than specific technological apparatus. This essence is thought as *das Gestell*, which we shall translate as *Enframing*.

The term *man* translates the German *der Mensch* (in French *l'homme*) which, though gendered masculine, is intended in the generic sense of 'human beings,' and is understood as *neutral*. The early Heidegger even stresses that he has not chosen, on purpose, the word *Mensch*, but the neutral term *Dasein* (GA26, p. 171). The present study makes it clear that Heidegger's thinking of 'essence'—always understood in the temporal or dynamic sense of essential unfolding or prevailing—dislocates this traditional concept of man by its claim that the *essence* of man is "nothing human."

The *Centre National des Lettres* (French Ministry of Culture) have pledged financial asssistance for the translation, and we thank them for their welcome support of this project

Finally, the translator owes a special word of thanks to Karen Feldman for her generous help with the proofs.

FOREWORD

Hubert L. Dreyfus

Heidegger and the Essence of Man is a welcome innovation in overviews of Heidegger's work. Up to now we have seen, both in Europe and the United States, a long line of Germanic treatises that have reverently repeated Heidegger's jargon, and numerous French-style essays that have irreverently attempted to deconstruct Heidegger and go beyond him. In this book, however, one finds oneself in a different world. Instead of piety or playfulness we find what Heidegger would call an *Erörterung*—a dedicated and subtle attempt to experience the place from which Heidegger is speaking and to place him in our contemporary world. We find the scrupulous attention to detail characteristic of the Germanic approach combined with the critical distance characteristic of the Latin one, but, above all, a sympathetic questioning that accepts Heidegger's self-understanding on its own terms and then attempts to reveal central tensions running through his work. It is fitting that this combination of what is best in both the German and French approaches should be the achievement of a geographical and linguistic neighbor of Heidegger's—an Alsacian who speaks Heidegger's dialect.

Rather than being overwhelmed by Heidegger's immense achievement or driven to overcome him, Michel Haar accepts the importance of Heidegger's work and then proceeds to problematize it. Of course, it is not enough simply to think up difficulties. If the result is to be illuminating rather than merely clever, one has to locate the right problems. This Haar does by focusing on the tension that Heidegger himself sets up between *Dasein* as a receiver of understandings of being, and man as the *"Da"* where these understandings occur. (I follow here Haar's helpful innovation of writing being with lowercase "b" when it refers to the event which gives epochal understandings of all that is, and with an uppercase "B" when it refers to the metaphysical ground of everything.) Haar asks: If man is defined solely as the place where an understanding of being occurs, and being is no more than its epochal arriving, how can we understand how being could be hidden and forgotten? This is the first of many variations on this basic question. But are all these *aporia* as hard as they are made out to be? It seems to me that simply remembering the phenomenon as it was already revealed in *Being and Time* would provide a structural answer to this first version of the question. As the ubiquitous background of intelligibility our preontological understanding of being is both nearest and farthest away. The same holds for the epochal understandings of being. The fundamental attunement of an age, its *Grundbefindlichkeit,* is so pervasive as to be transparent to that age. It will, as Heidegger tells us when he talks of the pre-Socratic thinkers, be *experienced* but not *thought.* Just because it determines *Dasein* through and through it must be hidden, and once hidden it can be forgotten.

The same sense of the phenomenon would enable Haar to answer the question he asks in Chapter 6, as to whether Sophocles could have thought the Heideggerian notion of the overwhelming power of being. Granted Sophocles did not and could not have *thought* it, being as close to it as he was, it does not follow that the only alternative is "admitting that 'Greek man' is not only what he has been, but also what he is today for *us.*" Haar himself later notes that the governing understanding of being in any epoch must be experienced preconceptually and not thought, and this same claim surely applies to the Greek experience.

The issues Haar raises get harder and deeper, however, as the book proceeds. With his usual ability to find the telling citation in some surprising corner of the vast Heideggerian corpus, Haar cites Heidegger's attempt to "determine the human essence in terms of its relation to being, and *only* in terms of the latter." He elaborates with his characteristic lyric lucidity:

Man "realizes" his essence in opening himself, in effacing himself, in abolishing himself so as to let being appear, speak, act. He is not so much bearer of the ontological difference as borne by it. He is the space into which light irrupts, the medium or instrument of manifestation. He can be only transparency, or an obstacle to transparency, more or less docile towards the light, cleared rather than actively clearing. (p. 61)

Yet again by sticking closely to the phenomena one can perhaps escape the tension which Haar brings out between the claim that being needs man and that the human essence is determined solely in terms of being. The epochal interpretation of what people and things show up as requires social practices, especially language, and a capacity for world-opening style or attunement—a response to entities as such and as a whole. As Heidegger put it: "Truth in each case demands a humanity through which it may be structured, grounded, communicated and thereby preserved." Thus being needs man while at the same time determining his sensibility and practices through and through.

But this argument leads to even harder questions. There must be a being, then, that has the capacity for shared social practices, who responds to the meaning in these practices, and who has the capacity to absorb and pass on a cultural sensibility. What can Heidegger say about these transhistorial capacities? If everything that shows up, including man himself, is already understood from the ground up in terms of the understanding of being of a particular historical epoch, how can Heidegger make room for what is thus transhistorial?

Before proceeding, it will be helpful to summarize a set of distinctions Haar employs but does not fully develop. We can first distinguish (1) the *historial* essence of man that changes from epoch to epoch in the West, from (2) the *transhistorial essence of Western man* that remains the same through the various epochs in the history of being. Then we can distinguish from both of these (3) the *nonhistorial* essence of *all* human beings, that is, of the mortals. Finally, there is (4) the *extrahistorial*—the capacities that mortals share with other living creatures.

Haar does us the great service of problematizing these distinct dimensions of human being—asking how Heidegger proposes to fit them all together and give each its proper place. The move to the transhistorial focuses on those capacities that are involved in Western man's capacity to receive total understandings of being. Again Haar asks just the right question:

Heidegger reverses the formula *anthropos : zoon logon echon,* which has come to read: "man, the animal who has reason," to give the following:..."being, as emergence and gathering, holding man."...Does not Heidegger thereby suggest that

> there is a true, *transhistorial* essence of man; namely that
> entity endowed with the gift of collecting the gifts of being, or
> that entity to whom the gift is given? (p. 164)

Whatever makes Western man's epochal understanding possible cannot itself be epochal. Heidegger thus owes us an account of the transhistorial structure of *Dasein*.

It is his transhistorial capacity to respond to the call of being, to develop more and more totalized practices, which has been the undoing of Western man. Since the history of being culminates in the total ordering in which man as orderer is also ordered, the question arises how there can be anything outside the system that can hold open the possibility of a new understanding of being, or, since ours, according to Heidegger, is the last total understanding, some form of meaningful existence that can resist technology. As usual for Haar, the problems proliferate:

> *Where,* in what world might this human being exist? How
> would he relate to the one world governed by con-sumption?
> Would he be a "marginal figure" like the Nietzschean Over-
> man? Would he be outside of History? (p. 148)

He concludes that the saving power must reside in some nonhistorial, cross-cultural capacity of human beings.

> The simplicity of the mortal, inhabiting the earth with others,
> exposed to the heavens, belongs neither to the dawn nor to the
> dusk; it is of all time, ageless; it is at once archaic and of an
> extreme, immemorial youth. (Ibid.)

This leads to further telling questions:

> Yet is it conceivable that man understood as "the mortal", not
> linked to any historial or historical tradition, could appear
> *only* in the epoch of Technology and "simultaneously" with it?
> Must he not necessarily have existed *before* the History that
> emerged from the Greek commencement, in particular in other
> civilizations beyond the limits of that History, and perhaps, in
> an underlying or marginal manner, even *within* that History?
> (p. 174)

Thus Haar arrives at the other great theme of the later Heidegger; alongside the history of being we have the account of things thinging, a form of gathering that must have taken place before Homer and is still going on in Bali and perhaps in the Black Forest. This is the archaic and the yet young. But, Haar asks, how is it possible in *our* world, a world which Heidegger clearly sees will never abandon the amenities offered by technology? How can we say yes and no to technology simultaneously? He finds Heidegger's answer in the phenomenon of dwelling.

> Dwelling instantiates an essential mode of the non-historial...to the extent that despite the whole variety of cultural forms of dwelling, something immemorial persists: the *shelter*. Sheltering oneself cannot be reduced to protection against bad weather, but establishes an intimacy around a "hearth."...The term expresses well the necessity for every human being to establish a place of peace, of rest, warmth and stillness, a center or *focal* point of familiarity from which he or she can go from an inside to an outside, from a private to a public realm. (p.178)

Such focal practices coexist with and resist the totalizing tendency of technology.

> Heidegger here invokes an immemorial whole that does not concern any precise epoch. This immemorial whole can or must be inserted—though this seems quite difficult nowadays!—into a historial world conceived as the entirety of options open to a particular culture together with its language, its institutions, its Technology, its ethical rules, its sacred and profane; yet it can never be identified with, or coincide with, any epoch or with any particular History. (Ibid.)

Staying close to the phenomenon Heidegger is pointing out, Haar contributes his own suggestive example.

> Both local enrootedness and noninstrumental relationality belong to the nonhistorial dimension. A train or airplane pertains to the historial world, but when, sitting in a train or on a plane, I serve myself or a friend a drink, the microcosm opened up by this gesture in part escapes the planetary universe. For trains and airplanes reach into the distance. The proximity belonging to drinking or eating, on the other hand, constitutes a break with the space–time captured by Technology.... (p. 179)

So things can thing not only in the Black Forest, but on the TGV. Haar presumably would not be shocked, as many romantic readers would surely be, by Heidegger's including the autobahn bridge among his examples of things that can "each in their own way" gather the fourfold.

> The highway bridge is tied into the network of long-distance traffic, paced as calculated for maximum yield. Always and ever differently the bridge escorts the lingering and hastening ways of men to and fro....The bridge *gathers*, as a passage that crosses, before the divinities—whether we explicitly think of, and visibly *give thanks for,* their presence, as in the figure of the saint of the bridge, or whether that divine presence is obstructed or even pushed wholly aside. (Building Dwelling Thinking" in *Poetry, Language, Thought,* Harper & Row, 1971, pp. 152–153)

The tension between the historial and the *extrahistorial*—a dimension of original passivity essential to human beings—is the deepest tension Haar finds running through Heidegger's work. In bringing into focus the necessary role of the extrahistorial, Haar returns to the concerns of his book, *The Song of the Earth.* Here his approach is avowedly Merleau-Pontyian:

> The human body, as a living body...is incontestably immersed into the nonhistorial, yet opens onto the historial. It is immersed in the nonhistorial because our sensory or motor possibilities are as ancient as life; it opens onto the historial because both our acquired habits in respect of particular actions and our "spontaneous" gestures are fashioned by cultural models. (pp. 179–180)

Indeed, all the factuality of our body is transformed by our culture, and *a fortiori* our epochal understanding of being. There is no sex without gender, and sexuality can, of course, be taken up as a resource to be studied, controlled, and enhanced. How, then, are nature and culture, our original passivity and the pervasive style in our social practices, to be distinguished and related?

As *Heidegger and the Essence of Man* unfolds, the dimensions of this tension are so subtly and sensitively revealed that one begins to think that there is no hope of finding a resolution. Heidegger seems to have pushed the historial so far as to have run up against its limits. "Can life, the Earth, nature, the body, and the affective moods be reduced to a relation to being?" Haar asks. Then, just when the problem seems overwhelming, Haar gives an original, at first surprising, but finally convincing account of *Ereignis,* as precisely the interlacing of these two fundamental aspects of human being. Heidegger's notion of *Ereignis*—of what comes into its own by belonging together—is filled out with the phenomenon that the later Merleau-Ponty calls the intertwining. "There is no pure nature, yet nor is there any pure History. There is only the world as enrooted and founded upon an Earth" (p. 180). Nature and meaning cannot be separated but they are mutually dependent aspects of the human being as that entity where being comes to be.

> The nonhistorial cannot be understood as a "state of nature" or a site of rest and withdrawal, sheltered from the convulsions of history. We can gain access to it only through History, just as we can gain access to the Earth only through world. (p. 181)

At first, one is tempted to say that this account cannot be right since it is meant to hold for all human beings, where *Ereignis* seems to have to do with the way total understandings of being define and are defined through the receptivity of *Western* man. But Haar has Heidegger on his side, since for Heidegger *Ereignis* is clearly a nonhistorial notion meant to describe the way meaning and language emerge in *any* culture.

> [*Ereignis*] yields the opening of the clearing in which present beings can persist and from which absent beings can depart while keeping their persistence in the withdrawal. This unknown-familiar something...is the earliest and most ancient at once. (*On the Way to Language,* Harper & Row, 1971, p. 127)

Ereignis is what makes possible human practices everywhere and thereby makes possible the historial, should it come to pass. Whether Heidegger's account of *Ereignis* succeeds in enabling us to understand this most basic essence of man, or whether *Ereignis* is just a new name for that interlacing that poses insurmountable difficulties to thought, Haar's book, whose purpose is to question Heidegger, not to praise or condemn him, fittingly leaves open.

PREFACE

For a long time man was certain of his essence: he was the living being endowed with *logos*, he was *the rational animal*. At the expense of a strange doubling, yet one that had become "obvious" on account of its banality, man's belonging to nature was included in this definition of him. The philosophical tradition endeavored as best it could to resolve the conflicts between body and soul, sensibility and reason, without stopping to question the fact that these opposing principles dwelt together in a single substantive being. Thus Nietzsche's inversion merely confirms this double identity by situating the body on the primary level as "grand reason," and by reducing the soul to a name for a dimension of the body.

Since Descartes, metaphysics has also been increasingly sure of the *central* place of man as *subjectum*, as the firm basis underlying every truth. And if for Kant the question "what is man?" contains the remaining three fundamental questions of philosophy,[1] this is because man alone unites the phenomenal determinations of nature and the noumenal determinations of freedom. Greek metaphysics had already constructed an anthropology, yet it linked the essence of man to the constitution of the being of entities as a whole, in keeping with the Aristotelian formula: *he psuche ta onta pos esti panta*, "in a certain sense, the soul is all entities."[2] "Something that man himself is," Heidegger comments, "and yet which exceeds him and extends beyond him, in each case comes into play for the purposes of determining entities as such as a whole."[3] *Psuche* in Plato and Aristotle, like the *logos* of Heraclitus, belongs to the "phusical" essence that moves all things. The modern meta-

---

1. *Critique of Pure Reason*, A805/B833; also Heidegger, KPM, pp. 200–201.
2. *De anima*, 431 b21; cited by Heidegger in GA 65, p. 313.
3. Ibid.

physics of subjectivity, on the other hand, presents a structure that is either anthropocentric or anthropomorphic. Either man himself is at the center, establishing by virtue of his judgment the norms of the true, the good, and the beautiful, and comparing everything before the tribunal of his representation for the purpose of examining and founding the legitimacy of his presentation. Or else the essence of the human subject, the will—via the threefold deployment of the will to knowledge, to love, and to power—becomes the most intimate essence of things, the being of entities.

However another tradition, resting on the account in Genesis, teaches that man was created in the image of God. He has not only a nature, but an essential relation to something supernatural, namely "transcendence" in the theological sense. "God said: Let us make man in our image [eikona] and likeness [homoiosin]."[4] Man carries in his essence, like the hallmark of the worker on his work, the image or corresponding analogy (homoiosis) of the All Powerful and Invisible. Christian theology adds "the idea of transcendence, according to which man is more than a being endowed with understanding,"[5] to reasonable animality, which it takes over from the Greek tradition without putting it in question, for man as ens creatum is a natural, substantial being. Secure in the certitude of revelation, theology produces a new conflictual scission within the human essence: between the side of nature and grace, body and spirit that are both held captive by the "worldly," and the side of the soul called to the "supernatural life."

Distancing itself from this dual tradition as old as the Western world, yet linking itself to it via the method of deconstruction, the analytic of Dasein as "being-in-the-world" initially introduces the extraordinarily novel and rich possibility of a unitary essence of man rid of his former conflicts. A new duality, that of the authentic and the inauthentic, of what is one's own and not one's own, of our own selves and the 'One,' indeed appears. But it precludes mixing the human essence with natural being. The question of man's belonging to nature is not suppressed either: it becomes transformed into that of "facticity." Thus the phenomenology of Dasein encounters the body only marginally, as a limit of the "world," or partially, as the hand capable of manipulating tools that are "ready to hand" (zuhanden) or of not intervening, of simply letting entities subsist, literally "at hand" (vorhanden). The human body has been

---

4. Genesis I:26, cited in SZ, p. 48.
5. SZ, p. 49.

extracted from any purely biological, vital, or animal definition, for the analysis shows it to be already inserted and taken up into an attunement, an affective mood or attunement that opens it and transports it outside itself into a situation, that penetrates it with transcendence. As Heidegger would later put it: "the human body is something *essentially other* than an animal organism."[6] In defining man as *zoon logon echon*, metaphysics would have defined him "zoologically," in a naturalistic and reified manner, as *homo animalis*, lacking the truely "ek-sistent" essence of *homo humanus*. It would, moreover, have forgotten the original meaning of *phusis*, namely, the luminous emergence of presence contained in the word *zoon*, as well as the primary meaning of *logos* as a gathering of presence, which would be completely concealed by translating it as *ratio*.

Yet the concept of *Dasein* also introduces the beginnings of a *decentering* of man's position. For the aim of the analytic is not to constitute a new anthropology, but to discern a way that permits the question of being to be posed anew. Since the period of *Being and Time*, the refusal of anthropology, which has become "a sort of dustbin for central philosophical problems,"[7] has been linked to the refusal of an ossified tradition, caught up in successive concealments and incapable of posing the question of the meaning of the being of what constitutes human nature: "life," "conscience," "reason." If Heidegger chose the term *Dasein*, avoiding the terms *man* and *subject,* this was done primarily so as not to reintroduce the presuppositions and prejudices that these terms carry. For *Dasein* is certainly quite other than man as the subject of modern metaphysics. *Dasein* is characterized by a relation to itself that is simultaneously a relation to being. *Dasein* indeed relates to its being as having to be this being. "This entity in its being is concerned with this being."[8] This particular relation that *Dasein* maintains with its being Heidegger calls *existence (Existenz)*. Yet this relation is not self-enclosed. It implies "equiprimordially"[9] an understanding of "world" as a totality of practical, defined possibilities, and an understanding of the being of intraworldly entities. *Dasein* is "in each case mine,"[10] but this "mineness" is simultaneously *Dasein*'s openness to world. For a being-in-the-world, *understanding being* simultaneously means understand-

---

6. Wm, pp. 321–322; tr., BW, p. 204.
7. KPM, p. 206.
8. SZ, p. 12.
9. Ibid., p. 13.
10. Ibid., p. 42.

ing its being in a "world" where it encounters entities that have and entities that do not have its mode of being. Note that this polysemy of being in the case of *Dasein* makes it the "exemplary entity" from which the analytic can orient itself towards the question of "being as such." Thus *Dasein*'s openness to itself is not that of reflection, for its openness always passes through world. At the same time, the traditional self-evidence of a necessary link between thought as representation and interiority is unsettled.

The *Da*, the "there" of *Dasein,* is its openness to being, the *Lichtung*: "it *is* itself the clearing."[11]

Whence the first de-construction of the definition of man as *zoon logon echon*: to take man, in his essence, in the first place as something "living" is to take him as *vorhanden,* as given at hand. It is to take him as an entity present at hand and as an intraworldly "process" (*Vorkommen*), to forget his "existence." In sum, the existential analytic undertakes a double decentering of man, both by relating to the question of being as such—though only in the program it announces—and by giving the world priority over being-mine. Yet will not this priority of world (as that "in which" *Dasein* always already is, as the inevitable horizon of its possible activities) be put into question anew when, in Division Two of *Being and Time,* in search of the condition of the possibility of authenticity, the analysis will encroach on the theme of the ek-static temporality of the self?

For this work as a whole is marked by an ambiguity in respect of the place of the self (is it truly decentered?), its definition (is it a singular, concrete self or a purely transcendental self?) and its function (is it truly the ultimate source as authentic temporality?). If, thanks to its unitary structure, being-in-the-world indeed exceeds the traditional dualisms of man, it nonetheless maintains—though certainly displacing it—the most important propriety of the subject: its relation to itself, which leaves a doubt hanging over its self-constitution and self-positing. The "openness" of *Dasein* remains ambiguous because it is both an openness towards being or world, and an openness towards oneself that is constitutive of the self.

It was undoubtedly to escape such ambiguity that the later Heidegger would be impelled to abandon all the elements of reflexivity that *Dasein* was left with, and even the very word itself, reverting simply to *man.* But who is this man? The obedient bearer of the word and guardian of being. The place of the clearing. The one who says being when addressed by it. And finally, a "mortal"

---

11. Ibid., p.133.

strangely divested of any *ego*, who no longer says "I" and no longer "possesses" any of the classical faculties of the subject. Is not this effort to break with the metaphysics of subjectivity that ends up with the tenuous, minimal, and bloodless figure of the "mortal" both excessive and, as Dominique Janicaud rightly says, "reactive"?[12] How far can the abandonment of interiority, reflection, and the relation to oneself that constitutes a unique, individual component be pushed? Can man be reduced to an openness that is ultimately anonymous, to a purely "ekstatic" dimension?

Before coming to these questions, we shall have to study—by way of a reading of Division Two of *Being and Time*, entitled "Dasein and Temporality"—the problems posed by the fundamental project of self-appropriation, of self-possession, of the absolute mastery of the self that is the project of authenticity. This project encounters at least *three limits* that are not explicitly thematized. These limits manifest themselves in certain tensions: the tension between the necessarily concrete, existen*tiel* character of the projection of the self, and the formal, existen*tial* character of the structures that make it possible; the tension between the movement of self-enabling, of self-temporalization instituting "being-towards-death," and the spontaneity of an originary temporality, more radical than authentic temporality or temporality proper, and which overrides it; and finally, the tension between the transparency of self-enabling and its limit, the opaqueness of facticity, which is acknowledged, yet which, as far as any possible enrootedness is concerned, is turned back into a natural, unfathomable past. Existential formalism distances the existentiel indefinitely; originary time furtively diminishes the reach of the authentic élan; facticity, even when refused, introduces a lack that cannot be possessed into the heart of the projection of self.

The three existentials we shall analyze—"being-towards-death," "the call of conscience" (*Ruf des Gewissens*), and "resoluteness" (*Entschlossenheit*)—appear to be three possibilities of self-possession that reverse themselves into encounters with self-dispossession. Being-towards-death, as the élan of running ahead to one's ownmost, unsurpassable possibility, opens the path to authentic temporality. Yet it will not tolerate being filled, merely providing a self without any existentiel content. The call of conscience, in the mood of anxiety, lets only one voice be heard, which says nothing, communi-

---

12. "L'analytique existentiale et la question de la subjectivité," p. 57, in the collection *Être et Temps de Martin Heidegger* (Sud, 1989).

cates no message, and casts *Dasein* back upon the singular naked-
ness of its existence. *Dasein* therefore merely appropriates itself as
pure form. These first two structures that can never be filled seem to
make the self recoil into something ungraspable. What is one's ownmost proves to be what is most remote, because it is constituted by
the limit of one's potentiality for death that cannot be appropriated.
The analysis of resoluteness in turn demonstrates the inability of
any existentiel content to ensure the "constancy" (*Stetigkeit*) of the
self. The unity and totality of one's own *Dasein* are guaranteed only
by a mode of authentic temporalization that represents the "faithfulness" of the self to itself as a projection of possibilities that have
already been chosen. Yet that "moment" when *Dasein* projects the
repetition of its ownmost possibilities is itself rooted in an "ekstatic
unity" of originary temporality that the projection itself does not
pose, but rather presupposes. Although an initial analysis suggests
that being-towards-death makes authentic temporality possible, the
latter, together with its form of repetition and the entire contents of
its resolution, is in turn made possible by originary temporality,
more profound than all mineness and all will to appropriate. *Dasein*
does not give itself originary temporality, which first makes possible
those possibilities that *Dasein* projects. It discovers itself as delivered over to this pure temporality, traversed by this power of possibility that bursts forth in it and that originarily dominates whoever
is "subject" to it. A dispossession is evident. We are dealing with a
true reversal that prefigures the "Turning" that leads from the phenomenology of *Dasein* to the primacy of being over man.

The primacy of being in fact emerged from a *hypertranscendental* step. At its extreme limit, the transcendental ceases to be
self-enabling. *Dasein* is decentered in relation to the temporal being
of the *Da*, which it neither produces nor absolutely masters. Even
when it is master of its own time, having assumed the authenticity
of its mortal finitude, *Dasein* is not the master of time. That temporality that cannot be appropriated draws the widest circle, encompassing all the structures, and secretly holds whoever believes he
holds it. This aspect of *Being and Time*, the reverse of its voluntarism, is not so explicit, yet it produces a gap that is quite fundamental and that undermines the quest for one's own self, condemns
it to fail at its very end.

If the analytic is conscious of the gap it opens up between the
originary and the authentic, it recognizes more tacitly and even
evades the enigma of *facticity*. Thrown into the world, *Dasein* is
obscurely and inextricably tied to the destiny of the being of natural

entities. This tie is facticity itself. The latter would not be enigmatic, were it not for the fact that it encroaches on the clearing, or if it could be entirely reduced to the transcendence of attunement. Heidegger fails to describe the ambiguous principle that links existence to natural being. He endeavors to extract death and even birth from their intricate involvement in life, and he does so by transforming them into pure extential possibilities. Within the overpure clarity of these existentials, we shall attempt to discern "the impenetrable heart of darkness" which will surely have left its trace.

"Every projection—and consequently all 'creative' activity of man as well—is *thrown*, i.e. determined by *Dasein*'s dependency upon entities which already are as a whole, a dependency which cannot be mastered."[13] *Entities as a whole* here means nature in the sense of *phusis*. Does not *being thrown* mean depending on nature for our very being? Although it is very heavily emphasized here, this "dependency" in respect of nature and life is never made explicit, neither in the work before nor after the Turning of the 1930s. The analysis of the Earth in *The Origin of the Work of Art* (1936) therefore places more emphasis on its power to make things possible in a nonworldly, nonhistorial way[14] than on man's inevitable submission to a dimension of original passivity. The analysis shows that the Earth as "nature" participates in world despite itself; it does not, however, show how man is subjected to it in undergoing its rhythms or cycles. During the period of *Being and Time*, Heidegger was above all concerned to disassociate himself from the then-dominant *Lebensphilosophie*, to distance himself from Bergson and Dilthey, whom he accused of having a substantialist view of "life." "Life is neither pure being at hand [*Vorhandensein*], nor is it *Dasein*."[15]

The determination of life is therefore essentially negative or privative. Intraworldliness is not part of the being of nature. "Intraworldliness merely *falls to* this entity, nature, once it has been *discovered* as an entity."[16] Yet we do not know what the being of this entity in itself is. Why does the being of that which is living simply elude a *direct* phenomenology, and why can it be attained only

---

13. KPM, p. 228.
14. See M. Haar, *Le Chant de la terre* (L'Herne, 1987), pp. 122–133. Trans. R. Lilly, *The Song of the Earth* (Indiana University Press, 1993).
15. SZ, p. 50.
16. GA 24, p. 240.

starting from a "reductive privation" undertaken from the point of
view of being-in-the-world? "The animal is poor in world," the
1929–30 course repeats as a leitmotiv.[17] Why can we not have direct
access to life, given that we are living entities? Or are we in fact not
living entities? What does the affirmation of including man in
nature signify, if all the efforts of the analytic of *Dasein*, whose
hypertranscendental tendency is intensified by the thought of
being, tend to extricate him from nature? We may concede that the
human body is not some extension of vital substance that supports
the mind, and that it cannot be reduced to a simple animal organism, as it does not have the mode of animality of animals narrowly
confined within their environment. Yet can our bodies nevertheless
be considered as "essentially other" than all living organisms?
From the fact that man is not a living entity like the others, can one
maintain that he is not a living entity at all, or that he is one that
escapes those determinations belonging to all other living entities?
Even if belonging to nature does not define man in his essence, it
gives him a certain *minimal essence*, a biological individuality, a
physical appearance, eyes, hair, a certain color of skin, a sexual
specificity, an age. Can these "terrestrial" features, which are evidently nonhistorial, be passed over in silence when describing
Dasein, under the pretext that they are "empirical" and without
any essential or "transcendental" significance? Are not sex or age
conditions of possibility for the existence of any *Dasein*?

Man has a nature, not simply because he has a biological individuality, but because he has needs: the need for air, for light, for
food, for clothes, for sleep....The earth allows us to meet these
needs. To that extent it sustains us. Does being also sustain us? Are
we held in being, or by it? *Does being make us be?* Does it give us
life? It presupposes life, but is unable to give it.

Does the clearing, that free site where we receive the light of
appearance, have the *force* to sustain us? Is it being that makes us
stand upright? Does it make our hearts beat? Is not the Earth as
natural influence, as "phusical" unfolding, the source of the clearing? In his reading of the Greek commencement, Heidegger always
traces *phusis*—conceived as that free, non-ontic surge that flows
back into itself—back to *aletheia*, to unconcealment, to uncovering.
He identifies the tumultuous movement of "natural" emergence
with, and reduces it to, the calm structure of manifestation or

---

17. See GA 29/30.

appearing. He assimilates the reserve of hidden power that *phusis* contains to the simple withdrawal of *aletheia*, to that temporal limitation of presence that always imposes itself so as to restrict its plenitude. He reduces the *physical* dimension to the *phanic* or *phantic* dimension. He forces the possibility of the Earth, which can never be illuminated, to enter the possibility of being, where the light administers to darkness its well-delimited role.

Heidegger's political engagement of 1933 was an aberration that is difficult to comprehend. What could be more aberrant, according to the very premises of Heideggerian thought at whatever stage one takes it, than *a human being* suddenly saluted as *being itself!* Neither the confused situation of the regime in its beginnings, nor even a certain hope that might have been permissible, can be regarded as excuses. Heidegger was by temperament, rather than by ideology, a conservative endowed with imagination, rather than a reactionary. He was not a nazi doctrinaire. He adhered neither to racism, because of his refusal of biologism, nor to the *Führerprinzip*, on account of his elitism and the idea that those who definitively govern an epoch are the poets and thinkers. One of the hidden motives for his engagement may have been a disastrous impatience. Impatience at having to pass via the long detour of de-construction to change man. The illusory temptation to produce a "new man" by an act of state authority. But it was also a nihilist temptation and a fall back into voluntarism: a waywardness he would attribute, in a somewhat cowardly manner perhaps, to the errancy of an entire era, marked by the will to will in "the sinister frenzy of unleashed technology and the rootless organization of normalized man,"[18] where all the "Führer" are consequences of the forgetting of being.[19]

In his large posthumous manuscript of 1936–38, the recently published *Beiträge zur Philosophie*, Heidegger underlines the *dangerous* character of the question "what is man?"[20] This question brings upon itself, he says further on—without indicating the meaning of the natural metaphor he appeals to here—"the storm of being."[21] Is this to say that a few flashes of truth must be paid for by a wind of destruction? No, for de-construction—according to a definition we shall come back to—does not destroy, but rather rebuilds

18. EM, p. 28; tr., p. 37.
19. VA, p. 89.
20. GA 65, p. 54.
21. Ibid., p. 300.

starting from a return to an experience of being that had fallen into forgottenness. If there is a threat of destruction, it is because the passage through the test of being, the abolishing of all foundation and all ontic certainty, is at once our original resource and a confrontation with the abyss. The abyss may be speculative, but it can also be political. The impatience of 1933 was a voluntarist excess, born of an ontic interpretation of *Entschlossenheit,* or "resoluteness."

Man does not "have" an essence like other entities, because he asks himself the question "who am I?" The entire tradition has said as much. What Heidegger tries to show is that this reflexive question hides our access to being. An "other man" would be one whose nonsubjective reflection, instead of turning him back towards himself, would open him to the free dimension of the clearing. This man would have everything, including his thought and including himself, before him like a face-to-face, and not like an object. He would no longer reflect on himself, but would reflect the world. But would he still be man?

"More original than man is the finitude of *Dasein* in him."[22] The final section of *Kant and the Problem of Metaphysics* impatiently repatriates a difference in man that *Being and Time* had understood more prudently as an extrinsic distinction, or an opposition between man of the tradition and being-in-the-world. *Dasein* henceforth appears as the intimate essence of man, whose true being has been reestablished. From 1929 to 1935 the return to man passes through a transitional phase where the two terms *Dasein* and *man* are conjoined in expressions such as "the *Dasein* in man,"[23] "the *Dasein* of historial man,"[24] "*Da-sein*" (with a hyphen) as the "being of man": "we call the being of man *Dasein.*"[25] This overhasty recuperation of the true essence of man participates in the same "naivety" as the contemporaneous project of "fundamental ontology" or of a "metaphysics of *Dasein.*" The word metaphysics signifies, as yet in a nonpejorative sense, all interrogation relating to the being of entities. The project of fundamental ontology in fact aims to "found" metaphysics by a restitution of the forgotten essence of man. The forgetting of being finds itself brought back to

22. KPM, p. 222.
23. Ibid., p. 227.
24. EM, p. 125; tr., p. 163.
25. GA 29/30, p. 95.

a *forgetting of the finitude* of man, where finitude means temporality, understanding of being, affective disposition, thrownness, "falling." It is a matter of showing that traditional metaphysics, in developing a doctrine of the being of entities as permanent presence, simply lost sight of and betrayed the finitude of *Dasein*. Once this missing piece has been added back on, metaphysics will once more be established on a firm base. This firm base is man! The inadequately deconstructed tradition takes revenge by imposing this new anthropocentrism. With the aid of *Greek man* prior to Plato, of man racked by *deinon*, by the worrying power of *phusis*, Heidegger would now rediscover a path towards a decisive decentering. The Turning has been accomplished: "Being itself throws man onto this path and tears him away, impelling him beyond himself and towards being as the one who is displaced, so as to set being into the work..."[26] It is being that throws, and not *phusis* as nature. It is not some blind necessity that weighs down on man to unsettle him from his place of repose in nature proper, but the historial light that orders him to set truth to work. Man as *der Ausrückende*, the one who is never settled, will rest no more. He will be disappropriated, undone by himself, broken open like the "breach" into which being irrupts, "a stranger in his own essence"[27]—yet not without essence.

The movement of dispossession and relinquishing of man would indeed be further radicalized following this Turning of the 1930s. The relation of man to being would find itself enclosed within the relation of being to man that tends to become not merely primary, but unique, exclusive. What remains for man stripped of his powers? Can he have an essence if he has virtually nothing of his own left to him? This problematic will constitute the theme of our second section. The *Kehre*, the turn, often enough begins to look like an *Umkehrung*, a turnaround. For a *reversal* is indeed expressed by this frequently recurring formulation: "It is not we who..." Therefore, "It is not we who play with words, but the being of language that plays with us."[28] "We never arrive at thoughts. They come to us."[29] It is not we who are free, it is freedom that pos-

---

26. EM, p. 125; tr., p. 163.
27. Ibid., p. 120; tr., p. 156.
28. WhD, p. 83; tr., p. 118.
29. ED, p. 11.

sesses us.[30] It is not we who are mistaken, but entities, in masking
other entities, lead us astray, or else it is being that refuses itself.[31]
It is not we who carry out an act of memory, but being that
addresses its recollection to us.[32] It is not we who produce works of
art as we please, but truth that sets itself to work. It is not we who
decide concerning the presence or absence of God, but the destiny of
being. It is not man who decides what configuration of truth is
granted to him as accessible and discovered. Rather this configuration is epochal in each case.

It seems, furthermore, that the essence of man is entirely
determined by the limits of each of the epochs of the History of
Being. From this perspective, the definition of man seems to be
exclusively historial. "The ek-sistence of man is, as ek-sistence, historial."[33] Is this legitimate? Certainly we know that contemporary
"planetary" man has little in common with Greek man, that the latter was very different in the epoch of Homer and in the classical
age, that Renaissance man is very distinct from Enlightenment
man....But can man be reduced to historial figures? Are there not
"perennially human" features that, if not ahistorial, would at least
be of a transhistorical order, and without which we would be speaking of a radically different essence each time? If there is an identity
and a continuity of being and its essence through its History, is
there not necessarily an identity and a continuity of the essence of
man? And if we are to concede this, must we have recourse to the
idea of "human nature," which Heidegger refuses as biologically
determined by a metaphysics of living substance? Did not he himself have tacit recourse to a *nonhistorial essence of man* when presenting man solely as the one who speaks, who gives signs, who
shows, who exists on the earth and beneath the heavens alongside
things nearby in the openness of a world? On one single occasion, in
the *Beiträge*, we encounter the following double definition of man:
"Only as historial *is* man nonhistorical."[34] In this particular context,
this is meant to refute the idea of a humanity in general. For Heidegger, man is man only when integrated into a people, or more
precisely into the world of a people at a determinate epoch of their
history, into a relation with a "native," that is, familiar Earth (for it

---

30. Wm, p. 187; tr., BW, p. 130.
31. Hw, pp. 41–42.
32. WhD, p. 97; tr. p. 151.
33. Wm, p.333; tr., BW, p. 216.
34. GA 65, p. 48.

can be an adopted one) where something immemorial and a historial tradition opened for us in projection are threaded together and conjoin.

Yet how could one dare to speak phenomenologically of something immemorial? How could one gain access to a nonhistoriality of man, while maintaining the primacy of the experience of *world*? Is it possible to recognize an immemorial human dimension, without reestablishing in us or beyond us some dubious, perennial, and elementary substance, without restoring the substantial, opaque permanence of a primitive or primordial nature?

PART ONE

The Self-Enabling of *Dasein* and Its Limits

Chapter 1

BEING-TOWARDS-DEATH AND THE LIMITS TO TOTALIZING ONE'S OWN POTENTIALITY FOR BEING

The first chapter of Division Two of *Being and Time*, which really opens our access to a phenomenology of temporality (something the analysis of Care had merely hinted at), is devoted to being-towards-death. Its theme is straightforward: only by way of a relation to its death can *Dasein* grasp its own temporality. This positive relation—as opposed to the *flight in the face of death* that in several ways characterizes the attitude of the 'One'—is called *vorlaufen*, "running ahead." What is meant by this movement of "running ahead" in the face of death? It is neither a "thinking about death" nor an investigation into actual death, but a way in which *Dasein* can *approach its extreme possibility*, one that is ultimate and "unsurpassable," because there can be no possibility beyond it. This pure possibility of no longer existing, Heidegger notes, cannot be interpreted as a lack, something yet to be added to *Dasein* to make it complete. For when this possibility falls due, *Dasein* no longer is its "there."

How is this anticipation of death possible? Given that we are not dealing with some kind of speculation about death here, what does it mean "in practice" to preserve a possibility *as* possibility, to meet it without effecting it? Does not *Vorlaufen* already presuppose the notion of that which is one's own? To run ahead of "my" death—is this not to project *my Dasein* as limited, as finite? Is not *my death* only another term for designating the finitude of my temporality whose futural horizon is indeterminate? Moreover, is not *being-towards-death* a name for the will to self-possession, to the self-appropriation of *Dasein*? Can such a will be satisfied?

3

However these questions stand, Heidegger attempts to extricate death from its dimension of generality (the mortality of man) and factuality (the biological fact): death as a possibility that *Dasein* always already *is* is not the fact of dying, of passing away, of "physical disappearance." This interpretation, which belongs to the 'One', betrays an "inauthentic," that is, nonproper, relation to death: one must distance oneself from it! One will die, but for the moment one is not dead! One thereby consoles or reassures oneself. As 'One', no one ever dies. To be authentic, that is, to be *ourselves*, it is necessary to posit the possibility of death as mine and as possible at any moment. Is this not nevertheless, no matter what Heidegger says, a "thinking about death"? Death is indeed theoretically possible at any moment, yet it is not true that I am objectively threatened at every moment. Thus the proximity of possible death can result only from an effort to imagine what is abstractly possible, but improbable most of the time.

Once again, it seems that death is an emphatic underlining of the finitude of presence. Being-"there" implies the potential for not being-"there." Yet this possibility of not being our "there" does not *of itself* seem to be a positive one, otherwise there would be no need for an effort, an élan, a will to *vorlaufen*.

In any case, the Heideggerian analysis rejects any *abstraction* from the potentiality for dying, so as to make it the core of authentic temporality. Being-towards-death is the indispensable mediation for passing from temporality as a unitary structure of the three dimensions of time to temporality as the opening of oneself for oneself as projection. Being-towards-death makes temporality possible. Temporality first presents itself as Care, that is, as the unity of the three "ekstases": projection, facticity and falling. Care makes possible being-towards-death, which is called a *concretion* of Care, no doubt insofar as the potentiality for dying—to the extent that it represents a contracting—contracts the *entire* concrete unity of existence into a single point in advance. Being-towards-death contains the possible totality of *Dasein*, not as a dead totality, but as a totality ahead of itself, a totality in the making. Being-towards-death exists authentically only as running ahead, as a projected totality of oneself.

A long tradition makes death into a passage towards the beyond or a leap into the nothing. As early as the 1925 course *Prolegomena to the History of the Concept of Time*,[1] Heidegger excludes

---

1. GA 20.

taking any stance on this issue. In the phenomenology of death "no decision is at stake regarding the question of knowing whether something else comes after death, or something in general, or whether nothing comes after it."[2] Is such neutrality possible without amputating "the face not turned towards us," as Rilke puts it, from the phenomenon of death? In any case, the analysis reduces death to the pure immanence of its meaning, to *Diesseitigkeit*, to "this-sidedness" that, once again, implies an exclusion of part of the phenomenon. We shall return to this point.

Thus the Socratic problem of immortality and, in principle, the fear of death, which precisely the tradition (Epicurus, the Stoics, Montaigne) attempted to evoke, are bracketed out. Death ceases to be that opaque wall down there at the end of the road. It becomes repatriated into the heart of existence, as a transparent possibility. It no longer represents adversity, obscurity, but—via running ahead—is to become the very source of time proper, that is, of freedom. Death is thus illuminated, metamorphosed into a principle. It is no longer the enigmatic symbol, itself fleeting, of the fleeting nature of time and annihilation, but a fixed point, a positive pole, the heart of temporality. Heidegger never regards death as a possibility of destruction on this side: the decaying of physical and mental faculties in growing old, the painful loss of loved ones, the possible absurdity of death that prematurely interrupts a life, congealing it into a state of radical incompletion. He does not explain how the principle of free temporality, once accepted, can also be the principle of pure adversity: physical and mental decay, bereavement, sclerosis, fossilization.

Is not the phenomenon of death thereby skillfully masked, metamorphosed, volatilized? Do we here not find a repetition of the dialectical optimism by which the negative is continually and uniformly converted into being? "Death, that unreality...," as Hegel said. Is not being-towards-death similar to "the life that bears death and maintains itself in death itself,"[3] to Hegelian negativity? Running ahead has something of the "magic power of the negative." Anticipating the *potential for no longer being* reinforces *absolutely* the potential to be, opens for *Dasein* its being-in-full-time, its being to the limit of its time.

There is, therefore, in *Vorlaufen*, this self-founding movement that makes it comparable to the *cogito*, making it a point of anchor-

---

2. Ibid., p. 434.
3. Hegel, Preface to the *Phenomenology*.

age, a primary, unshakeable certainty. Heidegger himself makes the comparison. However, we may say that it is only an analogy, for *Vorlaufen* is not a *Vorstellen*: the relation to death is not a representation; it is *Dasein*'s movement towards its "ownmost" possibility, not an imagining of the end or of the "final moments." "*Sum moribundus*, yet certainly not as gravely ill or seriously injured. I am *moribundus* insofar as I am—*the* moribundus *first gives the* sum *its meaning*."[4] A strange *cogito*, turned around.

In the "I am as having-to-die" (the gerund must be heard as a necessary and indeterminate future), the having-to-die *precedes* the *sum*, giving it its meaning in the first place (*allererst*). Death is a certain possibility, of a greater and more primordial certainty than the *I am*. The certainty of my death is older than "me"! "This certainty: that it is I myself in my going towards death, is the fundamental certainty of *Dasein* itself and is a genuine proposition concerning *Dasein*, whereas the *cogito* is merely the semblance of such a proposition."[5] What does this imply? That it is in the time of mortal finitude that being appears; that the being of the *sum*, which is given to me only in the narrow horizon of having-to-die, manifests itself as mine only in this way. The Heideggerian position is here close to Kierkegaardian existentialism. It is opposed to abstract universality: "There is no death in general."[6] It is in favor of a singularity that can find itself only in effecting itself.

Death makes me possible, and I remain "condemned," suspended in possibility until my effective death. *Dasein* completely joins being, in the sense of its own being, only in dying! "It is only in dying [*im Sterben*] that in a certain way I can say absolutely 'I am'."[7] A remarkable position! Death individualizes me, but until my de facto death I can preserve what is possible for me thanks to death as possibility. In this text, which dates from before *Being and Time*, Heidegger seems to oppose being to existence. Being, existence becoming a subsistent entity, would then be the ultimate fallout of existence. Or, to give a different interpretation: when I no longer exist, as it were, in dying, I rejoin my pure possibility of being that is about to disappear. Or again, I am what I am, I am identical to myself only unto death, and therefore death always precedes me as the open time where I am not yet, but where I have to be. For

---

4. GA 20, pp. 437–438 (Heidegger's emphasis).
5. Ibid., p. 437.
6. Ibid., p. 433.
7. Ibid., p. 440.

Dasein, being is time. Existing, it can never say "I am" in the sense of a self-identity. Heidegger acknowledges this indirectly in *Nietzsche II*. There, in a series of definitions of *existence*, just after Kierkegaard's concept of existence, he includes existence as defined in *Being and Time*.[8] In a sense, this definition signifies that I am never a subsisting entity, a *sum* in the Cartesian sense of substance, except when I no longer am. Thus my last word at the fateful moment would be, "I am," yet such that I have not been, having *existed*! I become a "subject" only at the hour of my death! To understand oneself in accordance with one's extreme possibility, to open oneself to one's own possibilities thanks to this extreme possibility, "to choose oneself,"[9] would signify at once, and in an entirely reversible way: *being-towards-death* and *existing*. Now if death is *Dasein*'s possibility of being ("*Dasein* thus essentially is its death"[10]), this possibility is reflected or echoed in all the structures of *Dasein*! Death as the potentiality for being becomes the equivalent of being-in-the-world in absolute singularity.

"Anxiety in the face of death is anxiety 'in the face of' one's ownmost, non-relational and unsurpassable potentiality for being. That which this anxiety is 'in the face of' is being-in-the-world itself."[11] Being-in-the-world becomes a synonym for death, and vice versa. In this way all the existentials become names for death. Thus an equivalence is established between death and *Geworfenheit* or thrownness, between death and *Verfallen*, falling. Thrownness, falling, inauthentic existence as a whole become other names for death, as do their opposites: projection, authentic repetition! "*Dasein* dies factically as long as it exists, yet at first and for the most part in the mode of falling."[12] However, as being-towards-the-end is a projection, so too death is a name for existence itself. Thus: "Existence, facticity, falling characterize being towards the end and are consequently constitutive of the existential concept of death."[13] Fleeing in the face of death is nothing other than fleeing in the face of one's own *Dasein*. Death is one's own *Dasein*, but also *Dasein* as disowned, because the 'One' is an evasive recognition of being-towards-death. Anxiety on the one hand, detaching *Dasein* and

---

8. Though reinterpreting such existence as the "clearing of the *There*"!
9. GA 20, p. 440.
10. Ibid., p. 433.
11. SZ, p. 251.
12. Ibid.
13. Ibid., p. 252.

pulling it back from being lost in the 'One', and false security on the other hand attest *equally* to the fact that death is the being of *Dasein*. Why, if death is always already present in the midst of *Dasein* as its being, is it still necessary to run "ahead" of it?

Running Ahead and Freedom

As pure possibility, original and "ownmost" possibility, "death gives nothing to be actualized" within *Dasein*, because its actualization marks its abolition.[14] What does it mean to run ahead of this possibility? What is meant by running ahead, and what does it add to this possibility? It is not meant to add anything to it, but merely "to leave it in place as possibility."[15] It is not a question of "making this possibility actual,"[16] and suicide is explicitly excluded. To commit suicide would be precisely to betray the possibility as such. "Through suicide, for example, I precisely relinquish the possibility as possibility."[17] Running ahead of death as possibility means *excessively* intensifying its possible being. Running ahead increases, exaggerates the possibility of death. It is certainly excessive, for example, without any concrete representation and beyond any cause or circumstance, to imagine death as possible at any moment. Yet running ahead has indeed something of this about it: it is a question of an *intensification of possibility* that remains remote from every concretization. Heidegger here rejects two ways of approaching death: on the one hand "thinking about death," and on the other, *expecting* it. For it to remain pure possibility, death must be as little manifest and palpable as possible. Running ahead means attaining a *nonpresent proximity*. The thought of death, ruminating and meditating on the moment or the manner in which it will arrive, "weakens death through a calculating will to dispose over death."[18] Expecting, for its part, does not anticipate the possible as such, but its realization. Something actual is expected, and thereby "expecting drags the possible into the actual."[19] In approaching death in running ahead, it is a matter of penetrating

---

14. Ibid., p. 262.
15. GA 20, p. 439.
16. Ibid.
17. Ibid.
18. SZ, p. 261.
19. Ibid., p. 262.

into and letting oneself be penetrated by pure possibility, via an effort to *understand* what this possibility comprises, in particular with respect to the certainty of death. To run ahead towards death is simply to understand it better, that is, not to "stare at some meaning, but to *understand oneself* in the potentiality for being..."[20]: "In running ahead towards this possibility, it becomes 'even greater', that is, it unveils itself as one that knows no measure whatsoever, no greater or lesser, but signifies the possibility of the immeasurable impossibility of existence."[21] "Immeasurable" because extreme, situated beyond every other, this possibility offers no additional "support" (*Anhalt*) on which to base whatever project, no basis for "portraying" something that could possibly be realized or for thereby "forgetting the possibility."[22] Unrepresentable, being-towards-death nurtures no imagination of the future. It seems impoverished, empty.

We now see it undergo a reversal. And the reversal is marked in the following way: running ahead into being-towards-death, now affirmed and grasped by *Dasein* in turn, becomes what makes the potentiality for death possible. "Being-towards-death as running ahead into possibility *makes possible* this possibility in the first place *and frees it* as such."[23] "In the first place" (*allererst*), prior to running ahead, death is not something truly possible; following this "movement," *Dasein* is *free*, face to face with it and face to face with itself. It has discovered its own truth. "In this unveiling of running ahead..., *Dasein* discloses itself to itself with respect to its most extreme possibility."[24] "Running ahead in becoming free for one's own death frees us from being lost in contingent possibilities..."[25] "Running ahead discloses...a renouncing of oneself and thereby shatters any ossifying in an existence already attained."[26] In other words, *Dasein* is liberated both from factual possibilities, from possibilities belonging to others, and from its own ossifying or becoming immobilized in choices already made. Yet why a "renouncing of oneself" (*Selbstaufgabe*)? Is it not paradoxical that supreme freedom should imply the "sacrifice" of oneself? Through running ahead, which places it before

---

20. Ibid., p. 263 (emphasis added).
21. Ibid., p. 262.
22. Ibid.
23. Ibid. Heidegger emphasizes *makes possible*; emphasis added: *and frees it*.
24. Ibid.
25. Ibid., p. 264.
26. Ibid.

death, *Dasein* is free from everything, including itself. In *Aufgabe* there is *Gabe*, the gift; *Aufgabe* means the "task." *Dasein* is capable of *giving* itself entirely over to its tasks, at the risk of losing itself. It has taken on the risk of death. It is no longer desperately attached to an 'I', to a *sum* that would precede the *moribundus*. Nor is it ossified in itself any more, ignorant of the possibilities of others. On the contrary, it can freely perceive them: "*Dasein* dispels the danger that it may...fail to recognize that it is being surpassed by the possibilities of existence belonging to others, or that it may misinterpret them and force them back upon its own."[27]

We can thus comprehend the ultimate significance of running ahead. It is *Dasein*'s turning back on itself in attaining the "absolute" point at which it can give itself what is possible for it. "*Dasein* can only *authentically* be *itself* if it makes this possible for itself of its own accord."[28] Do we not have a full-blown idealism? *Dasein* wants itself, posits itself in its most extreme possibility, like the absolute Hegelian Subject and like the Will to Power. *Dasein* takes every possibility back to itself and into itself by force, by an act of will. The four features of death—being one's ownmost, nonrelational, unsurpassable, and certain possibility—are quite explicitly the effects or results of an effort, something gained by running ahead. In fact, death becomes this absolute possibility only through "acts" of running ahead. For it to be one's *ownmost* possibility, it must be "torn" from the '*One*'. How can *Dasein* be torn from the 'One'? Because it "can in each case, in running ahead, tear itself free."[29] That which is one's own is proposed in advance. Likewise for the nonrelational character of this possibility: "Running ahead into its nonrelational possibility forces the entity running ahead into the possibility of taking on its ownmost being from out of itself of its own accord."[30] In other words, *Dasein* forces itself to posit itself in its own singularity. Similarly, once again, for the unsurpassable character of being-towards-death, by definition (it is almost tautological) running ahead frees us for a possibility that no other possibility could succeed. Running ahead also gives *Dasein* the possibility of projecting itself as an *existentiell totality*. "Because running ahead into this unsurpassable possibility also discloses all the possibilities lying ahead of it, it entails the possibility of an existentiell

27. Ibid.
28. Ibid., p. 263.
29. Ibid.
30. Ibid., pp. 263-264.

anticipation of the *whole* of *Dasein*, i.e. the possibility of existing as a *whole potentiality for being.*[31] From the summit of the ultimate possibility *Dasein* can *in advance* look upon its own concrete life as a completed whole. In the end the possibility can become *certain* only via running ahead itself: "The certain possibility of death only discloses *Dasein* as possibility through *Dasein*'s running ahead towards it thus *making* this possibility *possible* for itself as its ownmost potentiality for being."[32] Only the *indeterminate* character of the possibility does not result from running ahead. Yet running ahead assumes this indeterminacy to the point where it itself seems (though this is impossible) to be able to awaken the *anxiety* linked to the *threat* of death: "In running ahead to its indeterminate and certain death, *Dasein* opens itself to a constant *threat* springing from its own There."[33] And as anxiety is the mood of this threat, we ought to experience a constant anxiety! It is indeed a question of a voluntarism—the theme of resoluteness makes it even more evident—that can be translated by a will to will. Not a will to death, but a will to disclose oneself to the extreme limit, to the point of losing oneself, to the abyss of "freedom," that is, of a self-transcending transcendence. Not a will to death, but "taking death to be true," catching it at its own game, getting the better of it, beating it on its own ground. Does not the dizzy spiral of freedom into which *Dasein* is dragged (Sartre would find a way of adding even more) represent the victory of an idealization of death? "Freedom for death" is said to be "impassioned, released from the illusions of the 'One', factical, certain of itself and anxious." The least evident of these attributes is that it is "factical": what facticity can remain for a *Dasein* that has made itself wholly possible, has freed itself unto itself and for itself? Free "for death," is not *Dasein* both free "for nothing" and for the whole of itself? How can freedom be detached from the whole and clamped to the ipseity of an absolute and unattainable ownness? Freedom certainly has its "elementary concretion"[34] in anxiety, but anxiety makes us "free for the authentic and inauthentic"; anxiety once again *detaches* us, not only from the 'One', but from all prior engagement.

   Faced with this doctrine of freedom, it is difficult to prevent the impression of extreme rarefaction and abstraction, of *hypertranscen-*

---

31. Ibid., p. 264.
32. Ibid. (Heidegger's emphasis).
33. Ibid., p. 265.
34. Ibid., p. 191.

dentalism. Let us nevertheless attempt to defend it. Heidegger conceives freedom as the making possible, via one's ownmost possibility, of factical possibilities that on their own are falling and not free. How can such a supreme possibility, so pure and even intensified by a true understanding, bestow a character of "freedom" on everyday possibilities? Obviously, a mediation is required between this unique, "nonsubstitutable" possibility of my death and the everydayness that gets on with its tasks. This mediation must be on the order of an *experience* that exits from the everyday and yet has an intimate relation to it. This mediating experience is that of anxiety. Anxiety alone reveals *concretely* to *Dasein* its potentiality for death and does so via a withdrawal, a retreat, an unattainability pertaining to world as a totality of goal-related activities or practical paths referring to one another. Only through anxiety can being-towards-death appear as a concrete possibility, a "concretion."[35] Without anxiety, it would remain a simple form. Therefore I can "authentically" do what I ordinarily do only if I act, not under the sway of a constant anxiety (anxiety is rare and intrinsically paralyzing), but "on the basis of" this attunement, by keeping it in mind. What does this imply? That "I must" have reference to the possibility, experienced at a particular moment, of the *impossibility* of doing what I ordinarily do; for example, my job. I will do it "well" only if I securely grasp its precariousness and provisional character in the time of my existence and in the time of the world, and if I am not engaged in it as some job in general, but as mine at this hour. The "I must" does not express a universal moral objection, but a premoral necessity: "mineness." How far removed we are from the Kantian idea of an action that is moral because it can be universalized, because it is deindividualized! We have precisely the reverse. Yet is it absolutely necessary to designate this dimension of "mineness" as "death"?

Is death really what is at issue in being-towards-death? If death is a present possibility, why then situate it away in some more or less remote future? Why should it disclose the future, since it definitively closes it off?

A Critique of Being-Towards-Death

Death, says Rilke, possesses an "invisible face turned away from us," an enigmatic face, necessarily turned either towards the

---

35. Ibid., p. 251.

beyond or towards the nothing. This signifies that the *integral* phenomenon of death, in addition to its *Diesseitigkeit*, also comprises a *Jenseitigkeit*. The latter is not something invented by religion. Is not a phenomenology of death truncated and one-sided that overlooks its double character and treats it like a purely intraworldly phenomenon? By cutting death off from the side turned away from us, the side that escapes us, Heidegger entirely reintegrates death into *Dasein*. Furthermore, in making it the path of access to one's own, he transforms it into a transcendental faculty, into a possession and a potential, a certainty, a (scarcely abyssal!) foundation. Yet we can only ever take hold—if one can put it this way—of half of its being and its meaning, for we cannot know its other face.

What is more, in insisting on the potentiality for dying as an ontological possibility that is "exceptional, one's ownmost, non-relational, unsurpassable, and certain," Heidegger separates existential death from the phenomenon of life, which is relegated to straightforward facticity. The potentiality for dying can be identified only with the pure potentiality for being at the expense of a *forgetting of life*. However, it is clear that if *Dasein* were not a living being, it would not be a being, and that its potentiality for dying is therefore not an original potentiality for being. Unless one considers—and Heidegger is not far from doing so—that *Dasein* gives itself its own being. How can being-towards-death legitimately be situated "*prior* to every ontology of life"? Because life, like nature, is an entity in the world that can be understood only in its being as a lesser being-in-the-world, by way of "a reductive privation with respect to the ontology of *Dasein*."[36] In Heidegger we find a recoil in the face of life. No comportment of *Dasein* can be founded on life. *Urge* (*Drang*) and *inclination* (*Hang*), to the extent that they imply the temporal unity of being-ahead-of-oneself, already-being-in, and being-alongside, are founded in Care and in thrownness. The urge, which cannot be uprooted, to let oneself live, to let oneself be borne by the world, belongs to a nonfree Care. "In pure urge, Care has not yet become free."[37] It is impossible to annihilate the urge "to live."[38] Life is alienation, the temptation of existence to fall below itself. The urge "to live" is not primordially the fact of life, but the fact of temporality forgetting itself as projection and, losing its being-

---

36. Ibid., p. 194.
37. Ibid., p. 196.
38. Ibid.

ahead-of-itself, becoming enslaved to the "only ever already-along-side..."[39]

The Kantian theme of the condition of possibility always has priority over life. Vital spontaneity does not exist; it presupposes a prior possibility. The word *possibility* is sometimes hammered out in every sentence in certain sections of *Being and Time*; for example, in Section 53.

Yet how can possibility be that which gives potential? Does *Dasein* have the potential to make itself possible? The idea that it itself makes itself possible is incredible, no less remarkable than that of the *causa sui*. Would *Dasein* be like the Baron von Münchhausen, who took hold of his hair to lift himself into the air? Whence does the possibility—as it is not simply logical, but ontological—draw its power to make possible? *Dasein* makes possible only because it is. Can one say that it is, if it does not live? Heidegger separates being—which, however, is only the field in which entities appear—from life.

Is there not, however, a root common to being and to life, a point at which they can be identified with one another? It is true that, to the extent that it belongs to the essence of *Dasein*, death is a "possibility of being." Heidegger indeed admits that *Dasein* is "thrown" (*geworfen*) into this possibility, but he nowhere acknowledges that this possibility depends on life. Why could *Dasein* not be thrown into being by nature or life? Why must thrownness only concern being?

It seems that the origin of facticity, of *Geworfenheit*, must, for Heidegger, remain indeterminate. It would be crucial, however, to elucidate the phenomenon of death to know what power "throws" *Dasein* into existence. Heidegger grants that the concept of *facticity* presupposes that *Dasein* understand itself "as bound up in its 'destiny' with the being of those entities it encounters within its own world."[40] To what being of entities are we bound in our destiny—to life, to death—if not to the being of natural entities? Yet the entire effort of the existential analytic aims to extract us from the way we are intricately bound up with natural entities.

Does the fact that, contrary to the animal, we can and *must* "take over"[41] death as such, as possibility, suffice to conclude that we can thereby make possible the very possibility of death? Is that

---

39. Ibid., p. 195.
40. Ibid., p. 56.
41. Ibid., p. 250.

not wanting to leap over one's own shadow? And yet this is what Heidegger does when he speaks of running ahead as "making this possibility possible."[42] What does it mean to "become certain of the totality of one's potentiality for being"?[43] What can be meant by the "certainty" of a possible totality that goes before us in the future? The certainty of an unrealized possibility, even if it is yet to come, does not remove its coefficient of unreality.

Is not the very idea of running ahead ambiguous? "Projecting oneself towards," "running ahead of" the supreme possibility indeed seems to imply that it is somehow incompletely present, which is false. Running ahead does not entail any tension between a present and a future and therefore does not disclose any future. For as this élan for running ahead of death cannot be accompanied by any concrete "content" (whether thought, expectation, or suicide), "this being-towards-death that is existentially 'possible'," says Heidegger, "on the existentiell level remains a fantastical suggestion."[44] Is it not indeed a question of a movement occurring at an eminently *formal* level? For running ahead cannot mean *transporting oneself in advance*, in our imagination, over into the future at the moment when the possibility is about to be realized, that is, at the moment of death. Heidegger excludes this, and must do so. For in the instant that precedes factual death—where I would find myself in thought, if this is what were meant by running ahead—the possibility of dying would still remain a possibility. And if death arrived, its possibility would disappear.

At the end of the day, then, what are being-towards-death and running ahead if not the *forms* of *Dasein*'s self-appropriation, forms eternally devoid of content? To run ahead of one's essential possibility is quite simply to run ahead of oneself, of one's own truth. Running ahead could just as well be called *resoluteness*, and it will be called this because the latter will be the existential that can equally be existentiell in the form of a decision whose pure existential, without possible concretion, was running ahead. It seems that the two allow *Dasein* radically to take hold of its initial disclosedness, to capture its own light, to enter absolutely into possession of itself, of its "freedom," to learn to "choose its choice."[45] An extreme voluntarism.

---

42. Ibid., p. 266.
43. Ibid.
44. Ibid.
45. Ibid., p. 268.

Yet fairness obliges us to emphasize the reversal announced at the end of this very chapter. The first concrete, that is, ontic, existentiell content—which was absent from being-towards-death—will be found by the existential analytic not in resoluteness, but in the "call of conscience." The ontic potentiality for being a whole announced by this call does not proceed from a voluntary act. "The call is not, is never planned, nor prepared, nor accomplished voluntarily *by us ourselves*."[46] Through the call, as in anxiety, *Dasein* is brutally thrust towards its own potentiality for being, *without its having chosen it. Dasein* finds itself placed in the presence of itself by a superior power, and yet one that is none other than itself.

Does not the call of conscience, therefore, instead of giving *Dasein* absolute mastery of itself, in truth lead it towards an initial dispossession?

---

46. Ibid., p. 275.

Chapter 2

THE CALL OF CONSCIENCE, OR
THE LIMITS OF *DASEIN*'S SELF-APPROPRIATION
OF ITS POSSIBILITIES

Heidegger proceeds from the "voice of conscience" (*Stimme des Gewissens*) as a given fact belonging to "the everyday self-interpretation of *Dasein*." One must beware here of too rapidly identifying *Gewissen* with *moral* conscience, as does Vezin's "translation." For *Gewissen* would then be related precisely to *being indebted* and considered as an "existential condition of possibility of 'moral' good and evil,"[1] thus as something premoral. *Dasein* hears a voice or a call (*Ruf*) that makes it understand "something" (*etwas*) about what it itself has to *be* (and not, strangely enough, to *do*!) within its own situation ("the call does not give an ideal, universal potentiality-for-being to be understood"[2]). An obscure feeling of fault or debt (the word *Schuld* has both these senses) is thus connected with this strictly singular call. In addition, this call is *uncanny*, worrying. This uncanniness is partly connected with the fact that the call is *silent*. It is not expressed in an articulated discourse. "Conscience calls solely in remaining silent, i.e. the call comes from the silence of an uncanniness."[3] Finally, and this is initially the most disconcerting feature of the call, the call does not explicitly come from ourselves. "It" calls, against our expectations and against our

---

1. SZ, p. 286.
2. Ibid., p. 280.
3. Ibid., p. 296.

17

choice.[4] The irruption of this "foreign voice" (*fremde Stimme*)[5] into *Dasein* thus seems to interrupt or forbid the movement of self-appropriation and self-enabling that being-towards-death had straightaway pushed to its limit. How could *Dasein* be master of itself if it is inhabited by an alien voice?

The analysis indeed leaves us in no doubt concerning the nature of this voice. From the very beginning, it reveals its meaning, a meaning devoid of mystery and any effective dispossession. Who is it that is called? Everyday *Dasein*, always already dispersed into the 'One'. What does the voice call us towards? "Towards one's *own self*" (*Auf das* eigene Selbst).[6] The mystery is merely an apparent one. The call merely *seems* foreign because it is understood in terms of a banal, ordinary situation in which *Dasein* is *not* itself—because, that is, it is heard by a *Dasein* that is not one's own. The call nevertheless calls *Dasein* to itself in a very strange manner: it says nothing! The voice of conscience does not speak, does not indicate what one ought to do in this case or that. It does not pronounce any command, any moral maxim, any categorical or hypothetical imperative (are we dealing here with incontestable phenomenological evidence?[7]). Can the voice be only silent *and* indeterminate? Why? Does not conscience always "tell itself" something? When, for example, I tell myself: "I should be working"; "I must thank this or that person"; "I must visit a friend"; "I must change my conduct (or my clothes!)"—are these not calls of conscience? However things may stand, the call can come only from *Dasein* itself. "In conscience, *Dasein* calls itself."[8]

"*Dasein* is at once the caller and the one called."[9] It is illusory to interpret the force that is calling or the caller (*Rufer*) as a "foreign power invading *Dasein*,"[10] or as "some entity that would not

---

4. Ibid., p. 275.
5. Ibid., p. 277.
6. Ibid., p. 273.
7. For Husserl, on the contrary, the voice of conscience always *speaks* to itself, explicitly, for example by saying "you have acted badly," but it "does not communicate anything to itself," because it merely *imagines itself* as using words; it immediately grasps in reality what it properly intends to signify, without having need of signs (First *Logical Investigation*, Section 8). Cf. Derrida, *La voix et le phénomène*, Chapter 6. Trans. D. B. Allison, *Speech and Phenomena* (Evanston: Northwestern University Press, 1973).
8. SZ, p. 275.
9. Ibid., p. 277.
10. Ibid., p. 275.

have the character of *Dasein.*" "People ascribe a possessor to this power, or take this power itself to be a person (God) announcing their presence."[11] *Dasein,* however, is alone before this voice. No one, neither God nor someone other than *Dasein* itself, addresses itself *to Dasein within Dasein.* Heidegger affirms the autonomy of the voice, or rather its autoaffection, its autology. Conscience is not the "immortal and celestial voice" of Rousseau, nor the voice of God, nor that of nature. It is merely "the call of Care," which reveals the totality of *Dasein* as being-ahead-of-itself, already there, already thrown. The "debt" is turned towards an irrecoverable anteriority of *Dasein* that the latter, however, must take over. For although the call does not speak, although the voice says nothing, it nevertheless gives something to be *understood.* What does *Dasein* understand? It understands, first, that it "owes" something, that it is "indebted," not because of this or that situation or this or that act, but forever. It understands also (and simultaneously) that it must take on this archi-ancient debt once more and project it as far as its most distant future, thereby transfiguring it without being able to abolish it. From this unity of taking on one's being-indebted and of such projection is born *resoluteness:* "*this silent projecting oneself upon one's ownmost being indebted while ready for anxiety we call resoluteness [Entschlossenheit].*"[12] Yet what does it mean to be indebted? What is *debt (Schuld)?* The word *Schuld* is the substantive from *Sollen,* just as the French word *dette* is the substantive from *devoir. Schuld* simultaneously signifies *debt, fault, responsibility,* and *guilt* (and Heidegger constantly plays on this polysemy). The analysis attempts to go back from the factual sense of fault to the existential possibility of debt. The question that the sections on conscience pose is the following: when *Dasein* understands that it is indebted to someone for something, what is the origin of this phenomenon, and to whom is *Dasein* truly indebted? We cannot be dealing with a pure and simple fact. Thus Heidegger begins by analyzing the ordinary meanings of *debt* towards others: for example, we owe them some good, such as money, or we are responsible for a wrong against them, we have wronged them. In both cases we are responsible for a lack in the other *Dasein.* We can thus arrive at a formal concept of debt: "being the grounds for a lack in the *Dasein* of others." *Debt* in the ordinary sense is a factual lack, the lack of some subsisting entity. Yet nothing can be factually lacking in exis-

11. Ibid.
12. Ibid., p. 297.

tence without it having the intrinsic ontological possibility of this deficiency. "The idea of 'indebted' must be *formalized*."[13] This formalization is the passage to the notion of an ontological condition of possibility. To elaborate the *existential* concept of debt, Heidegger will fuse together two distinct traits of *being in debt*: on the one hand, the lack, the *not*; and on the other hand, the "responsibility," the fact of being a cause.

Being indebted means being responsible for a 'not', for a *nothingness* (*Nichtigkeit*). Heidegger retranslates the moral concept of responsibility into the ontological concept of *Grund*, "cause" or "ground." Being indebted means being the ground of a 'not'; it means, above all, being a ground that is affected by a 'not'. At this point the analysis is reversed.

The 'not' does not reveal a lack situated in any subsistent being or on the side of the existence of others, but one situated at the very heart of one's own *Dasein*. The original lack in *Dasein* is one that results from its being thrown. *Dasein* must *take over* the role of cause, principle and ground, though it cannot give itself and has not given itself the ground. It is not ground, but "only" the *being* of the ground; that is, the one who takes over being the ground. "The self that has to lay the ground of itself as such can *never* master this ground and yet has to take on being a ground by existing."[14] Hence the feeling of heaviness, the overwhelming mood it sometimes feels.

Heidegger hereafter no longer considers debt to be the result of a lack that has befallen the other through the fault of my *Dasein*. He traces being indebted back towards its principle: the constitution of the self of *Dasein*. "Being indebted is not the result of owing a debt, but of an originary being indebted."[15]

The "intersubjectivity" of debt vanishes. The 'not' that *Dasein* introduces into the world and among others must be found beforehand in *Dasein* itself. Whence the idea of an originary debt of *Dasein towards itself*, which is articulated in a dual manner:

1. *Dasein* must determine itself as an original potentiality for being, as "ground"; and yet it receives this ground as "thrown" ground, affected by *Nichtigkeit*. The primary debt of *Dasein* is to have received and therefore somehow always

---

13. Ibid., p. 283.
14. Ibid., p. 284.
15. Ibid.

already usurped being a ground. *Dasein* "owes" to its abandonment, to its facticity, the very possibility of freely projecting itself.

2. Thrownness is not an abstract principle, but the fact of finding oneself already situated in certain determinate possibilities. Therefore *Dasein*, which *must choose among* these possibilities, is "indebted" not only with respect to these possibilities, but in the very fact of choosing. It is free only if it chooses, yet by choosing it becomes exposed to the revenge of what it has not chosen. It must bear the consequences of both its choices and its nonchoices. The 'not' that the debt comes from is double: not having chosen one's "own" possibilities; and having to carry (*tragen*) the others, those it cannot choose or can no longer choose. *Dasein* is initially indebted as thrown into its possibilities and not because it can do wrong to another *Dasein*: "it in each case stands in one or the other possibility and constantly is *not* another one which it has renounced in its existentiell projection."[16]

Thus ontologized and formalized to the extreme, the Heideggerian analysis of *debt*, on which a large part of the ethical question depends, in truth ends up with a radical nonindebtedness, with a detachment in respect of all factical debt and every law or determinate duty. "The idea of debt...must be detached from any relation to a duty [*Sollen*] or a law [*Gesetz*] in respect of which someone at fault feels guilt [*Schuld*]."[17]

Having relativized debt and fault by underlining their ontic character, having traced all debt back to an originary indebtedness with respect to our own possibilities that exceed us and before which we are always indebted or overdue, Heidegger rejects approaching debt via notions of good and evil. For him, both the "good" and its privation are the concern of an ontology of subsisting entities. Being indebted as (ethical) fault, on the other hand, concerns a *mode of existence*. For him, morality presupposes originary being indebted; that is, the irrecoverable facticity of our possibilities, the "nothingness" of ground. And yet, what is the connection between "being the ground of a lack in the *Dasein* of another"[18] and

---

16. Ibid., p. 285.
17. Ibid., p. 283.
18. Ibid., p. 282.

"oneself being a thrown ground"? Can the fact that we are somehow always in default of our possibilities "make possible" the good or evil that we can do to others, and if so, how? The analysis does not tell us this, although it affirms that essential or originary being indebted is "the existential condition of the possibility of "moral" good and evil, in other words, of morality in general."[19] Every *Dasein*, whether it is at fault or not, is in the first instance indebted with respect to its own being-in-the-world or in the process of the proper becoming of its being-in-the-world. How is it thereby engaged and "responsible" in respect to others? It indeed seems that, far from conditioning morality, originary indebtedness can merely put it out of play.

The threat of an "existential solipsism" weighs on the Heideggerian ethic. Conscience calls to nothing, if not to one's ownmost self. "Hearing the call" for *Dasein* merely means understanding the existential necessity of choice subjected to the sole imperative of having in any case to "choose oneself." What Heidegger terms "wanting to have a conscience" implies no other "responsibility" than being ready to "want to hear" the call to be oneself. "Wanting to have a conscience" means passing from being indebted towards others to being indebted towards oneself! Furthermore, this "will" exerts itself like a force of self-enabling: "With this choice [of itself], Dasein makes possible for itself its ownmost being indebted."[20]

Here we find again the same formalism and the same tautology: wanting to have a conscience means wanting to be properly oneself. Yet how could the pure, nonrelative self accept any morality, that is, any *relation of reciprocity*? It is *Mitsein*, "with the other" or "with others" even when it is alone, just as much as it is in the world, but it is not with any determinate other. "Hearing the voice of the friend which every *Dasein* carries with it"[21] cannot mean the voice of a determinate, ontic friend, but only *Dasein*'s own *and* foreign voice.

One final mortgage completes the strain put on the Heideggerian ethic: Heidegger does not understand action as obedience to the voice of conscience." All action is factically necessarily 'without conscience' [*gewissenslos*]."[22] All action is "guilty," is a debt coming into effect and suspending the call. Action takes the plunge; it for-

---

19. Ibid., p. 286.
20. Ibid., p. 288.
21. Ibid., p. 163.
22. Ibid., p. 288.

gets "absolute" exigency and the purity of the call. Here Heidegger nowhere understands action—as he would in the *Letter on Humanism*—as the accomplishment of a possibility of being. In *Being and Time*, *Gewissen* is situated well *prior* to both good and bad conscience. The main objection that the analysis refutes in fact concerns the concept of bad conscience. It indeed seems as though the voice of conscience appears as remorse *after the act*. And so it is, one will say, when I have carried out an act for which I may reproach myself: is it not the factical guilt that gives rise to a factical conscience? "The voice follows the lived act."[23] Heidegger's response: neither the act nor especially the fault and the voice of conscience are merely *facts*. They have the mode of being of Care: they belong to a being-ahead-of-oneself that returns towards its having-been. The voice recalls a debt more ancient than the act at fault. Bad conscience calls on one to take on one's debt, thus calls to a future.

Likewise with good conscience. It does not boil down to the affirmation "I am good," but calls us to a certain absence of *Gewissen*, based on "I have nothing to reproach myself for." Taken as a fleeing in the face of conscience as such, good conscience amounts to the mode of being of the 'One', and thus to an existential possibility that is equiprimordial with that of *Gewissen*, given that authentic and inauthentic are equiprimordial.

What emerges from these interpretations is a strong impression of tautology, formal rigidity, and rarefaction. Once again, why can conscience provide no determinate injunction? For its "call" does not appear "in general," but always in a very precise situation. Heidegger's reply is circular: "If the call of conscience provides no 'practical' directives, this is solely because it calls *Dasein* to existence, to its ownmost potentiality for being a self."[24] If the voice has no content, it is because it expresses the pure possibility of taking on one's ownmost self. Yet, from the point of view of being indebted, is not what is ownmost that which is concretely, *factically* ownmost? Is it not *necessary* for conscience to propose particular acts? Nothing of the sort, Heidegger maintains, in the name of the same formal necessity: "If conscience provided the expected maxims which could be univocally calculated, it would refuse existence nothing less than the *possibility of acting*."[25] How does he arrive at the idea that the possibility of acting is weakened or suppressed by

---

23. Ibid., p. 291.
24. Ibid., p. 294.
25. Ibid.

a precise or preconceived projection or by commencing an action? The fact that conscience can propose nothing to the self except the form of the self excludes all existen*tial* morality. There is certainly an existentiell morality, but, because it is not founded on the voice or the call, it remains contingent! And conversely, does not the voice for its part remain powerless and ineffective? If listening to the voice of conscience means acting factically, yet factical action is the forgetting of conscience, or "absence of conscience," it seems that only the echo of the pure form of the self resounds in the call.

It is an empty form, in any case foreign to action, as witnessed by the *mood* of the call: anxiety. One's own potentiality for being calls itself in anxiety: "The caller is *Dasein* which is anxious in its thrownness."[26]

Anxiety indeed suspends action, just as it strikes us silent! The Heideggerian *Gewissen*, like Socrates' daimon, interrupts the impulse to act, rather than provoking it. This spontaneous voice is antispontaneity itself. It throws *Dasein* back into the pure uncanniness of its isolation.

The voice reveals only that *Dasein* is radically isolated and abandoned. Indeed. Are we dealing with a presupposition or with phenomenological evidence? It seems to be more of a presupposition. Why might being indebted, and thereby the condition of possibility of all morality, not rather be the call of *Mitsein* in *Dasein*? If *Dasein* is "essentially in itself being-with" and if "being-with is a determination of one's own *Dasein*,"[27] is it not possible that the call of being-with-the-other arises in us precisely when we are indebted? There is certainly a "solicitude that leaps ahead and liberates,"[28] in which we do not put ourselves in the place of the other and which, unlike a "solicitude that leaps in and dominates," "helps the other to become transparent *in* his or her Care and to *become free for it*."[29] Heidegger certainly recognizes and describes an "*authentic* solidarity...which frees the other, in his or her freedom, for themselves."[30] But ought he not also to recognize an "authentic" debt through which we give back to the other what we owe him or her, whether fairly or unfairly? For if we cannot give "something" back to the other, some ontic good, we can at least be grateful to

---

26. Ibid., p. 277.
27. Ibid., p. 121.
28. Ibid., p. 122.
29. Ibid.
30. Ibid.

that person in the attunement of acknowledgment. Does Heidegger judge this very high mood, that of *Danken*, to be too high to transpire between human beings? Or, as the *Postscript to "What is Metaphysics?"* (1943) would later show, does it merely proceed from man to being?

Chapter 3

THE LIMITS OF RESOLUTENESS AND THE INITIALLY LATENT, THEN EXPLICIT PRIMACY OF ORIGINARY TEMPORALITY OVER AUTHENTIC TEMPORALITY

"Resoluteness" (*Entschlossenheit*) is defined as an extension of being-towards-death and the call of conscience, insofar as it presupposes running ahead and the capacity of *Dasein* to take on its ownmost being indebted, and to do so with a view to a possible action. Resoluteness is to lead to *decision* (*Entschluss*), that is, to the projection of a factual possibility. The decision is the existentiell concretization of resoluteness. Resoluteness constitutes the existential structure of the most complete and the most originary disclosedness of *Dasein*. For *Entschlossenheit* discloses (*erschliesst*) *Dasein* most comprehensively. Resoluteness draws its possibility above all from running ahead, that is, from a unifying of the temporal field and from putting the possibilities offered into perspective. It is therefore, in a seemingly abstract way, the possibility of a possibility, but it thereby enjoys the highest existen*tial* determination. The theme of resoluteness at once introduces, in Section 60, a new critique of *action*. Heidegger raises "the precursory character" (*Vorläufigkeit*) of decision. It is a matter of knowing whether resolute running ahead towards death perhaps has a primacy—as the most certain and most complete existential possibility—over the factical possibility of decision. The relation between death and action is far

27

from obvious, and Heidegger asks: "What can death have in common with the 'concrete situation' of action?"[1]

The "situation" itself, in the sense intended by *Being and Time*, is not a preestablished framework, nor a coordinated set of circumstances, but rather the *There*, both spatial and temporal, in which events take on meaning, yet only in the perspective of resoluteness. There is a situation only for a resolute *Dasein*. The situation is not the content of events, but the manner in which they can be understood. It belongs to the realm of the possible. The situation, always determinate, concerns an existentiell truth whose meaning depends on an existential truth that itself is a pure form.

In itself, resoluteness indeed has no content. It modifies our *understanding* of world, others, and ourselves, but this modification is merely formal. In view of it, the world "does not become other in its 'content',"[2] but the possibilities are linked differently to one another and to *Dasein*. The fact that there is a supreme possibility casts a different perspective on the possibilities and gives them a different organization. Resolute *Dasein* does not withdraw from the world to float above it. On the contrary, it is "nothing other than *authentically being-in-the-world*,"[3] a formalism that is underlined a little later, "*Resoluteness is only the authenticity...of Care itself.*"[4] *Dasein* for the first time, because it is resolved to itself, no longer encroaches on the possibilities of others; it becomes capable of authentic relations with others, capable of that "solicitude which runs ahead" and liberates the other from himself or herself, "far from the ambiguous and jealous arrangements and the talkative fraternizing in the 'One'."[5] Resolved to the silence of itself, *Dasein* can authentically approach the other and truly talk to him or her, because it has gathered itself into itself and is no longer half-melted into the other.

Yet how can resoluteness pass over into an act and become a determinate decision? This is all the more difficult because it has no interest whatsoever in the content of the action. Is there not a break or leap between the "principle" and its "application"? Resoluteness, says Heidegger, is neither practical nor theoretical; insofar as it is bound to a care for what is one's own, it goes back to a totality prior to the division between theory and practice.

---

1. SZ, p. 302.
2. Ibid., p. 297.
3. Ibid., p. 298.
4. Ibid., p. 301.
5. Ibid., p. 298.

The "passage to action" is in no way problematic, because our understanding of the situation, as arising from the call, is not at all a *representation*. For *Dasein*, understanding a situation does not mean setting it before oneself (*Vorstellen*) or setting oneself before it, but on the contrary *placing oneself within it*. And placing oneself in a situation means acting: "as resolute, *Dasein* already *acts*."[6] *Dasein* "makes its factical existence possible for itself"![7] Is not this ability to make the concrete situation possible for oneself mysterious and quasi-magical? Heidegger spares himself analyzing its details and ontic implications.

For him, as for Hegel, what appears to common sense as the most concrete is the most abstract, and vice-versa!

In the phenomenon of resoluteness, the analysis first attains the true concretion it had sought from the beginning. It is the unity and totality of originary temporality. The potentiality for being a whole had already been unveiled in running ahead, but in that phenomenon, temporality was not taken in its full extent, in its whole being, but rather primarily with respect to its limit. *"Temporality is experienced in a phenomenally originary manner in Dasein's authentic being a whole—in the phenomenon of resoluteness as running ahead."*[8] Only resoluteness allows the élan of running ahead, and discovering one's own indebtedness, not to be particular moments of *Dasein's* existentiality, but *constants* in a projection that is not merely fundamental and constitutive, but *existentiell*. Only resoluteness projects itself simultaneously towards an archi-ancient past (the "debt") and towards an extreme future (death). Only resoluteness reveals the entire interval of time and its intimate connectedness. Confronted with the overly formal character of running ahead and being indebted, Heidegger searches for the *existentiell* content of these structures in the *reciprocity of resoluteness and decision*. The connection between resoluteness and decision is called a *taking back* (*Zurücknahme*). Every authentic, factical decision retains the character of *disclosedness* (*Erschlossenheit*) given it by *Entschlossenheit*. A resolute decision precisely does not "ossify" within the situation, but remains free to be taken again and perhaps differently. This possible withdrawal leads not to a lack of resoluteness, but on the contrary to the *possible repetition* of oneself.[9] *Dasein* keeps open a con-

6. Ibid., p. 300.
7. Ibid.
8. Ibid., p. 304.
9. Ibid., p. 308.

stant freedom of decision that draws its certainty from the certainty of death; that is, from the certainty of the possibility of one "taking oneself back" absolutely, withdrawing absolutely.

The analysis thus discovers, in the temporality of resoluteness, the concrete manner in which *temporality itself* intervenes to unify past, present and future and let them interact, and does so in every specific decision. To the extent that "resoluteness is not, but rather temporalizes" (to paraphrase the famous expression[10]), originary temporality will thus become—by an imperceptible and scarcely marked reversal—no longer the "object" that resoluteness must take hold of, but the true "subject" of the latter, and ultimately of *Dasein* itself! For the analysis will make it clear that it is not resoluteness that makes temporality possible, but that resoluteness on the contrary presupposes an originary structure of temporality. What does this primacy of temporality consist in? Is authentic temporality identical to originary temporality? What role remains for resoluteness, if it turns out that temporality *temporalizes itself of its own accord*, independent of *Dasein*'s authenticity or inauthenticity?

Situating Authentic and Resolute Temporality Relative to the "Spontaneity" of Originary Temporality

Originary temporality is defined by the radical "outside itself" of the three "ekstases": projection towards...(in the case of future), returning to...(in the case of past), and being alongside...(in the case of present)[11]—as opposed to an indefinite sequence of equal and above all leveled-down 'nows'. The discovery of this temporality seems to bring to a *halt* the self-enabling movement of *Dasein*. The unity of the three ekstases, as well as their totalization, which is operative in every instance and not certain "until" death, has no need of a resolute projection of *Dasein* to constitute itself, insofar as it is able to take over the extreme limits of its existence in both backward and forward directions. Resoluteness does not make temporality possible; rather temporality, in its "spontaneous" structure, makes resoluteness possible. Originary temporality temporalizes, that is, radically makes possible all the modes of being of

---

10. Ibid., p. 328.
11. Ibid., pp. 328ff.

Dasein, gives meaning to all the "existentials" (understanding, disposition, falling), but above all makes possible the authentic and the inauthentic. The entire conclusion of *Being and Time* will attempt to show this. Originary time, because it is "the fundamental possibility of authentic and inauthentic existence,"[12] "temporalizes itself" (*zeitigt sich*) out of the future, apparently irrespective of whether *Dasein* is resolute or not.

Yet if resoluteness merely condenses the intrinsic structure of temporality (which is what primarily temporalizes) to take it on and affirm it, does it effectively function as an existential condition of possibility? Does not resoluteness become the *ratio cognoscendi* of temporality as *ratio essendi*? Is not the necessity of the "position" of resoluteness relativized if, once again, temporality temporalizes itself of its own accord or if the finitude of originary time does not depend on a projection, but is what it is *of its own accord*? "*Temporality*," Heidegger says, "is the *originary 'outside of itself' in and for itself.*"[13] Resoluteness seems to lose its primordial function. Indeed, the conclusion of the initial analyses of temporality fails to mention authentic temporality: "Time originally is as the temporalizing of temporality which, as such, makes possible the constitution of the structure of Care. Temporality is essentially ekstatic. Temporality originarily temporalizes out of the future. Originary time is finite."[14] It seems that there is an autonomy to the self-production of originary time.

How could originary ekstatic temporality, however, as "making possible"[15] the unity of the three ekstases (existence, facticity, falling) that constitute Care, manifest itself and become a task for *Dasein* if not via authentic temporality, that of resoluteness? There seems to be some competition between the authentic and the originary. They sometimes manage to overlap and coincide, at least partially. For example when Heidegger writes: "*The primary phenomenon of originary and authentic temporality is the future,*"[16] or "*originary and authentic existing...*"[17] Yet the two dimensions must be distinct, for if the originary were absolutely dependent on the authentic, it would no longer be originary. Must we say that the

12. Ibid.
13. Ibid., p. 329.
14. Ibid., p. 331.
15. Ibid., p. 328.
16. Ibid., p. 329.
17. Ibid., p. 336.

authentic is a certain way of looking at the originary? Must we admit that the authentic is *derivative* on the originary, in the same way that the inauthentic is derivative on the authentic? There is certainly derivation, but the authentic is an intensification of the originary whereas the inauthentic is a degradation.

It seems that resoluteness no longer has a fundamentally active function of enabling, as with running ahead and the call of conscience, but a function of discovery, of the revelation of temporality such as it is originally given.

To make explicit this function of manifesting, we must ask: *How does resoluteness enter the constitution of authentic temporality? What does it reveal that is already originarily active and constitutive? In what way does the authentic in general also have a foundational function?* The analysis itself invites us to determine this by comparing the authentic and inauthentic modes of the three ekstases. Note that the authentic mode always entails an *ekstatic* character; that is, a *sighting* that departs from the straightforward leveling-down belonging to the time that has been made entirely public, "world-time." Thus an *ekstase (Entrückung)* of existence is at the very heart of the inauthentic present, namely, "making-present." "Even in the most extreme making-present, *Dasein* remains temporal, i.e. awaiting, forgetting. Even in making-present, *Dasein* still understands itself..."[18] Similarly with respect to the inauthentic past: "forgetting is an ekstatic mode of having-been."[19] The authentic mode always implies resolution and decision, that is, a relation to the future.

The inauthentic is constituted as deficiency, lack of future. In particular, it lacks running ahead, the relation to its ownmost possibility and to the structural totality of possible time. Inauthentic temporality is founded on a contraction of the field of the ekstases: it flees death and anxiety, but also debt. The "ordinary" understanding of time that posits an infinite time divided into identical moments stems from a refusal of the finitude of *originary* time, limited and constituted by both death and debt. Authentic and inauthentic are relations to what is originarily ekstatic: one takes it on, the other flees it. We must not lose sight of *this triplicity of levels* through which the analysis subtly avoids any dualism of the authentic and inauthentic. Such a dualism is excluded all the more because existence can never extricate itself *once and for all* from

---

18. Ibid., p. 348.
19. Ibid., p. 339.

the inauthentic mode belonging to the "at first and for the most part" (*zunächst und zumeist*); that is, to an unsurpassable and primordial—though not originary—facticity.

The Originary Future as Distinct from Its Two Modes

Let us begin with the ekstase of the future. How is the authentic future to be distinguished from the inauthentic future? And, to begin with, what is the phenomenal basis for the distinction between the originary future itself and the authentic future? Inasmuch as *Dasein* is a projection of that in view of which it exists (understanding always has a projective character), and a projection of itself in general, the future is originarily inscribed in *Dasein*'s existential structure, and not through resoluteness. Projection, as Section 31 already explained, does not issue from a thematically conceived "plan," but belongs to possibility as a "mode of being" (*Seinsart*) of *Dasein*. *Dasein*'s disclosedness is a disclosure-in-projection. It throws itself into its possibilities, whether or not it has attained the certainty of its ownmost possibility. "Projecting oneself upon the 'for the sake of oneself', as grounded in the future, is an essential characteristic of *existentiality. Its primary meaning is the future.*"[20] *All* the existentials, not merely understanding but also disposition (*Befindlichkeit*), for example, draw their meaning from the originary future. They flow from the future, even if they are not animated by any authentic decision. Resoluteness merely allows the future to *wholly* and simultaneously penetrate the projection itself, the present, and the past—with the intensity of the ultimate and distinguished possibility—thus giving birth to the *instant* (in which *Dasein* grasps the totality of its potentiality for being), and to *repetition*, in which *Dasein* turns back towards those possibilities it has already chosen so as to reactualize them. A *passion* for the future traverses *Dasein*, thrown *volens nolens* into its possibilities, a passion that resoluteness can only take up again and turn into pure activity, via the hierarchization of possibilities with respect to one's ownmost possibilities.

The future to come (*Zu-kunft*) is the originary "coming" (*Kunft*) to oneself by which we first arrive at our being and then possibly at our most singular potentiality for being. This future that has been actively taken up is already outlined in the temporal structure of Care:

20. Ibid., p. 327.

"being-ahead-of-oneself-already-alongside...." Resoluteness manifests the *whole* structure of Care, but does not make Care originarily possible. Originary temporality is undoubtedly antecedent to resoluteness: it itself makes the latter possible. "The 'before' and the 'ahead of' indicate the future which first makes it possible in general [*überhaupt*] for *Dasein* to be in such a way as to be concerned *about* its potentiality for being."[21] It is first of all necessary for *Dasein* to exist in such a way that it can come to itself, that it can "sustain [*aushalten*] possibility as possibility"[22] and relate it back to itself, in order for resoluteness to be able to affirm itself as the totality of existence.

When Heidegger writes: "Future makes ontologically possible an entity that is such that it can exist by way of understanding in its potentiality for being,"[23] or again, "*Dasein* is factically constantly ahead of itself, but non-constantly running ahead,"[24] he is describing the future as a possibility *prior* to authenticity. Running ahead and resoluteness endow *Dasein* authentically with future. But "factically" *Dasein* always already comes to itself. Existence itself, as possible, as "thrown projection," is therefore the originary phenomenon of the future.

The originary future, signifying that *Dasein* "is only possible as futural [*nur möglich als zukünftiges*],"[25] is *neutral* with respect to the authentic and inauthentic. This conclusion of the analysis is not only of methodological significance. The primacy of the originary future reveals the limit of freedom within freedom itself, a limit more profound than the facticity of being in a situation. We are dealing with a true turning in the analysis, one that signifies that *Dasein* is delivered over to time as to an ultimately anonymous power and is not, whatever it does, master and possessor of its own time.

This turning is barely highlighted, insofar as the analysis puts more emphasis on what resoluteness brings to *Dasein* and how it is necessary for it to conquer its increasingly straightforward dispersion into secondary and contingent intentions. The analysis thereby tends to forget the relativity and original dependency of the authentic future. The movement of self-possession and the will to

---

21. Ibid.
22. Ibid., p. 325.
23. Ibid., p. 336.
24. Ibid., p. 337.
25. Ibid., p. 325.

self-transparency sometimes lead it into giving the impression that resoluteness achieves absolute, incessant self-determination. For example, it is said that being-towards-death not only frees *Dasein* "from the contingencies of distraction" (*Unterhaltenwerden*), but allows it to "take *power* over existence" (*der Existenz mächtig zu werden*) "and to fundamentally disperse all fugitive self-conceal-ment." The highlighted term *mächtig* recalls the *Wille zur Macht*. Is it possible for *Dasein*, because it is resolute, to be free of all illusion (*illusionslos*, the text states) and sheltered from the phenomenon of covering over, yet to inhere within every manifestation of the true? Furthermore, it is stated that resoluteness "*gives itself* every facti-cal situation,"[26] thus absolutely overshadows facticity. Because authentic existence has "retrieved" (*eingeholt*) the possibility of death, it "can no longer be surpassed by anything" (*kann durch nichts mehr überholt werden*).[27] This giving oneself the situation, as the unlimited independence of existence, seems to lose sight of fini-tude and of the fact that *Dasein*, because it does not give itself orig-inary temporality, is somehow always preceded, that is, surpassed, by it. The nonresolute future brings into relief what resoluteness achieves, namely, a radical concern for oneself as one's own poten-tiality for being. This nonresolute future is not so much limited (no limit is as radical as being-towards-death) as *partial*, and above all *passively* expected. Its ekstatic mode (there are inauthentic ekstases) is an "awaiting," or better an "attentiveness" (*Gewärti-gen*). In "attentiveness" *Dasein attends to* the various matters of its everyday concern insofar as they are practicable, urgent, or oppor-tune. It forgets itself in favor of rules of action. "*Dasein* under-stands itself out of its potentiality for being, which is determined by success or failure, by the opportuneness or inopportuneness of its dealings with things....It is things, i.e. our dealings with them, as it were, which project our potentiality for being, and not primarily *Dasein* itself from out of its ownmost self..."[28] Thus "*Dasein* does not come primordially towards itself,"[29] but through the mediation of the things it is concerned with. It attends to what it can master and to what escapes it or resists it. It thereby turns away from itself in identifying itself with what it does. Our ordinary expectation is a derivative mode of "attentiveness." We can expect something or

26. Ibid., p. 307.
27. Ibid.
28. GA 24, p. 410.
29. SZ, p. 337.

someone only out of a horizon of "attentiveness"; that is, only if we are held out towards the possibility of something or someone arriving. In this expecting, we have completely forgotten that it is our coming to ourselves that makes possible the arrival of something. Does this mean that every partial expectation is doomed to inauthenticity? No, for if there is inauthenticity, it has to do not with the fact that the outcome of this or that expectation may possibly teach us nothing about our own potentiality for being, but with the fact that we comport ourselves as though the object of expectation had become what is essentially possible for us, as though it were to decide our very being.

Originary Present, "Instant" and Inauthentic Making-Present

The relativization of authentic—i.e. resolute—temporality with respect to originary time becomes more detailed shortly after *Being and Time* with the notion of *Praesens* or *praesentia* as "the horizonal schema of the ekstase of making-present,"[30] which is developed in the 1927 course, *The Basic Problems of Phenomenology*. The concept of "horizonal schema" had been introduced in Section 69(c) of the *Hauptwerk*, within the general framework of the question of the mode of temporalization pertaining to world as primarily constituted by a context of practical "ends" or correlative equipmental activities. The use and handling of tools has its own temporality whose mode belongs to inauthenticity. The handling of tools effectively requires that one forget one's own self. It presupposes an understanding that attends to the work to be carried out in accordance with the standards required; it presupposes a "making-present" of the tool and a "retention" of its goal. It is already strange in this context that the making-present which manipulates the tool should thereby inevitably be inauthentic, for, as Heidegger notes, we say that someone is "authentically" involved in his or her task.[31] The making-present of a tool ought to be neutral: it will become so by virtue of the schema of *praesens* in the 1927 course.

In *Being and Time*, indeed, making-present (*Gegenwärtigen*) is an *inauthentic* manner of making something present only by con-

---

30. GA 24, p. 431.
31. SZ, p. 354.

trast with an *authentic* present, which is called the *instant* (*Augenblick*[32]). Why is making-present inauthentic? Because it is deprived of any view of *Dasein*'s own future, closed in within the present. Making-present means wanting something to be merely present, incessantly, without future or past. Making-present certainly results from an act of formal unification of time around something, but it is a passive unity, entailing a cutting-off of time into a sucession of equal moments. The instant, on the contrary, entails the most profound unifying of *Dasein* itself, which initially always already finds itself dispersed. The instant is to be taken "in the active sense";[33] it is *stretched out* towards the past and the extreme future that it embraces in a "blink." It is *"held* in resoluteness,"[34] *held* in respect of future and past. The term *held* (*gehalten*) is repeated three times. It is a *held* ekstase, like a (musical) pause. In the instant the whole of temporality is collected and gathered together. The instant is the most ekstatic ekstase because it makes present resoluteness itself. It is the shortest time in which being-in-the-world perceives its situation "in a flash," "holds its world in view."[35] The instant is the sole and unique point, one that Heidegger links to the *kairos* referred to by Aristotle in Book VI of the *Nicomachean Ethics*. It is the point where originary temporality and authentic temporality coincide. "The instant is a primordial phenomenon of originary temporality, whereas the 'now' is merely a phenomenon of derivative time."[36]

As we have shown, resoluteness could not be both originary and authentic; it is not the full ekstase of the future. The instant, on the contrary, is the ekstatic point-source from which temporality as a whole springs: complete, undivided, enveloped in an atom, invisible to the commonplace of day, and as though eternally recommenced. "The instant is not the fleeting 'now', but the collision between future and past,"[37] writes Heidegger on the subject of the Eternal Return. The most difficult thing to understand in this doctrine, he adds, is that "eternity *is* in the instant." Yet how could it be thought that such an instantaneous source could spring from an effort, a tension of the will? Are we able to will or decide what or

---

32. Translator's note: Literally, the "look," "flash," or "blink" of an eye.
33. Ibid., p. 338.
34. Ibid.
35. GA 24, p. 408.
36. Ibid., p. 409.
37. NI, p. 312; tr., NI, vol. Two, p. 57.

when the instant must be? Is not the instant an instance that in the first place *holds itself* (*in-stans*) in itself as the heart and reserve of time? Those instants in which the entire situation of a *Dasein* is unveiled are rare. They cannot constitute a sequence in the way that there is a sequence of 'nows'. If it is true that the instant is the making-present pertaining to resoluteness, is the latter capable of making instants present at will? Heidegger does not say so, and such a thing seems rather improbable. We thus rediscover a spontaneity of the instant and originary time. The instant always emerges as a surprising novelty. The veil is torn. The integral character of time is revealed in a tiny fraction of time, only to withdraw.

The concept of the horizonal temporality of world decisively separates the originary from the proper, the two tending to merge in the instant. "Temporality as ekstatic unity has something like a horizon," *Being and Time* tells us.[38] Let us note in passing that the "ekstatic unity," or unity of the three ekstases, *is not and absolutely could not be* derived from any particular mode, authentic or not. It is radically originary. Each of the three ekstases has a different horizon. The schema of each horizon is somehow the direction taken by the ekstatic escape. In Section 69(c) Heidegger defines in turn the schema of the future, *Dasein*'s "for-the-sake-of-itself"; the schema of having-been, the "before-which" of thrownness; and the schema of the present, the "in order to." The ekstatic unity of the schemata makes possible the horizon of temporality, not only that of *Dasein*, but also that of *world*. The transcendence of world, in which intra-worldly entities appear, is not an ekstatic phenomenon but a horizonal one. Our dealings with intraworldly entities do not in fact depend only on *Dasein*, but essentially on the schema of the present, to which all making-present is subordinate.

In *The Basic Problems of Phenomenology* Heidegger therefore calls the horizonal schema of the ekstase of making-present *praesens*. Why, if it is true that temporality always temporalizes in and through the *unity* of the *three* ekstases, should one then grant a privilege to *presence* as horizon and originary schema? And what, in the first place, does the concept of schema add to the concept of ekstase? Heidegger attempts to show that the understanding and manipulation of a tool are not only made possible on the side of *Dasein* by the ekstatic unity of temporality, but somehow made possible "objectively" before *Dasein* via a horizon of presence that is *deposited in the world* or emerges on the side of world. On the one

---

38. SZ, p. 365.

hand, indeed, understanding the being of equipmental entities and of an instrumental context presupposes an act of making-present that consists of recalling the function of the tool and at the same time anticipating its purpose; that is, it presupposes the unity of a threefold ekstase on the side of *Dasein*. On the other hand, however, the present of this act of making-present points back to a horizon of presence within which an equipmental entity can offer itself in general to the act of making-present. The present of this equipmental making-present is neither the objectified and fallen present (the simple 'now'), nor the authentic present (the *instant*). This neutral horizon of presence is not explicitly posited by the act of making-present the tool; on the contrary, such an act presupposes it as its correlate and as the leeway of the "in order to." *Praesens* is a *schema*; that is, a permanent, nonsensible, and nonintelligible horizon of world. It also escapes the dualism of the authentic and inauthentic. It is originary, without ever having been authentic. Unlike the 'now' or the very act of manipulating the tool, it is not a moment unfolding in a derivative time. The tool has been at our disposal, it is so now, it will be again. But the horizon or the schema of equipmentality that makes this type of understanding possible is not susceptible to sliding into the past or emerging solely in the future. The schema is that towards which temporality first advances or is ekstatic when it goes outside itself, beyond itself. *Praesens* is thus just as originary as the act of making-present. Is not what Heidegger calls *Temporalität* the originary schematization of *Zeitlichkeit*? In Husserlian terms, one could say that *praesens* is the fact that active, preoccupied temporality points or aims *into the void*, a form that awaits various determinate contents.

The notion of equipmental presence brings to light a quasi-"objective" aspect of temporality that is distinct from the "resolute self-projection" of *Dasein*: it is the being of the intraworldly entity that, whether at our disposal or not, itself presents itself as something possible, practicable or impracticable. The 'not' plays an essential role in the phenomenological demonstration of the permanence of *praesens*. Whenever something usable or manipulable fails us or breaks down, when an instrument slips out of our grip or quite simply refuses to function, this failing is not 'nothing', nor an absence of the horizon of equipmentality, but a *horizon of modified presence*: *Praesens*, says Heidegger, is affected by a particular "modification." In the relative or total absence of an instrument, the modified *praesens* is maintained. Neutral, indifferent to one's own *Dasein* and its projections, the schema of the present at our disposal could be neither interrupted nor begun. This feature, which was judged inauthentic in *Being and Time*, here becomes originary. Heidegger lends no pejorative character to this stable present. Yet does it not remind us of the permanent presence belonging to metaphysics, prefiguring the presence of "standing reserve" (*Bestand*) constituted by the will to will in the "Enframing" of Technology?

Why this privilege of the present? If we compare the understanding of the being of intraworldly entities from out of the horizonal schema of *praesens* with the understanding in *Being and Time*, we can observe a shift of the future in the direction of the present. In *Being and Time*, understanding is determined primarily from out of the future. As authentic, it becomes that resoluteness which is capable of running ahead of death as the limit of its potentiality for being. As inauthentic, it is defined as straightforward awaiting or rather as attentiveness (*Gewärtigen*) through which *Dasein* understands itself in terms of its practical preoccupations. "Inauthentic understanding projects itself upon that with which one can concern oneself, upon what is feasible, urgent or indispensable in our everyday business."[39] Heidegger emphasizes that making-present is a modification of understanding in the sense of a greater dispersion (*Zerstreuung*) and incapacity to remain where one is (*Unverweilen*). The present that is subjected in a restricted and factical manner to the exigencies of praxis is even more "falling" than inauthentic understanding. In *Being and Time* the opposition between originary and derivative passes through the opposition between future and present: "the future [*Zukunft*: literally, 'coming to oneself'] is the primary phenomenon of originary and authentic temporality."[40]

Thus, from the summer of 1927 onward, the importance of the distinction between authentic and inauthentic, originary and derivative, becomes attenuated; *Dasein* moves towards *neutrality*.[41] Yet Heidegger maintains the notion of ordinary time as a forgetting of essential finitude. Authentic time, however, founded on the primacy of the

---

39. Ibid., p. 337.
40. Ibid., p. 329.
41. Cf. the 1928 course, *The Metaphysical Foundations of Logic* (GA 26, pp. 171–172), dealing with the "neutrality" of *Dasein* also in respect of traditional determinations of man such as individuality, the carnal body (*Leib*), and sexuality. Cf. J. Derrida, "*Geschlecht*: différence sexuelle, différence ontologique," in *Psychè* (Galilee, 1987); translated as "*Geschlecht*: sexual difference, ontological difference," *Research in Phenomenology* 13 (1983).

future, is no longer considered a "self-projection." The temporality of world comes to be detached from the temporality that is mine.

If we consider that the Turning of the 1930s is the displacement of the origin of the temporality of *Dasein* towards a temporality of being, must we not discern in the phenomenology of *praesens* the first beginnings of such displacement?

Originary Past (Birth and Thrownness), Repetition and Forgetting

The analysis of the ekstatic past does not seem to corroborate this evolution towards a primacy of a neutral originary. It is marked by a climate in which resoluteness dominates, a climate of anxiety.

Only authentic and resolute temporality delivers (*überliefert*) *Dasein* to its "fate" and makes *repetition* possible, that is, the project of explicitly taking over and renewing possibilities of existence that have already been chosen in the past. "Authentic repetition of a possibility of past existence—*Dasein* choosing its hero—is founded existentially in resoluteness as running ahead; for in the latter the choice is first made which liberates *Dasein* for the ensuing struggle and faithfulness to what can be repeated."[42] The past that can be repeated, made possible anew, is decisively detached from what is simply and factually past (*Vergangenes*) and gradually enters a totality of *Dasein*'s fate. But what precisely is meant by fate in this context? *Fate* (*Schicksal*) is defined as "the originary happening of *Dasein*" (*das ursprüngliche Geschehen des Daseins*) that becomes unified because it is taken up into resoluteness. Fate is the affirmative taking up of the originary possibilities of one's own *Dasein*, the resolute repetition of oneself, the constant future of a past. Having a fate means explicitly wanting what has originarily come to oneself. Does the authentic then take precedence over the originary? Before answering this question, let us note that the individual *Schicksal* is distinguished from *Geschick*, the shared destiny or "codestiny" that is the happening of being-with, the fate of the community or people.[43] We should also note that this term *Geschick*, which will come to designate the destiny of being as the origin of History, is initially used with a particular, concrete connotation. There will be only one History of Being, whereas there may be as many destinies as there

42. SZ, p. 385.
43. Ibid., p. 384.

are individuals and peoples, although destiny in the active sense is merely the authentic *form* of our relation to the past. Someone who is not resolute, we are told, has no destiny.

Yet is destiny pure activity? It would be paradoxical for Heidegger to completely reverse the traditional meaning of the term, which contains the idea of a submission or dependency in respect of a "fate" despite our will, the idea of a sequential cohesion of existence that imposes itself or is always already made for us whether we want it or not.

What lies at the basis of destiny is the *originary past* of *thrownness* (*Geworfenheit*), the radical possibility of *facticity*. One must distinguish here—though this distinction is not always made clear in the texts—between facticity as the inauthentic understanding of oneself as a thing or subsisting entity and facticity as the authentic yet obscure understanding of the intimate link between *Dasein* and subsisting entities, the fact that in some way *Dasein is itself both!* *Geworfenheit* in effect constitutes the opaque and unexplorable basis and fund of destiny. No project of repetition, even if it were to take it on entirely, can ever definitively illuminate it. For *being* thrown concerns the obscure and original connection between the ekstatic essence of *Dasein* and the being of those entities unlike *Dasein*. Being-in-the-world that is comprehensively grasped and illuminated by the "meaningful character" of world *is also* a *factual entity*, states Heidegger; namely, *die Tatsächlichkeit des Faktums Dasein*, a strange redoubling of the term "the factuality of the *factum Dasein*"![44] "The concept of facticity entails the being-in-the-world of an 'intraworldly' entity such that this entity can understand itself as bound up in its 'destiny' with the being of those entities it encounters within its own world."[45] The terms used are particularly forceful: we are using "bound up with" to translate *verhaftet mit*, where the word *verhaften* means *to keep prisoner, detain.* The use of *Geschick* indicates the possibility of a destiny *common* to *Dasein* and the being of intraworldly entities. The existential analytic remains silent about this common destiny, for how is one to describe this ambiguous principle that connects and *unites* existence to a "being" quite other? How do things stand concerning this *other being* to which we are so closely connected that we may be captive to it? The problem is much like that of the union of soul and body in Descartes: easier to experience than to conceive. Would Hei-

---

44. Ibid., p. 56.
45. Ibid.

degger be Cartesian in the sense that he is afraid of confusing different kinds of being? This *other being* is of course the being of natural entities. Nature, says Heidegger in *The Basic Problems of Phenomenology*, could *be* even if there were no world. In other words, "intraworldliness does not belong to the being of nature." "Nature can be even if no *Dasein* exists."[46] Heidegger remains Kantian on this point: all we know of nature is what we see of it, or can say about it or do with it *in terms of the light of world*. Its being in itself will always escape us. Our approaching nature or life is dependent on a *privative* view with respect to world. Thus the animal will be characterized as *weltarm*, "poor in world."

This *other being*, however, somehow retains part of our secret. We are the *detainees* of nature. Are we not hanging, quite alert, onto the back of a tiger? Heidegger refrains from saying so, and undoubtedly from thinking so too!

Our being detained by a being other than ours is coupled with another worrying phenomenon: the *Wurf*, the throw or cast. Every *Entwurf* is a response to a *Wurf*, whereby *Geworfenheit* is obscurely produced. What power "throws" *Dasein* in this way? Later, Heidegger will say that being itself throws us into its own light. Yet would this not rid us of all facticity? "To the facticity of *Dasein* there belongs the fact that *Dasein, as long* as it is, remains in this throw [*Wurf*]. *Dasein* exists factically."[47] But what is it to "exist factically"? It means taking into one's projection the *anteriority* of an originary throw, of an originary past that remains absolutely *closed off* from us in respect of its source. "Thrownness, which *Dasein* can be *authentically brought before*, so as to understand itself authentically in it, nonetheless remains closed off [*verschlossen*] from it in respect of its ontic 'whence' and 'how'."[48] Facticity entails *not knowing* our most ancient provenance. Is it not surprising that such ignorance affects even the *ontic* domain? The science of the human phylogenetic descendency is apparently of no interest as regards *Dasein*! Perhaps because such study would only hide "the ekstatic character of the *abandonment* [*Überlassenheit*] of existence to the nothingness of its ground,"[49] that is, hide the fact that *Dasein* must ground things without having been able to ground itself! Yet is this not at least to recognize that *Dasein* is in some way "grounded" on

---

46. GA 24, p. 241.
47. SZ, p. 179.
48. Ibid., p. 348.
49. Ibid.

an impenetrable facticity? Voluntarily blind as to its provenance, therefore, thrownness is interpreted as *violent abandonment to the world.* "*Dasein* is suddenly torn [*mitgerissen*] into thrownness, in other words, as thrown into the world it loses itself in the world in being factically directed towards what it is concerned with."⁵⁰ The throw, originarily extraworldly, becomes the purely intraworldly fact of devoting oneself merely to the inauthenticity of one's concerns, and to the 'One' in general. The very movement of the *Wurf* is identified with the "turbulence" (*Wirbel*) of inauthenticity. "It belongs to its facticity that *Dasein*, *as long as* it is what it is, remains in this throw and is dragged by this turbulence into the inauthenticity of the 'One'."⁵¹ Yet *Dasein* is certainly not thrown into the world by the 'One'! The fact that the 'One' can capture and profit from the movement of this throw gives a pseudo-transparency to this movement. It would indeed be tempting to then identify the rupture with the 'One' with a surpassing of thrownness, yet the latter is wholly unsurpassable.

This temptation to wholly subsume facticity within existence *by reducing its enigma to a comprehensible and controllable meaning* appears in those rare passages of *Being and Time* where *birth* is at issue. Is not birth our originary past? Does not birth *link us back* to a nature within us older than our intraworldly possibilities? Curiously, birth is not traced back to indebtedness. Yet if there is a debt we can never pay off, nor even measure, it is surely that debt we contracted in being born. As concretion of the entire natural past that we bear within us, birth is more opaque than death for the analytic of *Dasein*. How can it be taken up into a projection? Is it likely to shelter within it a possibility that, like being-towards-death, could itself be made possible by resoluteness?

"Understood existentially, birth is never something past in the sense of something no longer present at hand....Factical *Dasein* exists in being born, and in being born it is also already dying in the sense of being-towards-death....In the unity of thrownness and being-towards-death—whether fleeing or running ahead—birth and death 'are linked' in the manner of *Dasein*. As Care, *Dasein is* the 'between'."⁵² Birth here receives the status of a possibility that is closely implicated *within* that of being-towards-death! Existence includes birth as "being towards the commencement" (*Sein zum*

---

50. Ibid.
51. Ibid., p. 179.
52. Ibid., p. 374.

Anfang) by removing its natural substance and effacing the obscure side of the commencement. The two extremes definitively clash in terms of their primacy: the possibility of being-there and that of no longer being-there. Heidegger writes: "Death is only *one* end of *Dasein*. The other 'end' is its commencement, its birth."[53] Both birth and death shelter finitude, limit. Yet Heidegger thereby effaces the specificity of the limit of birth. For birth does not simply have one face, turned towards us. The other side of birth is *its anterior face*, which thrusts us in the direction of our parents, heredity (what biology understands by the concept of "genetic program"), both "descending" in the direction of the whole line of living beings and what we maintain as generically human, and "ascending" within us in the form of our gifts, our "natural" talents, our "innate" dispositions (which the analytic *disregards* in favor of possibilities provided by the world). By making birth into a possibility of being thrown *into the world*, the analytic forgets that birth is in no way a commencement *ex nihilo*. It forgets *Dasein*'s enrootedness in life. The prenatal, which is included in the natal and not limited to gestation, is our entire life starting from its primitive forms, the life that continues to live in us. This other side of birth, its dark face, symmetrical with the beyond and yet less closed than the latter, this vital primitivity in us—this is all excluded by the analytic, not even noticed by it. It disregards it.

What interests the analytic is that resoluteness reaches out so as to recover the whole "stretching" (*Erstreckung*) of the time "between" birth and death. This reaching out and *stretching* of the self that reaches out to meet its extreme possibilities is the very definition of its "future," of its historiality (*Geschehen*).[54] *Dasein* must endeavor to conquer the true span of existence and its "stretched constancy" by the "inclusion" of birth as well as death. "The resoluteness of the self against the inconstancy of dispersion is in itself the *stretched constancy* [*erstreckte Ständigkeit*] in which *Dasein* as fate keeps birth and death and their 'between' 'included' in its existence..."[55] Note in passing that the "stretched" or "ex-tended" [*é-tendue*] constancy is nothing other than *repetition*, which indicates that the latter is not at all a straightforward ekstase of the past, but rather the authentic unity of the three ekstases. "Possibility only returns if existence is *instantaneously*

---

53. Ibid., p. 373.
54. Cf. Ibid., p. 375.
55. Ibid, pp. 390f.

open for it in the manner of fate and in resolute repetition."[56] Repetition includes the possibility of birth and combines it with that
of death *in the instant*. "Birth" (the quotation marks indicate that
it is something possible) "*is taken up into existence* in returning
from the unsurpassable possibility of death."[57]

What does resoluteness effectively "include"? Possibilities. Yet
the double face of birth, the face that is abyssally open to life, is no
more susceptible to being included or taken up than the double face
of death. Can *Dasein* include its own childhood, that palpable trace
of its birth? The analytic neither gives us the means for doing so
nor shows us the method. The analytic is concerned only with a
Dasein in its prime, which, deciding to give itself a vocation,
detaches itself from, and yet by way of, the possibilities of the whole
culture of its world, a *Dasein* that forgets and annuls its vital roots
and the opacity of its destiny, while claiming to dominate them.
Resoluteness is proper to man in his maturity, in "the middle of
life's way," man who is ready to act, rather than to ponder the
enigma of being. A child *Dasein* or an aged *Dasein* would not find
the strength to draw from their limits (weakness, dependency,
fragility) that self-enabling which *Dasein* draws from the extreme
weakness of being born and being able to die.

Does not *repetition* teach a *wisdom* that would consist in each
Dasein wanting to become what it already is, wanting to calmly
reiterate the possibilities it has already made its own? To say this
would undoubtedly be to minimize the role of anxiety, through
which resoluteness is acquired anew, put back into question by the
'already there' that it never has behind it as a resolute past. It
would also be to lose sight of *forgetting* as a possibility of "fleeing in
the face of one's ownmost having-been."[58]

During the period of *Being and Time*, forgetting is mainly and
seemingly restrictively defined as "inauthentic" past; that is, as a
refusal of having-been. But we can refuse the past only because the
past as having-been refuses itself in the first place and always
already does so, whatever our abandonment of resoluteness. Forgetting is *originary* in the first place, before being able to be inauthentic. "What we are...what we have been, somehow lies behind
us, *forgotten*."[59] It lies there and is not effaced, for forgetting must

---

56. Ibid., pp. 391–392 (emphasis added).
57. Ibid., p. 391.
58. GA 24, p. 411.
59. Ibid.

not be understood according to the ordinary concept of the past; whereas the bygone past is supposed to have simply disappeared, having-been remains, albeit forgotten, and forgotten in respect of its very forgottenness. For what is proper to forgetting is that it forgets itself. That which has been and is to come cannot disappear, even as forgotten. "It is only on the basis of this *originary forgetting*,"[60] which must be understood as a *positive* ecstatic mode,[61] that the ekstase of inauthentic having-been, which closes itself off from its own having-been, is possible, as well as retention or a memory. "Remembering is only possible on the basis of forgetting."[62] All inauthenticity or loss of self in the 'One' may be considered as a forgetting, essentially a forgetting or fleeing in the face of death. Resolute existence means to be forgetful as little as possible; it is that existence that "holds" *its* time in forgetting neither birth nor death nor those possibilities it has decisively appropriated.

Anxiety and Resolute Existence

Yet why must such an existence continue to be anxious, to be still "ready for anxiety"? Why is it anxiety alone that "brings us before repeatability"?[63] Why does "anxiety alone bring us into the mood for possible decision"?[64] Anxiety is certainly the source of authenticity, as it brings *Dasein* before its ownmost possibility. Anxiety is originarily founded in having-been, for all attunement relates to the already established "situation" of *Dasein*. The most elementary having-been is thrownness. Anxiety "brings us back to the pure 'that' of one's ownmost, individuated thrownness."[65] *Dasein* can no longer evade or elude its thrownness through forgetting nor form a theoretical representation of it. Existence is "naked," doomed to the worrying uncanniness of being "thrown-there," torn from every projection or concern founded within the world, whose insignificance bursts forth. Heidegger attributes a lucidity to anxiety, a capacity for superior revelation, a liberating power. In the "clear night" of anxiety the *possibility* of an instantaneous decision is unveiled, the

---

60. Emphasis added.
61. SZ, p. 339.
62. GA 24, p. 412.
63. SZ, p. 343.
64. Ibid., p. 344.
65. Ibid., p. 343.

possibility of a radical repetition that, in order to be authentic, must return to the most elementary conditions of thrownness. Whereas fear arises from an entity in the world, anxiety arises from being-in-the-world as such. However, the text points out, "properly speaking, anxiety can only arise in a resolute *Dasein*....Whoever is resolute precisely understands the possibility of anxiety as *that Stimmung* which neither inhibits nor confuses him."[66] There is somehow a kind of circle here, or else a lofty election by anxiety that leads to the certainty of resoluteness whoever has already arrived there. From this perspective, only those whom anxiety renders free and sure of themselves are anxious.

Must one not distinguish from authentic anxiety an inauthentic anxiety, perhaps a simple anxiousness, though perhaps more profound? Neither in *Being and Time*, nor indeed in the *Zollikon Seminars* forty years later (1959–1969),[67] does Heidegger compare existential categories with psychoanalytic concepts. Being-towards-death seems to be the opposite of the "death drive," repetition the opposite of the "neurotic repetition compulsion." As with anxiety, these are entirely positive categories whose negative counterpart merely has to do with forgetting and fleeing into the 'One'. Yet why might there not be an "inauthentic" anxiety, different from fear, that would lead to a "negative" repetition, anxious yet not projecting? Without even going as far as the anxious neurotic, on which side—from the point of view of *Being and Time*—should we align phenomena such as compulsive repetition, obsessive memories, melancholic and anxious repetition of the past by imagination alone, stereotyped yet conscious acts, nonliberating repetition of past possibilities, which may be mixed with a nonproductive, merely inhibitive anxiety? Heidegger would undoubtedly reply that these seemingly nonforgetful phenomena nevertheless forget one's ownmost possibility, that they lose themselves in the maze of a past or a present reified by the incapacity radically to run ahead to the future. The truest anxiety, because it opens *Dasein* most extensively to its potentiality for being, would necessarily be fecund.

This does not prevent this optimistic, active interpretation of anxiety being marked by a hiatus or an internal antinomy. On the one hand, anxiety in fact removes any signification or significability from world in its totality. Its "practical" signification (the *Um-zu*, the 'in order to' constitutive of the tool) becomes zero and is

---

66. Ibid., p. 344.
67. *Zollikoner Seminare* (Frankfurt: Klostermann, 1987).

deprived of any importance. "The 'world' has nothing more to offer..."[68] except the 'nothing' of its unused tools or its unmobilized means. That in the face of which anxiety is anxious, being-in-the-world as such, itself remains indeterminate, ungraspable; it has become a "nothing and nowhere"[69] in which even the elementary meanings of "here" and "there" dissolve. Entities as a whole slip away, slide into an abyss of nonmeaning, become radically *uncanny*. In addition, "anxiety strikes us silent....All 'is'-saying falls silent in its presence."[70] How in this void could *Dasein*, in the very moment when this "nihilation" (*Nichten*) reigns, rediscover precisely its *ownmost* potentiality for being, its freedom? Isolated, pure *Dasein*, thrown into its "There," is thrown back, Heidegger tells us, on its potentiality for being in the authentic world; it becomes "*free for* the freedom to chose itself and to grasp itself."[71] It can no longer understand itself in terms of world or the 'One', in terms of anonymous and established interpretations stemming from "idle talk" and received ideas. Yet precisely if it no longer understands anything in the world, how can it understand itself as being-in-the-world? Does not the melting away of significations and of the identity of world entail the melting away of one's own identity? Anxiety, says Heidegger, does not deliver *Dasein* over to the solitude of an "existential solipsism," precisely because it now finds itself before the *world as world*, and at the same time before itself *as* pure being-in-the-world. Yet if the world is at that moment devoid of meaning, how can the meaning of world *as* world, of world *as such* survive the shipwreck of all significations? The pure possibility of being-in-the-world, beyond all content, must be unaffected yet *intensified* by anxiety. Anxiety brings being and the 'nothing' into communication with one another. It announces the discovery of being under the veil of the 'nothing'. "The 'nothing' unveils itself as belonging to the being of entities."[72] If anxiety is nothing but the suddenly accentuated meaning of being, then the antinomy between the radical indeterminacy of the 'nothing' on the side of world and the renewal of the pure and proper identity of *Dasein* is resolved, but at the expense of a circularity or that "lofty election" of which we spoke earlier. Anxiety is absolute uncanniness *for the*

68. SZ, p. 187.
69. Ibid., p. 186.
70. *What is Metaphysics?* in Wm, p. 111; tr., BW, p. 103.
71. SZ, p. 188.
72. Wm, p. 119; tr., BW, p. 110.

'One', a return to absolute propriety for one's own *Dasein*. "The falling flight *into* the 'at-home' of publicness is a flight *in the face of* the 'not-at-home'*, i.e. the uncanniness which lies in *Dasein* as thrown being-in-the-world delivered over to itself in its being."[73] In other words, anxiety is the passage from the false familiarity to the true uncanniness of *Dasein* with respect to itself, the return to one's radically disturbing self as radical potentiality for being. The "flight" or loss of self in the 'One' is an *originary* flight in the face of the anxiety of the self. To repeat, anxiety affects only whoever *already* has the "meaning of being" as the potentiality to be authentic. This meaning of being as the source of a prior making-possible—a meaning that itself perhaps already belongs to one's own—is not abolished by anxiety, but intensified. Yet the floating and melting of significations described as omnipresent remains *entirely relative*, limited to the *everyday* familiarity that is shattered, because in *Being and Time* there is no *anxiety in respect of being*—which neither floats, nor melts, nor refuses itself—but only in respect of the possible signification of world, whenever the system of everydayness at our disposal withdraws, vacillates, or when its foundations shake.

"Originary Anxiety," or Anxiety with Respect to Being

Instead of arising in *Dasein* alone as the index of its ownmost potentiality for being, anxiety, from *What is Metaphysics?* (1929) onward, would appear as "an event of being itself," as attestation of that power in man which is more elementary than his ownmost possibility. In that text it is therefore constantly named *originary anxiety* (*ursprüngliche Angst*), and, in the later 1934 *Postscript*, *essential anxiety* (*wesentliche Angst*), that is, *with respect to being*.

From the 1929 lecture onward, anxiety goes more hand in glove with the nothing, via various forms of "nihilative comportment" (*nichtendes Verhalten*) of *Dasein* in general than with what is proper to each particular *Dasein*. It goes more hand in glove with the strange power of negation that man bears within—without his being able to either ground or master it completely—than with "mineness." The nonhuman origin of nihilation (*Nichten*), the powerful trace of thrownness, overrides the assumption of self-enabling via death. This text is marked by all the signs of a reversal, in

---

73. SZ, p. 189.

which the link between anxiety and the self-manifestation of being is substituted for the linking of anxiety with extreme, individual enabling. There is a drift from phenomenology to the thinking of being. Indeed from the moment when "the nihilating of the nothing happens in the being of entities,"[74] the thoughts and acts of negation, as well as the transcendence of *Dasein* beyond entities as a whole, come to be rooted in the force of nihilation and *no longer in the tension of resoluteness*. Originary anxiety reveals merely a making-possible on the part of the nothing as coming from being. It no longer sets us on the path of an authentic self-enabling. The movement towards the intensification of *Dasein*'s "transcendental" faculties is suddenly arrested. "The nothing is the making-possible of the manifestness of entities as such for human *Dasein*."[75] Note the timid reappearance of the *human*: man as rediscovered is more limited and even more stripped than *Dasein*; he has lost all aspiration to an ipseity of his own and is reduced to the quasi-skeletal figure of the one who "holds the place of the nothing."

Originary anxiety appears as the point of focus and point of revelation of all "nihilative" conduct. "*Dasein*'s being permeated by nihilative comportment attests the constant though obscured manifestness of the nothing which anxiety alone originarily unveils."[76] Indeed, anxiety is like the *akme* or plenitude of the self-revelation of the nothing that manifests itself in man via various forms of his thought and his action: "the measured negation of thought," "unyielding antagonism," "stinging rebuke," yet also "the pain of failure," "the severity of prohibition," "bitter privation." Both the activity and passivity of man are here paralyzed by a negativity that does not stem from man and that is more radical than being active or passive. In all such conduct, and in reality in all transcendence, anxiety is there, "slumbering" or kept on edge. For "originary anxiety is for the most part suppressed [*niedergehalten*] in *Dasein*."[77] As a fundamental mood, or even fundamental texture, anxiety is no more the property of someone audacious than it is absent in ordinary or passive activity. It is always underlying. It is no longer specially associated with a crisis or a choice between the authentic and the inauthentic. "It stands—on this side of such oppositions—in a secret alliance with serenity and the gentleness

74. Wm, p. 114; tr., BW, p. 106.
75. Ibid.
76. Ibid., p. 116; tr., BW, p. 108.
77. Ibid.

of creative aspiration."[78] Despite its omnipresence, even as it underlies joy, it cannot become banal, for it is always "on this side," always secret. If it inhabits the act of creating above all, it does so because this act always runs counter to whatever is established, acquired, habitual, or normal. No one can create without encountering the nothing: "the creator ventures into the unsaid and irrupts into the unthought."[79]

Dasein does not originally draw its powers and creations from itself, but from the work of nihilation and from the anxiety that possesses it. Its power to deny therefore does not come from its faculty of judgment; instead, negation is grounded in the 'not' that has its origin in the nihilation of the nothing. Likewise for its freedom. Running ahead allowed *Dasein* to approach its freedom at will and attempt to appropriate for itself the possibility of radical impossibility. Yet it remains in vain in the neighborhood of the nothing, keeping its place open for it, and cannot (unlike the Sartrean conscience that identifies itself with "nihilating") make its ekstatic cohabitation with the nothing into a power *of its own* that it could dispose over as it liked. The nothing strips *Dasein* of the free employment of its transcendental faculties. It prevents it from foreseeing and calculating the irruption of its freedom. Without the nothing, no transcendence, no freedom in the sense of disengaging oneself from entities. Yet man can do nothing about the nothing that alone frees his capacities. He can neither foresee the occasion when it will arise, always unexpectedly, nor can he summon it to render himself free, nor can he decide on the extent of its effects. "We are so finite that we precisely cannot bring ourselves originarily before the nothing through our own decision or will."[80] Finitude is not to be understood as a secure limit, outside of the entity that we are, where we will sometimes happen to encounter the nothing, but is an internal-external movement of abyssal "finitization" (*Verendlichung*). "Finitization digs [*gräbt*] so abyssally in *Dasein* that the most proper and most profound finitude refuses itself to our freedom."[81] This "finitization," on this side of the adopted finitude that characterized authentic *Dasein*, opens a new dimension that is still called *our freedom,* but that is already the freedom of being in us. This dimension corresponds to a melting away of the proper, eroded and undermined by the nothing.

---

78. Ibid., p. 117; tr., BW, p. 108.
79. EM, p. 123; tr., p. 161.
80. Wm, p. 117; tr., BW, p. 108.
81. Ibid.

The possibility of metaphysical questioning as such hangs on this erosion, which is more anguishing than anxiety concerning what is one's own, an erosion in which *Dasein* loses any footing on the secure ground of mineness. "Only because the nothing is manifest in the ground of *Dasein* [*through originary anxiety*] can the entire strangeness of entities come over us."[82] The astonishment that gives rise to the "why?" and to metaphysics itself here appears as derived from originary anxiety in the face of this complete strangeness of entities. Originary anxiety thus seems more constant than the diversity of specifically epochal attunements, such as astonishment itself, which Heidegger would later assign solely to the Greek epoch. Is not the fundamental *Stimmung* here already transhistorial, even before the History of being is worked out? In any case, metaphysical questioning now becomes the "fundamental happening" (*Geschehen*) of *Dasein*. What is essential is no longer the happening of coming *to oneself*, the historiality of the proper. "*Die Metaphysik ist das Grundgeschehen im Dasein. Sie ist das Dasein selbst.*" It is the end of the primacy of resoluteness, the "Turning" before it is spelt out! The question of the being of entities henceforth definitively eclipses the question of authenticity, although what is at issue in metaphysics is still that which is fundamental *in Dasein*, that is, its essence, or as Kant (who is cited) puts it, the "nature of man."

The 1943 *Postscript* underlines and rejects the interpretive error that would separate anxiety from its relation to the nihilation of being by treating it psychologically as one "feeling" among others. Anxiety is termed *essential* (*wesenhaft*) because it comes from being itself, because it manifests being in the verbal sense (*wesen*) in its pure difference from entities. "Being...destines us the nothing in essential anxiety."[83] It is a matter of hearing, via the mood of anxiety, the "address" or "claim" (*Anspruch*) of being that calls man towards it from his fallenness or errancy alongside beings. Anxiety has the role of instantaneously effecting a *separation* (*Abschied*)— so difficult to think—from entities. Being itself "sends" anxiety (should we say it is "willed" by being?) with the *aim* that man may learn to think it after having been claimed by it: "so that man may learn to experience being in the nothing."[84] There is nothing mystical about this "intention" of being. What is disconcerting is the nonanthropocentric, totally depsychologized formulation of the

---

82. Ibid., p. 120; tr., BW, p. 111.
83. Ibid., p. 304.
84. Ibid., p. 305.

very meaning of attunement. Yet why is it necessary to have recourse to anthropomorphic formulas to express the *contrary* of an anthropocentrism? Thus the "voice" (*Stimme*) of being, as the capacity to dispose (*stimmen*) man towards thinking it via anxiety, signifies man's incapacity to transport himself into radical openness. The gift of thought is henceforth called a *favor* (*Gunst*) of being. Does this metaphor not express once more the idea of a "lofty election"? Only the chosen ones receive a favor.

However things may stand in this respect, the appropriate human "response" to this anguishing favor is quite similar to resoluteness, although the response to anxiety as a response to being would henceforth define thought itself and no longer decision. Or rather, Heidegger would refuse the distinction between contemplation and action: "essential thought," he says, "is also an acting."[85] In effect, man must sustain and actively take on essential anxiety, and not only to receive the gift of thought. Thus, the qualities of that thinking which is open to this test will be "being disposed to anxiety" (resoluteness too was *angstbereit*, "ready for anxiety"), courage, "freedom to make the sacrifice" (*Opfer*). *Sacrifice* defined as "the separation from entities" is evidently not some concrete act, but an *act that is thought*. It has a radicality but also an "abstractness" that are worrying, since it is not concerned with this or that category of entities, but with entities as such. "The thinking of being seeks no support among entities"![86] (How is this possible? What meaning can the sacrifice of *all entities* have, given that entities never are without being? Why introduce, by the very word *sacrifice*, a religious connotation?) However things stand, thinking "offers up" (for *Opfer* also means an *offering*) entities to being, even as it takes leave of them. It requires more than courage and *valiance* (*Tapferkeit*) to confront the *terror* and horror in the face of "the abyss of being." The attunement of terror constitutes the anxiety belonging to the epoch of Technology, well after the end of the reign of the great metaphysical principles. Those who experience terror are those rare contemporaries who are capable of understanding that what is dominant today is insensitivity in the face of the abyss (the groundlessness of being) in the form of the "distress of the absence of distress."[87] Yet Heidegger did not explain this here, letting a kind of initiatory, purified, extremely rarefied atmosphere

---

85. Ibid., p. 308.
86. Ibid., p. 366.
87. NII, p. 391; tr., NII, vol. Four, p. 245.

hang over this *Postscript*. Man scarcely has any identity left, unless to be the one who welcomes the coming of being with anxiety and courage. His essence is balanced between marvel and terror. Inhabited by the horror of the abyss, he approaches the "indestructible" (*Unzerstörbaren*), awaits the "inevitable" (*Unabwendbaren*). These mysterious, elliptical terms—which seem to point to a new assuredness, a new foundation—are not elucidated. The thought that is guided by anxiety enters a quasi-mutism in which the dimensions of awaiting and expectation are accentuated.

The 1949 *Introduction*, "The Return to the Ground of Metaphysics," reaffirms the fundamental vocation of anxiety to reveal being, to restore thought despite the dominant forgetfulness of the epoch. Anxiety and terror make manifest not merely the forgetting of being, but the urgency and destitution of the contemporary situation in which man remains "almost abandoned" by being and in which this abandonment is itself veiled. Anxiety also translates the impotence of thought to change anything in the irresistible unfolding of the History of Being: thought "can do nothing other than to anxiously bear this destiny of being, so as to first place thought in the presence of the forgetting of being."[88] A doubt arises as to knowing whether man will again be *capable* of "ontological" anxiety, or whether, on the contrary, anxiety will not be increasingly deflected towards subjectivity alone. It is as though the main difficulty with anxiety were that it still has too much to do with ipseity!

Roughly a decade after *Being and Time*, from 1936 onward, anxiety is identified with thought itself, taken at its source. This is attested by a brief remark from *Holzwege* regarding *true nihilism*. Such nihilism is "anxiety in the face of thought." Yet this anxiety is nothing other than "anxiety in the face of anxiety": *die Angst vor der Angst*.[89] Fleeing from anxiety and fleeing from thought concern the same flight in the face of being.

Likewise, from 1936 on, in *The Origin of the Work of Art*, resoluteness becomes reinterpreted in keeping with its etymological sense as dis-closedness (*Ent-schlossenheit*), openness to the gift of being. "Resoluteness as thought in *Being and Time* is not the decided action [*die decidierte Aktion*] of a subject, but *Dasein* opening itself from its being caught up in entities towards the openness of being."[90] This self-interpretation hardens nuances with the aid of half-truths:

88. Wm, p. 366.
89. Hw, p. 246.
90. Ibid., p. 55.

certainly resoluteness was never "the decided action of a subject," since it was the possibility of being-in-the-world (which is not closed in on itself like a subject) choosing its own ipseity, yet the self-appropriation of *Dasein* was not yet the "ekstatic abandonment of existing man to the unconcealment of being,"[91] that is, transpropriation to being, to which man agrees radically to entrust himself. What we are here translating by "abandonment," *Sich einlassen*, means not so much actively engaging as giving oneself over, leaving oneself to, letting oneself be taken up into the relation of being to man. In *Being and Time* there was no way in which resoluteness could mean being open to the openness of being, that is, to the primacy of the truth or unfolding of being over all human thought, understanding or action. Resoluteness was the very search for the pure form of the self in one's ownmost temporality, just as anxiety was a nonvoluntary running ahead towards the possibility of death.

The hermeneutic violence of this self-interpretation nonetheless remains faithful to a *fundamental truth*: *anxiety* makes being-towards-death possible, which is to say, *temporality itself*, not as resolutely disclosed, but temporality whose remotest horizon discloses itself of its own accord, suddenly and unexpectedly, at certain instants—this temporality projects us in our being. Even while saying "time is mine," Heidegger in 1924 was asking: "Am I time?" and he already affirmed: "Time is temporal."[92] The priority or self-temporalization of time was not yet thematized, but already implicit, assumed, or intimated.

---

91. Ibid.
92. BZ, pp. 26–27; tr., pp. 21–22.

PART TWO

The Poverty of *Homo humanus,*
or Man Without Faculties

From the analytic of *Dasein* to his final meditations on "mortals" Heidegger assigns a singularly ambitious and disconcerting task to thought: *to change the essence of man*[1] and to this end understand him *otherwise* than the entire tradition hitherto. "For someone who has grasped the history of man as the history of the *essence* of man, the question of who man is can only signify the necessity of removing man, by way of questioning, from his hitherto metaphysical realm of abode, of directing him by way of questioning *towards another essence,* and of thereby overcoming this question itself."[2] Yet why such a project? Why must man be determined otherwise than as an amalgam of soul and body, or as that "living entity endowed with language," *zoon logon echon,* which for centuries has been called the *rational animal* and which Technology has recently transformed into its last avatar, "the living entity that calculates" or "works," "the beast of labor"?[3] These representations, says Heidegger, are not false, but they have lost sight of the essential trait of man. Schematically, the whole Heideggerian trial of metaphysical "humanism" boils down to two charges: substantialism and anthropocentrism. Man is not in the first instance an animated,

---

1. Returning to the ground of metaphysics ought to permit a "mutation [*Wandel*] in the essence of man" (Wm, p. 363).
2. GA 65, p. 491.
3. VA, pp. 68–69.

corporeal substance, nor the unity of two substances, but *ek-sis-tence*, which is to say: openness, transcendence, an ek-static relation to being. Such is his essential trait. Man does not bear his properties and powers of his own accord; he does not give himself being, nor his relation to being. He is not the center of entities; he maintains himself "in the midst of entities" without being their *middle*; far from possessing the secret of his own essence, he perhaps never accedes to it.

Nietzsche had diagnosed a disgust and prophesied a mutation: "We are tired of man."[4] For him, faced with a long-term weakening that had arisen from the will's nihilistic turning back against itself, it was a matter of restoring to man an excess of affirmative force. Yet only someone *other than* man, the Overman, would be capable of this excess. The Heideggerian step is here located as precisely the reverse of Nietzsche's. Man has increased the idea of his power disproportionately. He has become too pervaded by self-certainty, master and possessor of the universe to an excessively illusory extent. We are nowadays tired of Promethean or triumphant nineteenth century man. What is at issue, therefore, is not raising us beyond ourselves, towards the superhuman, but returning to the other side, towards our primary conditions and elementary resources. A return upstream, a return to the sources, a return to what the tradition discovered, then covered over again: such is Heidegger's continual movement. To find once more what is elementary in man is to find what makes him possible again even prior to biology, to find that in terms of which he is. To be within one's element is to be oneself. Man's element, his abyssal ground, is *being*, that strange medium which, rather than simply carrying him, carries him along and carries him away. To return to the elementary is to return to man's fundamental situation with respect to being, with respect to his being. This situation, where man is *thrown* into time, into a world and upon an earth whose facticity he necessarily espouses, into an epoch of History inevitable for him—this is not a situation of mastery, domination or centrality, but of dependency, submission, and decentering. Must we accentuate even further this dependency, submit ourselves even further to this submission, renounce all will to control in order to become more authentically who we are? This is one of the major questions posed by the Heideggerian unsettling of human attributes, properties, and powers.

---

4. *Genealogy of Morals*, I, Section 12.

To what extent can man be stripped of his traditional essence, of an essence that was edified, consolidated, and kept illustrious for so long and so nobly? Can he do without subjectivity, interiority, reflexivity or even individuality, as seems to be the case with the "mortal" in the later Heidegger?

The History of man from the Greeks to our time is indeed the History of the ever more firm and autonomous self-positing of the essence of man. For Protagoras the sophist, man is certainly "measure of all things," but he obeys the law of a *sophia* that imposes the strict frontiers of his reign and his knowledge. Cartesian and Kantian man delimits and assumes the finitude of a will to knowledge, a will nonetheless infinite in principle. Man of the human sciences, giving way to the will to will, exploits his own funds, sections himself into sectors that can be objectified and measured, and projects the grand, unattainable film of unlimited activism. The History of man is that of an absolute emancipation. From what has man not liberated himself? He has delivered himself from any relation to an Other than himself, to God, to nature, to being. He has become the entire relation, the pure medium, the sole object, the sole study of the unique subject: himself. Man nourishes and exhausts himself in this immense tautology, with which he is nevertheless contented; even if he has not expelled anxiety and death from himself, he professes to have cleared them of their archaic, metaphysical weight and to have reduced them to psychological or medical questions, that is, to techniques. Technical questions are not questions, but clear-cut problems, solvable or at least cleared of any enigma.

The whole of metaphysics from the dawn of modern times is either anthropocentric, that is, positing the essence of man, the subject, as the ground and unshakeable foundation of all knowledge; or it is anthropomorphic, transferring to an absolute Subject the properties and faculties of man, in particular the will. Yet since Plato, metaphysics has been "humanist,"[5] because its main preoccupation has been the salvation of the human soul, and because the doctrine of the two substances composing the rational animal has already been firmly established. In every case, man as substance and man as subject are considered as subsisting entities, *vorhanden*, given there before us as things of nature having once and for all their own consistency, their specific qualities, their virtues, and their richness.

Yet what metaphysics forgets, in an ever-increasing fashion, is the *poverty* of man. Man is not what he is, and does not have what

5. Cf. Wm, p. 234.

he has. According to Plato, it was necessary for man to remember this. Man is always lacking in something. This something is not some entity, but his very being: that relation to being that he cannot possess, but only exhibit in the ek-static movement of existence. He is the entity that he is only in having lost being and in finding it again, so as to lose it anew. Man is *Dasein*, an entity whose being-in-the-world, as well as the modes of being of entities other than himself, are "eternally" in question in his own being: "in question": in the possibility of meaning or whose meaning is in suspension. The Turning of the 1930s does not abandon this position of *Being and Time*. Heidegger merely shows that the relation to being is not decided *in Dasein's own being*, in accordance with *Dasein's* inclinations, but is determined from out of being itself, insofar as the latter uncovers itself and gives itself as "true"; that is, as un-concealed, manifestly issued from its concealment.

"Heidegger Two" radicalizes what *Being and Time* called the necessary presupposition of the *there is* or the opening. The displacement that, after the Turning, transfers to being all the former properties of man is to a large extent initiated in the magnum opus when, for example, it is stated that: "It is not we who presuppose 'truth', rather *the latter* makes it ontologically possible in general for us to *be* in such a way as to 'presuppose' something."[6] The formulation *it is not we who* (it is not we who give ourselves freedom, language, thought…) is the fundamental formulation of the poverty of man. The dispossession of the traditional faculties, to which the thought of being will apply itself (and in which it will perhaps *indulge itself* excessively, to the point of vertigo, to the point of *Verwesung*, according to Trakl's word, to the point of the *decomposition of the essence* of man)—this dispossessing or this deposing is nonetheless presented as the opposite of any grace, "favor" or lofty election. For man alone knows or rather understands that he is. Man alone has a relation to the nothing, as being able not to be. "Man alone exists."[7] A provocative statement, all the more so when followed by this one: "God is, but he does not exist." Would man thereby be graced with a superiority to God? God is "only" an entity. Like a stone or a tree, he is lacking in nothing. He is what he is. A strange Heideggerian theology that forbids God what is possible for man: to exit from himself. Why, for example, might not God have an ek-static relation to man? "The proposition: 'Man alone exists'

6. SZ, p. 227.
7. Wm, p. 370.

means: 'Man is that entity whose being is marked by a privilege [*ausgezeichnet*] of and in being, through his being openly maintained in the unconcealment of being'."[8] This somewhat redundant definition makes a pure gift out of ekstatic openness, a pure feat of being that "maintains" man in the open, guards man as the servant and guardian of himself—himself: the alpha and omega. What good is the marvel of existing if it is to "incarnate" the height of passivity? For man "realizes" his essence in opening himself, in effacing himself, in abolishing himself so as to let being appear, speak, act. He is not so much bearer of the ontological difference as borne by it. He is the space into which light irrupts, the medium or instrument of manifestation. He can be only transparency, or an obstacle to transparency, more or less docile towards the light, cleared rather than actively clearing. On this point there is a complete modification with respect to *Being and Time*, where *Dasein* was essentially both "disclosive" and the *Lichtung*, the clearing light brought to bear by *Dasein*.

An extreme poverty of man, who has nothing that would not be granted to him: freedom, action, speech, thought, the affective dispositions. Who neither adopts nor is ever in possession of what thus *passes* through him. What, then, do these new names of man signify: the "guardian," the "witness," the "shepherd," the "neighbor" of being? Are these not euphemisms that hide poorly a pallid translucidity, a spectral attenuation, a medium-like pallor of his essence? Is there not an excessive and fantastic omnipotence of being as well as an excessive depotentializing and desubstantializing of man, which would resemble an inversion of the excess of substance that metaphysics has conferred on him? Does not the impoverishment of man entail a *danger*, and undoubtedly more than one? It may be that all the aberrations of history do not merely flow into the insubstantiality and impotence of man. Yet must they not necessarily be accepted by him as what being sends to him, destines for him? Who is to judge, if the "who," the "being-a-self," is merely a moment in the self-disclosure of being?

What henceforth becomes enigmatic, more so than being itself, is that *part* of the relation to being that truly belongs to man. Can his *own* role be isolated, circumscribed, defined? Where does man reside? In being ekstatic, does he not become evanescent? The essence of man resides in his ek-sistence, and ek-sistence is the clearing *of being*. Be that as it may. Yet can man ever rejoin this

---

8. Ibid.

essence, so as finally to be the "there" of being? Indeed, if man were to coincide with the clearing of being, how could being be distinguished from him, remain hidden from him; how could he himself forget it? What difference would there be between him and being? If, on the other hand, it is necessary to admit and preserve a distance between the "there" of being (man) and "being itself," it seems inevitable that being will be set aside, hypostatized, if not substantialized. Too great a proximity of man to being would make him melt into being and render the relation incomprehensible; too great a distance of being from man would situate them facing one another in an abstract opposition. How are we to think the "relation to being" *harmoniously*, that is, in such a way as not to absolutize being and render man inessential? How are we to prevent the relation leaning to one side and congealing in a sterile identity? The thought of *Ereignis* tries to overcome this aporia. Does it succeed? We cannot be certain, as the next section will try to show.

If man is not merely a natural entity endowed with spirit, something living capable of speech and reason, in short, if *rational animal*—according to what is said in the *Letter on Humanism*—represents the *homo animalis* only by being opposed to the one termed *homo humanus*, open to being; if man is *in the first instance* openness, how are we to conceive ontologically of that which concerns life in him? For, as Heidegger repeats, the metaphysical representations are not false, but simply do not go far enough. Who can deny that man is *also* something living? Is there a phenomenological or even scientific experiment that would allow one to corroborate the Heideggerian thesis that the human body is separated from the body of the animal by an *abyssal* distance and by a difference of *essence*? Heidegger thereby affirms that the human body is traversed by an opening onto world and by transcendence to the extent of being *entirely other* than the body of the animal. It is being-in-the-world as a whole that is "body" and "soul." In terms of which phenomena can he begin to justify this assertion? Is *homo humanus* to replace the reasoning animal or merely complete and deepen it? If, as it appears, it is to replace it entirely, is not this new unitary concept of human essence established at the expense of the body and somehow founded on an occultation or denial of life? Is the ideal unity of the human essence (as opposed to traditional dualism)—a unity obtained solely in and through the ekstatic relation to being—not lacking if it implicates a remainder that cannot be assimilated to the ekstatic? Is the attempt tenable that, according to Heidegger, was undertaken from *Being and Time* onward;

namely, to "determine the human essence in terms of its relation to being, and *only* in terms of the latter,"[9] an attempt from which he did not waver? Can life, the Earth, nature, the body, and the affective moods be reduced to a relation to being? If these elements resist such reduction, then the radical monism of *homo humanus*—despite the radical extroversion of being-in-the-world; despite the quasi-negation of interiority; despite the link of "transpropriation" between man thought of as "mortal" and earth, sky, and gods; despite the insistence on the new human's rediscovered relation to the near, the simple, the small—such a monism would only be a new version of the idealism and transcendentalism belonging to phenomenology since its origin.

Yet what is this "relation to being"? Can it be a univocal, unilateral relation?

The False Symmetry of the Double Relation Between Man and Being

The relation between man and being is evidently meant in a double sense: it runs from man to being and from being to man. Are these two sides symmetrical? Are they coordinate or subordinate? As we shall see by the end of this section, the whole thought of *Ereignis* is founded on the principle of a *mutual, reciprocal "belonging together"* of man and being. The relation of being to man is so originally determinative, having such primordiality or antecedence, and is so preponderant that there could not be the slightest equilibrium between the two sides of the relation. Does not man receive all his faculties from being? What is absolutely proper to him, other than to "remember" this? Are not all his most eminent qualities inscribed, if not in a schema of *passivity*, at least in one of *radical receptivity*: listening (*hören*), obedience (*Gehör*), submission (*Gehören*), the appropriate response (*Entsprechen*), the "gathering" in language that is none other than the act of bringing to language what the silent *logos* of being has already gathered? If the essence of man is his relation to being, does not this relation amount to the capacity to faithfully correspond to being's relation to him? Does the human essence not vanish into being?

Would being not then be the fictive, utopian site where, outside of man, the venerable transcendental faculties whose owner-

9. NII, p. 194; tr,. NII vol. Four, p. 141 (emphasis added).

ship the subject has lost are projected and reunited? To be sure, being itself neither wishes nor acts, neither thinks nor reasons. Yet being "addresses" (*anspricht*), "disposes" (*stimmt*), and "determines" (*bestimmt*) man to wish, act, think, or reason. Thus, in the epoch of *Gestell*, of the Order of Technology, the human will is merely the agent of a "will to will" inscribed in being. Yet being is thereby more than a transcendental condition of possibility that would be posed outside of man in a neutral manner. Being, at once "in" man as "in" every entity and beyond his grasp, has a view of man, manifests an intention, imprints a direction from which man cannot extricate himself. Being "uses" man: *braucht ihn*. Man is not simply "maintained" [*"main-tenu"*], but literally *manipulated* by being, because the relation that is termed *Brauch* translates or transposes Anaximander's *Chreon* (from *cheir*, the hand [*la main*]). We shall return to this a little later. In this Heideggerian theme, as in many others, do we not find the transposed taking up again of a religious theme and its current expressions: "we are in the hand of God," or "God has need of man" (*brauchen* means both "to need" and "to use"), or again, "Man proposes, God disposes"?

However things may stand, the balance between the two questions—"What does being mean?" and "Who or what is man?"—cannot be equal. The response to the second question always presupposes the response to the first, whether in the metaphysical mode of "What are entities as such?" (in this case man is a species of entities as such) or in accordance with that thinking which respects non-ontic presence and the temporality of being. Man *"is" nothing* but the free space for the presence of being. Such is his primary definition, which in Heidegger's eyes is not restrictive:

> What is distinctive about man resides in the fact that, as the one whose essence it is to think, open towards being, he is placed before the latter, remains related to being and thus corresponds to it. Man properly *is* this relation of correspondence, and he is only this. 'Only': this does not mean a limitation, but an overabundance. In man there prevails a belonging to being, a belonging [*Gehören*] which listens to [*hört auf*] being, because it is appropriated over [*übereignet*] to being.[10]

The essence of man is to depend on being, to correspond to it and to belong to it as *proper to it* (*eigen*). Immediately following this

---

10. ID, p. 18; tr., p. 31.

passage, the text of *Identity and Difference* seems to introduce a reservation and make apparent an equal dependency of being with respect to man. Indeed, would being come to presence without man? Apparently not. "Being essences and endures only insofar as it attains to man through the claim of its address [*Anspruch*]. For it is man, open for being, who first lets being arrive as presencing."[11] Yet there is an immediate corrective: "this does not at all mean that being is first posited by man and only through him."[12] The inequality of the relation is that man does not posit himself, but is put in the world by being; being, on the other hand, is never something fabricated by man. Being produces man; man cannot produce being, nor can he produce himself.

Nor is being something facing us, face to face with man. Being is not in front of us, but before us. The very idea of subjectivity, which is that of man's self-positing and positing the outside as object, rests on the idea of something facing. Yet is the thought of being not then simply a reversal of the metaphysics of subjectivity, insofar as it would simply turn the subject's self-positing around into the self-positing of being? Moreover, is not the fact that being somehow reassumes and takes on all the functions of the subject the index of this reversal?

To reply to this objection, according to which the subject-object relation would merely be inverted—being becoming the true subject and man its object—Heidegger develops the difficult notion of *Ereignis*, which is to think the tie between man and being in a quite different way. Their joining would precisely not be a link in the sense of a relation "with or without dialectic," in the sense of an *attachment* of two terms originally separated, but of an initial Identity, a full and unlimited "belonging together," a "constellation," an "interlacing," or "intertwining" (*Verflechtung*). *Ereignis* as an inter-belonging of being and man, as "the belonging together of call and obedience" (*das Zusammengehören von Ruf und Gehör*),[13] would be more original than the relation considered in terms of its two moments. Only a "leap" of thinking, a leap that "leaps away from being,"[14] would allow us to understand this wholly reciprocal appropriation, allow us to see that being *belongs as much to us* as we belong to it, since "being itself belongs to us; for only in us can it

11. Ibid., p. 19; tr., p. 31.
12. Ibid.
13. Wm, p. 402; tr., QB, p. 77.
14. ID, p. 20; tr., p. 32.

essence, i.e. presence as being [*denn nur bei uns kann es als Sein wesen, d.h. an-wesen*]."[15] "The leap is the abrupt entry into that realm from out of which man and being have always already reached one another in their essence, because both are appropriated over to one another out of a reaching-towards [*Zureichung*]. The entry into the realm of this transpropriation first attunes and determines [*stimmt und be-stimmt*] the experience of thinking."[16]

If the principle of *Ereignis* is a truly *mutual* belonging together of man and being, such mutuality or reciprocity is admissible only at the price of a *false symmetry*. For if the essence of man consists only in belonging and corresponding to being, how can this belonging (*gehören*) be equal on the side of man's relation to being, given that being can never truly "belong" to man in the way in which being possesses man, since being cannot depend on man as much as man depends on being? *Ereignis*, as equality and reciprocity of the two sides of the double relation, contradicts the absolute preponderance and antecedence of being over man. Heidegger fails to attain the simplicity that ought to characterize *Ereignis*, as *singulare tantum*. Indeed the "co-appropriation" (to attempt a translation of *Ereignis*) is, in the description given, doubled once more into two modes of appropriation that repeat the two asymmetrical sides of the relation. On the one side, "*man is appropriated unto being* [*dem Sein...vereignet*]"; on the other, "*being however is appropriated unto [zugeeignet] the essence of man.*"[17]It must be conceded that the leap into *Ereignis*, as an Identity in which the terms founding themselves lose their previous identity, that is, "those determinations that metaphysics has conferred on them,"[18] has not been successful, because being has not been removed and man still retains a *distinct* essence. To be called the *mortal*, must he not continue to be differentiated—from being, from the world, or from the gods? Strictly speaking, the priority of being renders unthinkable any true reciprocity of its relation to man.

How, then, can we imagine that in *Gestell* there is manifest a "*mutual* confrontation of man and being" (*wechselweisen Sichstellen von Mensch und Sein*)?[19] Is there not, on the contrary, precisely in Technology, a flagrant inequality and nonreciprocity? Man

---

15. Ibid., tr., p. 33.
16. Ibid.
17. Ibid., p. 24; tr., p. 36 (emphasis added).
18. Ibid., p. 26; tr., p. 37.
19. Ibid., pp. 23–24; tr., p. 35 (emphasis added).

is certainly *confronted* by *Gestell,* in the sense that he is summoned to calculate, produce, amass energy, bend to the mode of unconcealment proper to *Gestell.* Yet man is evidently incapable of confronting *Gestell,* whether in the sense of challenging it or in the sense of putting it into question, because the question of the being of entities has been resolved in advance, or rather is not even capable of being posed. "We overhear the address of being which speaks in the essence of Technology."[20] In confronting man, the *Gestell* confronts itself. Yet one cannot affirm, as does Heidegger, that "man is challenged, i.e. confronted, *im selben Masse wie das Sein,* to the same extent as being."[21] *Ereignis,* as much as being, even as *Gestell,* retains a "freedom" infinitely superior to that of man. Man can merely *await Ereignis* that, like the Turning, is already and is not yet, as *Gestell* is only the prelude.[22] *Ereignis* is therefore the name given by way of anticipation to a possible "identification" between man and being, beyond metaphysics. In awaiting a new commencement, a new History, *Ereignis* in Heidegger's last writings disposes over man to the same extent and with the same total sovereignty as does being. In particular, it reveals that man is "used," that he speaks only inasmuch as he listens to language and belongs to it. "*Ereignis* appropriates man to the usage [*Brauch*] it makes of him."[23] All schemas of freedom, activity, and power that were those of being are transferred to *Ereignis,* in the face of which man keeps the same determinations of quasi-passivity and dependency. The thought of *Ereignis* therefore does not fundamentally change the definition of man's essence as resulting from his relation to being, and from being's relation to him.

Man finds himself situated at the intersection of two movements: his own that transports him into being, and the movement via which being retracts human transcendence into itself. We therefore now need to analyze in turn the two sides of this double relation that is not suppressed by *Ereignis* and that is a central theme of all the writings following the Turning.

---

20. Ibid., p. 22; tr., p. 34.
21. Ibid., p. 23; tr., p. 35.
22. Ibid., p. 25; tr., p. 36.
23. US, p. 261; tr., OWL, p. 130.

Chapter 4

MAN'S RELATION TO BEING

Is it legitimate to describe this relation (*Bezug*) separately? In one sense, yes, for we can show how, on the one hand, the ekstatic movement towards being is presented from the point of view of man. On the other hand, man's essence, as Heidegger emphasizes often enough, is *nothing other* than this relation of openness. Can the whole of human facticity, and in particular the body, be embraced in this ekstatic dimension? If man were to exit from himself to the extent of leaving no remainder behind him, would he not vanish into the transparency of this relation, which would cease to be a liaison and become an absorption? For man to remain man, and not to be purely a link, is it not necessary that there be limits to his ekstasy, something this side of it which withdraws? Yet, in another sense, it is impossible not to recall at once—and Heidegger does so continually— that the relation to being is not a commencement, that man does not command or produce this relation, does not hold the initiative over it. It has a derivative character. It cannot sustain itself unless being gives rise to it or maintains it. In fact it is situated *within* the more originary relation of being to man, onto which it is somehow grafted. "Man stands within the relation of being itself to him, man."[1] Man himself does not decide about this relational essence defining him, rather his relation to being responds or corresponds to being's relation to him, which is always prior. Man is in a situation of receptivity, if not passivity. He is above all *correspondence*: *Entsprechung*, which for Heidegger also means "speaking in return," the response to a

---

1. NII, p. 358; tr., NII, vol. Four, p. 217.

silent "address" of being (*Zuspruch, Anspruch*). Correspondence is the counterpart to a "request" of being: Heidegger plays on the word *Anspruch*, which means "exigency," "claim." This leads to the following primordial definition of the essence of man: "man in the end *is* this relation of correspondence, and is only this."[2]

The relation to being that characterizes the essence of man is at the outset specified as a correspondence—which is always epochal—to the destining of being (*Geschick des Seins*). But the correspondence is not limited to the fact of belonging and adhering to an epochal opening. *Entsprechung* is at once belonging and speaking back. All belonging to a total or epochal situation and all saying are permeated by a mood that determines them. *Entsprechung heisst bestimmt sein*, "correspondence means being disposed."[3] "Only on the basis of being attuned (disposition) does the saying of correspondence receive its precision, its specific attunement."[4] The three fundamental dimensions constitutive of a relation to being, *Entsprechung—Stimmung—Sagen* (*Denken*), here appear closely interwoven. The three moments of being open to being, experiencing a disposition, and saying being in accordance with a disposition can be distinguished for the purposes of analysis, but are equioriginary. Somehow, there is always "mediation" "between" corresponding and the saying that thinks it, at least when it is a matter of essential thinking, of a *fundamental attunement*. There is no correspondence that would not be "disposed" or that could not be brought to language.

Everything starts from correspondence, which somehow occupies the place and plays the role of a *transcendental aesthetic*. Thinking, traditionally the function of understanding, apprehends and gathers into unity (as *noein* and *legein*), conveys correspondence in the element of language: *das Denken als Entsprechen steht im Dienst der Sprache*, "thinking as corresponding stands in the service of language."[5] Thinking does not create anything, but defines a correspondence. The attunement is the milieu, the interval or instrument of this defining. Attunement is situated between correspondence and thought in the manner of a *transcendental schematism*. It is via the mood of astonishment, therefore, that the specifically Greek relation to being can be grasped and expressed. *Fundamental Stimmung* and thought are degrees of correspondence.

---

2. ID, p. 18; tr., p. 31.
3. W. Phil., pp. 23–24.
4. Ibid. (*disposition* is quoted by Heidegger in French).
5. W. Phil., p. 44.

Undoubtedly there are other essential characteristics of thought in addition to this basic formula, *correspondence* + *disposition* + *language,* which, we note, takes up and condenses once more the "existentials" of *Being and Time*: disclosedness and understanding, thrownness and disposition, interpretation and discourse. Thus, thought is commissioned with "preserving" being (*Wahrnis*), with "remembering" being (*Andenken, Gedächtnis*), with accomplishing a "leap" (*Sprung*) to fulfill its function. But these other characteristics are in one way or another variations on this basic formula.

Viewed from the side of being, the three moments of the relation correspond to three major "initiatives" of being: being "claims" man (*Anspruch*) by its "address" (*Zuspruch*), "determines" him by the "throw" (*Wurf*) while disposing over him (*Be-stimmung*), and "calls" him to thinking (*Ruf, Geheiss*).

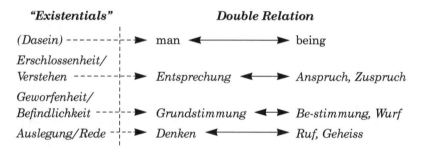

Certainly there are other "powers" of being: *Gabe* (gift), *Gunst* (favor), *Brauch* (usage, main-tenance), *Geschick* (destining), but they are more specific forms of these primordial powers. We shall later endeavor to explicate these various "powers" and, if possible, outline their organic links.

The preceding schema must not lead us to forget that, as we have seen, there is a certain disproportion between man's relation to being and the inverse relation.

Relation and Connection:
A Glance at Heidegger and Hegel

The vocabulary, as ever extremely rigorous, clearly indicates the dissymmetry. Heidegger never uses *Verhältnis* to designate the relation of being to man, but always *Bezug.* There is no *Verhältnis* of being to man, for *Verhalten* implies a comportment, distinctly "relative" and variable. The word *Bezug*, on the contrary, signifies that being "draws" something essential from man (*be-ziehen*),[6] uses him, or needs him (*braucht ihn*). On the one side, there is, if one may say such a thing, a relative relation (such as the relation to entities that is always *Verhältnis*);[7] on the other, an "essential relation" (*Wesensbezug*), that is, one that originally defines the essence of man.

However, Heidegger more rarely employs *Verhältnis* in an even stronger sense than *Bezug* to designate that which holds together the two sides of the double relation. He then writes the word, underlining and detaching the root *halten* (to hold), as *Ver-hältnis*; and here we are dealing with a concept quite different from that of relation, one we shall translate as *Connection*. The *Ver-hältnis* "entertains" [*"entre-tient"*] the double relation, unites its two moments to the point where they cannot be dissociated or thought separately, attaches them in a nonrepresentational way (in the sense that neither being nor man can be set opposite one another) and in a nondialectical way (their reciprocity is not the passage from one into the other that would negate them then to "sublate" them). More rarely, we find an equivalent of *Ver-hältnis* in the expression *das ganze Verhältnis*,[8] "the whole relation."

The notion of *Connection* partakes of the effort to avoid the relation of man and being falling back into the schema of the subject-object relation. The man-being relation does not have the character of a link (*Beziehung*) established between two entities that could exist separately, but constitutes an original ensemble whose division into two distinct relations is the work of representation. The *Ver-hältnis* has the same finality and the same scope as *Ereignis*: to remove the metaphysical idea of a simple "link" (*Beziehung*) from man to being or even inversely. "The Connection [*Ver-hältnis*] is here thought everywhere in terms of *Ereignis*, and is no longer represented in the form of a mere link [*blosse Beziehung*]."[9] *Ereignis* is defined in the same passage as the "Connection of all connections."

The following hierarchy of relations is thus established, from the closest to the most remote from being:

---

6. Wm, p. 401; tr., QB, p.75.
7. NII, p. 203; tr., NII vol. Four, p. 150.
8. WhD, p. 74; tr., p. 80.
9. US, p. 267; tr., p. 135.

- *Ver-hältnis*: original Connection
  (or *ganzes Verhältnis*)

- *Bezug*: essential relation
  (proceeding both from man and from being)

- *Verhältnis*: relation of comportment
  (proper to man)

- *Beziehung*: neutral, abstract, or dialectical link

The attempt that is thought in the name of *Ver-hältnis* aims at refusing any bid to bring being and man into a link (*Beziehung*) in the abstract or dialectical sense. At the limit (but is such an identity even thinkable?), it aims at bringing us into a "belonging together" (*Zusammengehören*), so that the old terms that were formerly linked would come to be effaced, to disappear, even as separate names. From the moment "the question of link" (*die Frage nach der Beziehung*) is shown to be "insufficient," "we would have to abandon [*fahren lassen*, drop] the isolating and divisive word 'being' just as decisively as the name 'man'."[10] But is abandoning the word *man* itself a *sufficient strategy*? Does it suffice to say "the mortal" to bring about the sudden emergence of what has been forgotten for so many centuries of metaphysics? Especially given that what metaphysics has forgotten is not some *property* that man would possess, something that would not have been on the inventory hitherto? However things stand, it is by no means the least of the paradoxes of the Heideggerian position that, on the one hand, he abundantly describes the relation, the *Bezug* or *Verhältnis* in each direction, whereas, on the other hand, via a critique of the futility of all *Beziehung*, he tries to merge relational thinking into a totality (*Ereignis* or *Ver-hältnis*) at the heart of which he must nevertheless name once more the terms of the old relation! This is witnessed by an important passage from *What Is Called Thinking?* that we must quote (almost) in its entirety:

> Every philosophical, i.e. thoughtful doctrine of the essence of man is already in itself a doctrine of the being of entities. Every doctrine of being is already in itself a doctrine of the essence of man....Why this is so, and what this relation [*Verhältnis*] between the essence of man and the being of entities

---

10. Wm, p. 402; tr., QB, p. 77.

ultimately rests on..., this question is abyssal in its difficulty....We are asking about the link [*Beziehung*] between the
human essence and the being of entities. But as soon as I
thoughtfully say "human essence," I have thereby already
stated a relation [*Bezug*] to being. Likewise, as soon as I
thoughtfully say "being of entities," a relation [*Bezug*] to the
human essence has thereby already been named. In each of
the two terms of the link [*Beziehung*] between human essence
and being we already find the link itself. To speak in terms of
the matter itself: there are neither terms of the relation nor
this link [*Beziehung*] taken by itself. This is why the relation
[*Verhältnis*] named here between human essence and being of
entities in no way tolerates any dialectical maneuver that
would play off one term against the other. This state of affairs,
the fact that all dialectic not only fails here, but that no place
even remains for a failure of this kind, is probably what most
balks and disconcerts today's habits of representation and the
skilled acrobatics of its empty astuteness.

No path of thought, not even that of metaphysics, starts
from the essence of man and from there passes over to being,
or inversely starts from being and from there goes back to
man. Rather every path of thought always already *moves
within* the whole relation [*ganzen Verhältnisses*] of being and
human essence, otherwise it is no thought.[11]

Man cannot be thought as a separate entity. Philosophy, in
fact, has never thought him in isolation. The *zoon politikon*, the
creature made in the image of God, the subject that bears its own
law (the moral law)—these definitions of man, like all others, in
each case refer to a totality: that of the *polis*, that of creation, that
of objects submitted to laws....Metaphysics situates man in his
relation to a totality and the nature of things; all the more so when,
like Spinoza, it takes its point of departure in this totality. Phenomenology, in grasping man as being-in-the-world—even though it
thinks world as horizon or network of relations and not as objective
totality—only radicalizes the metaphysical approach. For the latter, there is no "abyss of difficulties" here. This abyss only opens
once we are no longer concerned with a purely ontic concept of man.
Man ceases to be an *entity* of which one could make a separate
study, he ceases to be the *object* of anthropology, whether or not he
is subsequently ordered within the totality.

---

11. WhD, pp. 73–74; tr., pp. 79–80.

Yet if man "is" his relation to being, where is he *properly* situated? For this relation extends both "from the side" of man and "from the side" of being. This is one of the difficulties. The simple link (*Beziehung*) of two mutually exterior terms fails as an untenable abstraction. The *Bezug*, for its part, is integrated into a "whole relation." What distinguishes the "whole relation" from a dialectical relation? The dialectic also seems to start out from a whole relation.

Here, the proximity to Hegel seems formidable. What is the difference between Hegelian totality and the "whole relation"? Without going into the complex details of the link with Hegel,[12] we can outline two essential differences. First, Hegel proceeds from a totality that is always already completed in itself and that, from the most impoverished beginning, anticipates itself as completed. Heidegger, on the other hand, proceeds from the *Connection*, from a *Ver-hältnis* (or from *Da-sein*) that as such remains open, cannot be completed, and could not be interpreted as a kind of Whole superior to the parts that constitute it. In other words, the Connection does not embrace being and man in a synthesis higher than them. They are not submitted to a third term that would be the Absolute, the existing Concept. A second difference is that thought is not what is proper to the Absolute. Although it arises out of a requisition of being and results from a submission to the solicitation of being, thought remains what is proper to man. It is not the conceptual self-movement of the Absolute. The Heideggerian "totality" (if totality there is, namely the Connection being-thought) is not transparent to thought. There is certainly a "Sameness," a tautology of being and thinking, but only to the extent that thought is *logos*, the gathering of being itself—and this without any hinterworld. For no human thought can rise above being, and a fortiori above the Connection. Hegel posits totality as transparent to thinking, as spirit, and spirit as totalization of the totality. Heidegger—closer to Kant in this—retains the difference, in Sameness, between being and thinking, that is, affirms the specular or speculative nonreversibility of being and thinking. Being always conceals itself from thought, and perhaps this characterizes its essential trait (*Zug*): that it is drawn, roused, transformed by this movement of withdrawal (*Entzug*). "We are underway towards that which draws us in withdrawing."[13]

Certainly Heidegger in all his texts makes thought radically dependent on the "initiative" of being and even proclaims, at the

---

12. Cf. ID, "The Onto-theo-logical Constitution of Metaphysics"; and *Le Chant de la Terre*, pp. 141–158.
13. WhD, p. 5; tr., p. 9.

end of the *Letter on Humanism*, the wish that thinking regard itself
as the thinking and language of being "like the clouds are the
clouds of the sky."[14] But what is at issue is a metaphor of correspondence, of belonging, and not of a way of raising being to the status
of the subject of thought, something that would determine the latter, as is the case with the metaphysics of the absolute Subject.
Once again, it is only too evident: no thinking is *adequate* to being.
Thinking may be attentive to forgetting, faithful to the unthought,
careful to care for what remains in reserve. But there is no possible
adequation to withdrawal. The Hegelian totality, like the Kantian
totality, is for Heidegger a totality of the entity. Neither being in
itself nor man together with being can constitute the object of any
totalization. Even the demand of Technology retains a nonobjec-
tivizable element that is its proper destiny in the History of Being.

Man is not inserted into a total Grand Being, he is not part of
a whole, for being and totality are antinomic. Heidegger expressly
rejects the idea that being would be the all-encompassing,[15] con-
taining all entities, and thus man as one entity among others, such
as plants and animals. On account of the Connection, man's relation to being inhabits him more profoundly than his own self and
the link to the other. The thought of the Connection abandons the
dialectical conception of the relation between interior and exterior.
Man as *Dasein* is always already "outside," in the world, but he has
not had to exit from himself, because he *is* outside himself by his
essence. Being is more interior to him than any subjective interiority, and more exterior than any entity in the world.

Thinking as the Essence of Man, and the Question of the "Physical" in Man: The Treatment of Perception

The three "moments," which are inseparable, in the relation to
being—Correspondence, disposition, and speech—are superim-
posed or interwoven to form "thought": correspondence that speaks
in accordance with an affective disposition. *Entsprechen* is a
Sprechen.[16] "Thought" is not some inner procession of ideas, a

---

14. Wm, p. 360; tr., BW, p. 242.
15. Ibid., p. 401: *"das Allumfassende."*
16. W. Phil., p. 29.

reflecting (yet how, then, do things stand with reflection?), but speaking in response to a gift of being, the illumination in words of a situation always already comprehended without words.

> To be man means to be a sayer [*ein Sagender*]. Man...in the ground of his being is a sayer, the sayer [*der Sager*]. This is his distinction and at the same time his distress [*Not*]. It distinguishes him from stone, plant, animal, but also from the gods. Even if we had a thousand eyes and a thousand ears and many other senses and organs, our essence would not stand in the power of language. Every entity would then remain closed to us: that entity that we ourselves are, no less than those entities we are not."[17]

This text, like many others, underlines the absolute preponderance of thought-speech over the other faculties of man, in particular his faculties of "sense perception," his sensory, organic, biológical, and corporeal powers. No opening, that is, no access to entities as such comes to us from our sense organs! *The sole relation to being, and therefore the sole essence of man, would be "thought"*. Despite the fundamental "incarnation" of thought in language, one cannot prevent the feeling of abstraction here. Is there not, not so much an overestimation, but an exclusive valorization of the "phantic" capacity of man, of his power to show (what is properly human in man is "that he shows in the direction of being"[18]), in short, an idealism? What about physical man? How can the quality of being alive not constitute part of the essence of man? No one denies that man is a thinking being, yet how can we doubt that he is *also a living being* belonging to nature, whatever notion we have of it? How can we doubt that life is *equally essential* to him? Is not the ekstatic sayer arbitrarily separated from his own living physiological structure, the structure responsible, for example, for the fact that his mouth emits sounds, that it is still sonic vibrations that strike his tympans? What becomes of the dimension of *aisthesis*, of sensory receptivity in Heidegger? We know that the body or the flesh are not denied, but described as always already permeated by an attunement, that is, taken into a transcendence, into an embracing figure of world. In affirming, from *Being and Time* onward, that *Dasein* is always "more" than what it "factually" is (*tatsächlich*),

---

17. EM, pp. 62f; tr., p. 82.
18. WhD, pp. 95–96; tr., p. 149.

does not Heidegger detach man from the cosmic, material order of things? All human perception indeed always has a *sense of world*: I do not in the first instance perceive a pure noise that is then interpreted or judged, but a car engine, raindrops pattering on the window, a roll of thunder, the song of a bird, the step of someone familiar or unfamiliar. However, is this not to absorb or empty factuality (*Tatsächlichkeit*) into facticity (*Faktizität*), itself understood as a way of being of freedom?[19] There may indeed be no "brute" sensory data. "*Dasein* hears [*hört*] because it understands [*versteht*]," as is said in *Being and Time*. And all understanding is affectively disposed. *However*, does physical man in his sensory discovery of things encounter only what he has already understood? Do we encounter only meaning, within a multitude of innerworldly references to constituted things? Do we encounter only the play of things and world? Do we not also have contact with textures, surfaces, lights and shadows, with a grain, an infinite scattering of disparate sensible qualities suspended, so to speak, around things— qualities perfectly manifest and yet *deprived of meaning* or at least *awaiting definition*? Heidegger takes perceptual contact with things back to the uncovering of an ordered world, already organized because already understood. He makes perception into a mode of correspondence, that is, a mode of thought. *Unser Vernehmen ist in sich ein Entsprechen*. What Merleau-Ponty called raw *Being*, a mixture of nature and world, ambiguous being that would be neither pure life nor pure humanity, is thereby excluded.

The hesitation of forms on the threshold of the body, their latency, the clear obscurity of the sensible and sense is dismissed, refused even before being examined. As Jacques Taminiaux indeed rightly shows, Heidegger takes up, without questioning it, a concept of perception inherited from the tradition, without "asking whether perceiving...ever consisted in apprehending the subsistent base of a certain number of properties."[20] In the context of *Being and Time*, simple perception would effectively result from a suspension of equipmental comportment and a reduced, contracted, abstract view that reduces the "ready-to-hand" (*zuhanden*) entity to an entity subsisting "at-hand" (*vorhanden*). There is no originary role or autonomy of the act of perceiving. Perception is not an original relation to being. It is always derived. We would perceive only by grace of action being arrested or of our pragmatic relation to

---

19. See later, "Freedom as a Property Little Shared by Being."
20. *Lectures de l'ontologie fondamentale* (Millon, 1989), p. 130.

entities that determines our primary understanding of things. Whatever there is that is perceivable, it must already have been discovered. Now this discovery "makes sense" only thanks to an understanding of the being of the disposable entity, that is, thanks to thought ("and the essence of thought is the understanding of being."[21]). Perception would thus be derived from thought. Although the definition of thought would be quite other than in Descartes and Kant, the *subordination* of perception (in the latter cases to a judgment, in Heidegger to our pragmatic understanding of world) is the same.

What is given to us by way of sight and hearing is inscribed in our relation to being that in advance prescribes, preforms the eidetic of the visible and the audible, decides what will be a "sense object." "What the ear perceives and the way in which it perceives it are already qualified and determined by what *we* hear."[22]"Our human, mortal hearing and sight do not possess what is proper to them in mere sensory impression...."[23] "What addresses itself to us can only become perceptible through our corresponding."[24] The sense of what we perceive is not *defined* in terms of our sensory impressions. Heidegger sees proof of this in the fact that the Greeks were able to recognize the god Apollo in the statue of a young man. The physiological determination of the organs that allow us to hear and see is certainly a "necessary condition," according to the text, but not a "sufficient condition" for hearing and sight. Understanding, that is, correspondence or discovery of sense and meaning, precedes and makes possible hearing and seeing. "We do not hear because we have ears, but we have and are able to have ears because we hear."[25] It is always a faculty anterior to the physiological—an apriori faculty that definitively leads back to thought as correspondence to being—that is endowed with organs, and not the organs that make possible such and such a faculty. This reasoning, developed at length in the Course on animality of 1929–30,[26] rests, it seems, on a strange *petitio principii*. For what pure faculty, without organs, would exist prior to the organs, for example a faculty of vision without eyes? Does not the idea of a faculty not yet provided with organs and anterior to them proceed from a retrospective illusion? In any case, it proceeds from the antecedence of understand-

21. NII, p. 359; tr., NII vol. Four, p. 218.
22. SvG, p. 87.
23. Ibid.
24. Ibid.
25. GA 55, p. 247.
26. GA 29/30, Part Two (see my analysis in *Le Chant de la Terre*, p. 65).

ing over any "sensible" encounter with things. Not only all perception, but all sensation, however fragmentary and insignificant it might be, already finds itself included within the great principle of understanding, that is, within thought!

The Deconstruction of the "Rational Animal" and the Subject

At least three powerful motifs combine to "authorize" the deconstruction of man conceived as rational "animal," *zoon logon echon*— a deconstruction undertaken from *Being and Time* onward and pursued to the very end. (We find it again, for example, in *What Is Called Thinking?* and in *On the Way to Language*). It is one of those "red veins" that run through his entire work. First there is the idea that man's metaphysical essence is diminished by his being identified with an animal itself understood as a *subsistent entity*, because this entails a failure to recognize the living as such. Then we have the idea that the *logos*, which soon becomes translated into *ratio* (i.e. reduced to a simple human faculty), loses its initial reach, that is, its ekstatic relation to being, and forgets its dependency on a more original *logos*, that of being itself. Finally, we discover the idea that the rational animal is merely one particular case of the metaphysics of the *sub-jectum* whereby man projects his own objectivized image upon the scene of representation, that is, projects it before him as a central and self-grounding entity. To these three dominant motifs that preside over the deconstruction of the traditional essence of man we should undoubtedly add one latent motif: rediscovering the unity of being-in-the-world that had been lost by the tradition.

Every deconstruction implies bringing to light again or demonstrating anew an experience of being that has been dissimulated, buried, or covered by those very concepts by way of which it is to be exhibited. In the same year *Being and Time* was published (1927), Heidegger, in his course *The Basic Problems of Phenomenology*, spelled out the meaning of the "task" of a *Destruktion* of the history of traditional ontology as announced in Section 6 of *Being and Time*. The destruction of the tradition is in no sense a negation of it, but is meant to be a "positive appropriation of this tradition," by way of a "critical de-construction [*Abbau*] of received concepts...for the purpose of returning to the sources from which they

have been drawn."[27] De-construction is not an analysis, a disman-
tling or aimless taking to pieces of acquired concepts whose meaning has become banal, obvious, or self-evident, "*selbstverständlich.*"
Rather it implies a *double return*, a "double step back" that is con-
structive and founding: a return to the tradition, a return "to the
sources" of the tradition, that is, to this or that way of experiencing
being that has given birth to this or that conceptual order. Decon-
structing in fact means reconstructing, because it is a matter of
rediscovering an originary ground or phenomenal site for the concepts employed, a matter of "reattaining those experiences of being
which lie at the origin of metaphysics, by way of a de-construction
of representations which have become commonplace and empty."[28]
Thirty years after *Being and Time*, this text from *On the Question
of Being* (1955) assigns the *same* double task to de-construction: on
the one hand, *genealogical*, not in a Nietzschean, but in a Husserlian sense, that is, the return to an *originary experience*, a return
that, we may say in passing, has long since defaulted to Derridean
deconstruction; and on the other hand, *appropriative*, in the sense
that the task is not aimed at overcoming but at "saving metaphysics in its essence"[29] by way of a *Verwindung* that espouses and
prolongs from the inside the metaphysical movement of transcendence beyond entities. The essential thing about de-construction,
without which it would be reduced to reworking sedimentations of
meaning, consists in the reattainment of an originary and simple
experience of being; that is, in a phenomenological uncovering
through which it is again possible to *see* a forgotten elementary
structure of being-in-the-world. This phenomenological demonstration "must be *explicitly* accomplished, even at the risk of explaining
something 'self-evident'."[30]

Two examples taken from *Being and Time* will allow us both
to illustrate this method and to return to the question of the rational animal.

First is the meaning of *I am*. The being that understands and
attributes *Dasein* to itself (and does so independent of, and even
prior to, the Cartesian pronouncement of the *ego sum*) has become

---

27. GA 24, p. 31.
28. Originally, "*im Abbau geläufig und leer gewordener Vorstellungen die
ursprünglichen Seinserfahrungen der Metaphysik zurückgewinnen.*" Wm,
p. 411; tr., QB, p. 93.
29. Ibid.
30. SZ, p. 55.

an abstract and empty term, although it implies the meaning of *being together with*, being in relation with. "The expression *bin* [*am*] is connected to the word *bei* [*alongside*]; *'Ich bin'* [*I am*] in turn means: I dwell, reside alongside...the world such as it is familiar to me. *Sein* [*being*] as the infinitive of the *Ich bin* [*I am*]...means dwelling alongside..., being familiar with..."[31] *I am* etymologically means (note that de-construction is always rooted in a new listening to and understanding of language) not "I am in" in the sense of spatial enclosure, but "I am together with"...space, together with my own body, together with the world. *In-Sein* and *Sein-bei*, Heidegger tells us, if we retrace the linguistic roots of *in* and *bei*,[32] both go back to meanings that have to do with staying, with familiarity with places and beings. The connection between the linguistic *etymon* and the primordial phenomenological experience is presupposed rather than analyzed by Heidegger. It seems to be "something self-evident"! In any case, whenever the *I am* is deconstructed in this way it is not shattered or contracted, but opened up to a wider dimension, that of the "original dispersion" of *Dasein* into a multiplicity of spatial and temporal relations, a multiplicity of activities, affairs and concerns....The sole aim of this description is to show that the *sum* is originally not some substance closed in on itself, some entity given before us—one that only subsequently would enter into a relation with the world—but is relational from the start.

Likewise for *zoon logon echon.* "The later interpretation of this definition of man in the sense of *animal rationale*, 'the living being that has reason', is indeed not 'wrong', but it covers over the phenomenal ground from which this definition of *Dasein* has been taken."[33] What is this "phenomenal ground" that must be rediscovered? "Man shows himself as an entity that speaks."[34] The subsequent interpretation of the *logos* as rational statement or logical proposition eclipses the phenomenon or primordial experience of man as the living being (Heidegger is content to say "entity" [*Seiendes*]) *that has speech* or rather that is *held by language* into the light of the world. Reason understood as a faculty in the definition of man eclipses speech as the dimension of being-in-the-world.

---

31. Ibid., p. 54.
32. Ibid. *"in stammt von innan, wohnen, habitare, sich aufhalten."*
33. Ibid., p. 165. Translator's note: *the living being that has reason* translates *vernünftiges Lebewesen.*
34. Ibid.

However, this short passage from *Being and Time* not only leaves aside the deconstruction of man as a living being, as animal, but even points to an imperceptible recoil in the face of life: "man shows himself as an *entity* that speaks." This *recoil in the face of life,* the choice of a transcendental path, undoubtedly goes back in Heidegger's itinerary to the moment in 1923 when he abandoned the then central concept of "factical life" *(faktisches Leben),*[35] supported by references to Nietzsche, Bergson, and Dilthey, to lead *Dasein*'s facticity back to its *Grundphänomen:* temporality.[36] This first Turning (before this term was coined) from life to temporality remains to be studied.

In *Being and Time* there also appears to be some perplexity as to the ontological status of the living being. On the one hand, a negative and wholly aporetic definition of life is given: "Life is neither a subsisting entity, nor *Dasein.*"[37] The being of the living seems to elude a direct phenomenology, which seems to indicate that we are not part "of it." On the other hand, we are told that a description of the living being can be elaborated only *indirectly,* in terms of a "reductive privation" with respect to *Dasein.* This method will be extensively developed in the 1929–30 course (GA 29/30) in terms of the leitmotiv "the animal is poor in world." The animal enjoys a "lesser openness." Being and life, then, will not be in a relation of opposition or exclusion, but in a relation of more to less. For Heidegger, the "greater," that is, the clearing of being, founds the "lesser," life, and not the reverse. Being does not depend on life, rather if life is life, this is because it can manage to have a certain very limited mode of openness.

Heidegger will always remain faithful to this position, but he will subsequently considerably expand it by showing, in the Heraclitus course for example (1943–44),[38] that the essence of *phusis* is emergence, unconcealment, coming to presence out of withdrawal, that is, that its essence consists in *aletheia!* Thus the *phusis* of the Presocratics is defined as that which returns to itself in its flourishing, as an arising that shelters a self-concealing. And the Greek word *zoon* would originally signify nothing other than this capacity

---

35. GA 61 (*Interpretationen zu Aristoteles*), pp. 79ff. In this 1921–22 course Care had already been described, though as a "fundamental category of life."
36. GA 63, pp. 94, 101.
37. SZ, p. 50.
38. GA 55.

for self-uncovering. *Zoon* would merely be a kind of *phusis*, taken in the ontological sense of un-covering, which is why the gods can be called *zoa*. Living beings are those that arise and emerge. *Phusis* is *light*—whence the Heraclitean "fire"—a phanic power, a power to make appear, to bring into the open. Rightly or wrongly, Heidegger links the root of the word *phusis* to the word *phaos*, light,[39] and associates the root of the word *za*, *zoe*, with this same meaning: to appear, to come to light of one's own accord. "*Za* for the Greeks means pure emergence within the modes of arising and appearing."[40] "Animality for the Greeks is defined in terms of *zoon*, of an arising which then properly rests in itself in not expressing itself" (*indem es sich nicht ausspricht*).[41] This luminous, physical essence of animality *as phantic or phanic*, in short as aletheiological, constitutes the phenomenological experience that is to serve as a counterweight to the deconstruction of the living being conceived metaphysically as a subsisting entity. This phenomenological experience is not derived, Heidegger assures us, from images of the sunrise, of buds opening out, or of the birth of animals, but is the original experience of a relation to light, of a passage from the veiled to the unveiled, of an exiting from the hidden.

Yet what is thereby deconstructed is *animality as such* and in general—via the expedient of a de-construction of the substantialist concept of nature—and not the animality *of man*! Although it is relatively easy to deconstruct the way in which the *logos* becomes *ratio*, it remains difficult to deconstruct man's belonging to life, which is not without its own motifs in the tradition.

The Heideggerian position is ambiguous here. Does it effectively consist in affirming—to pose a first hypothesis—that life is not the essential trait of man; that man is not *merely* a living being, an animal; that "the *essence* of man does not consist in being an animal organism"?[42] Or, a second hypothesis, is it compelled to "think man as a *human* being *and not* as a living being,"[43] that is, to think a radical alterity between man and the "animal" in him and outside of him: "The human body is something essentially other than an animal organism";[44] "the living being is separated by an abyss from our

---

39. Ibid., p. 96.
40. Ibid., p. 94.
41. Ibid., p. 95.
42. Wm, p. 322; tr., BW, p. 205.
43. WhD, p. 95; tr., pp. 148–149 (emphasis added: *and not*).
44. Wm, pp. 321–322; tr., BW, p. 204.

eksistent essence"?[45] In the first case, life is something inessential in the human being. Yet what then is the relation of subordination or coordination between the essential, the ek-static, and this inessential aspect? Here we find once more another form of the traditional problem of the union between soul and body. In the second case, life is pure alterity for man; it is alien to the relation to being. But what, then, is the nature of the "corporeal relationship"[46] between the animal and ourselves that Heidegger maintains owing to the constraints of the phenomenon itself? The *Letter on Humanism* describes it as "unfathomable, scarcely thinkable."[47] Yet what this text calls "the enigma of the living being"[48] becomes enigmatic only from the perspective of a preliminary separation of man and life. This enigma is the straightforward counterpart of the exclusively ek-static character of man. "It might seem as though the essence of the divine is closer to us than this strangely impenetrable character of living beings."[49] An antiphenomenological idealism—fortunately rare in Heidegger—brings us near to an essence that we are visibly remote from and distances us from an essence that we visibly are, at least partially! For we have no phenomenological experience of the mode of being of a god, whereas we have some experience of nourishment, pleasure and pain, and sleep, which are undoubtedly not identical in the case of the animal, yet are not radically different either. The idea that the human body is *essentially* different from an animal organism also contradicts scientific, and especially medical, experience. Even if the structure of animal comportment is both simpler and more restrictively immersed in the environment, it is possible to show—as Marc Richir has done[50]—with support from the work of Köhler and Lorenz, that the animal has some recognition of the thing as thing, as well as an elementary attunement, and therefore a certain openness or the beginnings of an openness to a world, though indeed without language. In which case the "abyss" between man and animal would be nonexistent. Moreover, if the animal is "poor in world," must we not acknowledge that it has, nevertheless, a world in which it encounters *phenomena as such?*

---

45. Ibid., p. 323; tr., BW, p. 206.
46. Ibid.
47. Ibid.
48. Ibid., p. 324.
49. Ibid., p. 323.
50. *Phénoménologie et institution symbolique* (Millon, 1988), pp. 265ff.

However things stand, prior to Nietzsche metaphysics considers life as that element which does *not* differentiate man: life is *not the property* of man. In the *rational animal*, the tradition retains and develops rationality above all. As for animality—the animal-machine in Descartes—it itself becomes rationalized via the purely mathematical notion of extended substance, *partes extra partes*. However, one must not think that the *subject* of modern times is simply the *heir* of the ancient *zoon logon echon*. There is undoubtedly a continuity between the two. But the ancient idea of the rational animal will be progressively adapted to the new thought of the subject. The arrival of the subject, for Heidegger, does not result from a mutation in the essence of man as rational animal, but from a mutation in *the essence of truth*. It is not as though man one fine day decides to become a subject. Descartes, searching for the *subjectum*—that is, the thing that "bears" its own qualities (the word *subject* means "support"), the most stable and solid *subjectum*, the one most constantly present, but above all the truest, most certain one—situates it not within man (who is always taken to be a composite), but in the "I," the soul, reason, thought, which are all equivalent terms. It is truth defined in terms of a certainty for conscience (and no longer in terms of the *eidos, energeia,* or *actualitas*) that demands a "subject" in which the *adequation* of evidence can be grasped in the infallible self-presence of the instant. There is a metaphysics of the subject only if true being is understood in the first place as being certain, i.e. as a modality of being-known. However, this new metaphysics takes up the schema of substance from the old anthropology of the rational animal, with the necessary doubling of substance posited by Descartes. The rational animal is thereby confirmed and consolidated within the horizon of self-certainty. Man remains a subsisting entity and will remain so even after the critique of the substantiality of the soul conducted by Kant.

The principle of the de-construction of the subject is a double one. We shall have to be content with merely outlining it here, because to analyze this de-construction in detail would lead us into an examination of gradual developments in the philosophical lineage extending back to Descartes. *In the first instance* it entails the idea that the essence of the subject depends on the essence of truth in the epoch of modernity (Descartes to Kant) and then in the epoch of absolute metaphysics (Hegel to Nietzsche), epochs that themselves assume more ancient mutations in the essence of truth. The essence of modern man is thus inscribed in the *History of Being.* It depends on a *destiny*, on a *constraint* of being, in the face of which the idea

that man is his own maker becomes redundant. Man is not free to
determine his own metaphysical ground. The subject is a historial
figure that, as we shall see later, is condemned to soon being effaced
under the constraint of structures pertaining to the epoch of Technology. There is a Hegelianism here which we shall have to question. In particular, we must ask whether interiority, that reflection
which is the mark of the classical subject, simply remains a relic of
a more ancient epoch for us human beings of the end of the twentieth century. Does the progressive abandonment of interiority and
reflection as a return to the self—from *Dasein* to that thought
which remains "faithful" to being—also occur under the pressure of
the epoch, or does it happen through some necessity for phenomenological rigor? Can one conceive of a human being without his or
her "own," self-referential and self-centered subjectivity, who would
nevertheless still be "free," rather than a calculating slave to
Gestell?

On the other hand, the de-construction of the subject follows
the guiding thread of *representation*. The term *re-presentation,* in
the critical sense accorded it, belongs to an interpretation, or
rather to an *unthought* of the essence of the subject, because neither Descartes, nor Kant, nor indeed Hegel or Nietzsche explicitly
defines the subject by representation. What is implied in representation is in the first place an unlimited objectivization of every
entity, which necessarily entails the self-objectivization of the subject. The subject is the "stage" on which every entity, including
itself, must appear in order to be known and confirmed with certainty. Thinking understood as re-presentation means positing the
totality of entities as opposed, as standing opposite (*Gegenstand*),
but also presenting oneself before oneself as an objectivized subject. In the second place, this double presentation entails the
necessity of submitting oneself to truth as certainty, that is, to the
guarantee of a calculation. Representation is a calculative method
that ensures that whatever can be calculated has an incessant grip
on constant presence. This calculative method implies an aggres-
sion, an "attack" on entities as a whole. "Representation is an
objectivizing that investigates and controls."[51] This indicates that
representation is an inquiring and indiscriminate investigation
that aims to take hold of an entity in its entirety through calculative rationality. The Cartesian method; the Kantian investigation
into conditions of the possibility of objectivity in general, the self-

---

51. Hw, p. 100; tr., QT, p. 150.

presentation and self-conception of the absolute Concept in Hegel; the "calculation" of the Will to power that posits values ensuring its permanent preservation and enhancement—all these must be deciphered as figures of the increasing aggressivity of representation. Cautiously at first, then with increasing assurance and speed, representation places itself directly under the command of a will to domination that, through a new transformation, will become the "will to will," the unthought metaphysical essence of the planetary Enframing of Technology.

The Dissolution of the Subject in Technology; Politics and Subjectivity

In this will to domination that has been unleashed, and that becomes an unconditional will to will, the subject founders and is effaced. When deconstruction begins, the subject has already been destroyed, ruined, yet not abolished. When every entity is effectively reduced to the sole status of object, it constitutes a standing reserve (*Bestand*), an unlimited base and reserve of objectivity in which the subject dissolves. When everything becomes object, there is of course no longer any object for a subject; we can no longer even isolate any object, but are merely faced with an Enframing, a vast net of instrumental relations and interchangeable energetics, in which man, space, and time are swallowed up. We can no longer talk of *objectivity*, but only of *objectity*. Calculability and especially technological manipulability (entirely distinct from the manipulation of tools: in robotics, there is no longer any being-to-hand!) ultimately explode representation. Paradoxically, this does not, however, mean the end of the rational animal. Having become a "calculative beast," a "technicized beast," man is, or risks becoming, entirely subservient to Enframing.

The rational animal becomes *exclusively* rational. His animal drives can be calculated and serve to promote generalized consumption. This pessimistic view of Technological man leads Heidegger to pose the question, which we shall examine later, of a "deadly danger" threatening the essence of man.

Can man lose his essence? Can he abandon his relation to being? It seems not. For precisely the "servant of Technology" merely responds to the call of being that claims him through the will to will. Certainly, to the extent that his essence would thereby be *fixed,* if not forever, at least for centuries—two and a half thousand years perhaps, suggests Heidegger—this essence would no longer be "free." Yet what does freedom mean in any case for man who is restrictively subject to the "destiny of being," that is, to epochal configurations?

Before the subject abolishes itself under the pressure of Enframing, it has had, and still has before it, some fine days, a few days of glory. The metaphysics of subjectivity indeed founds and determines eighteenth century universalism, nineteenth century nationalism, and the "imperialism" of world powers in the twentieth century. These images are not past. They can be repeated and rejuvenated to the point of exhaustion in their paradigmatic force. Thus world domination can mutate into the conquest of space or exploration of the cosmos, all of which leaves a vast field yet to come! On the negative side, many ethnic specificities, those belonging to subcultures, to *local* establishments, to conduct or practices that cannot be standardized, such as customs, religions, and so on—all these would be, or will be (depending on whether one considers universal technologization as unstoppable and inevitable), necessarily destroyed to establish what Heidegger calls "the leveling-down of organized uniformity."[52] As for the movements of resistance to the imposition of state uniformity and to bureaucratic centralization of the economic machine (as manifest in this century, for example, in the countries of Eastern Europe and in various republics of the former Soviet Union)—are they simply a rear-guard defense, resurgences of the nineteenth century? Are they due solely to the poor functioning of state apparatus, or are they signs of a transformation that might announce a truly new future? It is difficult to decide. Yet the odds are that the awakening of various nationalities will likewise be inscribed within the metaphysics of the subject. For Heidegger, the integration or recruitment of individuals into the We of a People or a Nation has just as much to do with subjectivism as the voluntarist, idealist and universalist demand for the "rights of man" that is meant to defend—and quite rightly so—both the citizen and the individual (= *x*) against any state oppression.

One might reply by asking whether there is not an "authenticity" of a People or a Nation that would be nonsubjectivist, that is, nondominating? Is there not also a "freedom" of man to be affirmed and defended, a freedom that could come to be realized in a concrete political regime?

---

52. Ibid., p. 103; tr., QT, p. 152.

Heidegger gives us few positive hints on these questions, for most of his remarks—notably concerning democracy as a system badly adapted to Technology[53]—are critical and aporetic. Because the reign of Technology is *the* incontestable fact of our epoch, it seems that for Heidegger every political system, to be viable, would be forced to correspond to it and therefore to obey it. Heidegger is unwilling to believe or envisage that politicians, or indeed even philosophers, might become conscious of the "danger." And even if they were, they would be unable to reorient their politics in a truly "saving" way. An essential Turning cannot ensue from even the most profound human lucidity, but only from a transformation of being in its originary depths. Yet why should we exclude the possibility that improvements within technology, such as the systematic protection of the environment, for example, might be able to attenuate its devastating effects? Heidegger thinks that the idea of a technological control of Technology (especially any limitation of its growth) via the human will is an illusion that undoubtedly proceeds from a leftover of subjectivism and ignorance as to the unlimited essence of the will to will.

The more recently published *Beiträge* perhaps provide the beginnings of an answer to the first question in a short section entitled *"Da-sein und Volk"*.[54] Here we indeed find two phenomenological remarks on "the essence of a people," remarks whose political consequences are obvious and important, but not explicitly drawn. On the one hand, "The essence of a people is only to be conceived in terms of *Da-sein*." Just as *Dasein*, to be itself in its unity and totality, must reassume its originally "thrown," factical possibilities, so the essence of the people is to project its own tradition, to give back or take back to the future its own way of understanding being and determining itself with respect to other peoples. This means in particular that the essential meaning of a people does not accrue from "geopolitical" facts, but concerns freedom of projection, or in any case of self-interpretation. Like *Dasein*, the people cannot be founded on race, nor on the entirety of its socio-geographico-historical determinations, nor even on the political constitution that this people might have chosen at a particular moment of its history. A people, like a work of art (a work of art that modifies itself through time), is the site of a *struggle* between an Earth (a nonhistorial, quasi-natural side) and a world (i.e. a totality of choices relative to

---

53. Interview published in *Der Spiegel*, 31. May, 1976.
54. GA 65, p. 319.

modes of existence within a determinate epoch). Under what terms can a people conceive of its own finitude or its being-towards-death? The text does not tell us this. However, those who are capable of *thinking* this essence of a people as mortal—as tied to a destiny that is not eternal but stretches over several centuries—are only a few rare individuals. Hence the second remark: "The essence of a people is its 'voice'." Now this "voice" does not speak in "ordinary human beings" (there is an elitism here, to be sure, hardly "democratic"), but "only in a small number." Therefore, we can infer, though it is not stated explicitly, that the voice of the people for Heidegger, as for Hölderlin, is the voice of poets and thinkers! The self-understanding of a people as brought to language does not belong to the 'One', but to those who experience the provenance and future of their people as an intimate question. Every *Dasein* is necessarily in question in its very being. For the people to be *Dasein*, it must— at least for a few—be in question in its very essence! This plural and this questioning exclude, at least from 1936 onward, any totalitarian option. For a totalitarian regime by its essence cannot accept that the very definition of the people be subject to the interrogation of a few, amid a plurality of thoughtful words whose convergence is necessarily problematic. If it is true from the evidence that Heidegger is not a democrat, it is impossible, nevertheless, for him to be a totalitarian. He would be closer to the ancient oligarchic, philosophico-mythical thought of "philosopher-kings," but with the slight difference that we would be dealing with kings who would have permanently renounced political power and whose sole secret authority or sole invisible privilege would be concerned not exactly with the fact that they would speak "for the people," "in their place," but that the people would think through them. But who would govern this people? And according to what constitution? How could the voice or word of these mediators, thinkers or poets, be heard by the people and those governing them? Refusing the contemporary State as subservient to Technology, refusing to confront the ontic problem of institutions, Heidegger's political thinking escapes totalitarianism only to give way to a utopia, to the dream of a quite other site for the City.[55]

---

55. See my essay "L'impensé ambivalent du Surhomme et la double pensée politique de Heidegger," in *Phénoménologie et Politique, Recueil offert en hommage à Jacques Taminiaux* (Ousia, 1989).

The Acts of Thought

If thought as such has no political vocation, what then is its proper vocation? Is its proper vocation not limited precisely to being merely a *vocation*, that is, a being-called? Is not the essence of thought passivity, submission, quasi-transcendence with regard to That which calls it, addresses its *Anspruch* to it, claims it? "Thought accomplishes the relation of being to the essence of man."[56] Does not thought as the supreme accomplishment of the *Verhältnis*, of the complete Relation both of being to man and of man to being, become reduced to the abandonment of any spontaneity of man?

Although defining thought as listening (the *hören* of *zusammengehören*), offering itself, owing something to being ("thought lets itself be claimed by being in order to say the truth of being"[57]), Heidegger maintains that thought not only has an active character, but that it is *action* itself! "Thinking acts insofar as it thinks."[58] How is this possible? How can thought both abandon itself to a relation to being that takes hold of it before it can grasp this relation, and "act"—that is, have a movement of its own—of its own accord? Is thought free? Can it "act" without being free? What is a freedom that would no longer be that of a subject? How can we think a freedom that would be nonautonomous, a freedom that would not be self-determined? Let us leave these questions suspended for a moment. Let us say only, and provisionally, that the notion of "freedom of thought" in the sense of the free thinker of the eighteenth century or the "free spirit" of Nietzsche from *Human, All Too Human*, that the notion of a thought that would place itself outside of a tradition so as to critique or overthrow that tradition scarcely has any meaning for Heidegger. For Heidegger, all thought is a recovering, *Wiederholung*. Wanting to escape from the tradition is the surest way of becoming inextricably imprisoned within it. All thought not only responds to a necessity, but is *Not*; that is, simultaneously urgency, constraint and distress. The "necessary" character of a philosophy comes from its corresponding to the necessity of the things themselves. All thought that does not express the position of an individual, but translates an epochal configuration of being, is inscribed in a historial necessity where past, present, and future are knotted in a compelling and strictly determined fashion.

---

56. Wm, p. 311; tr., BW, p. 193.
57. Ibid., tr., BW, p. 194.
58. Ibid., tr., BW, p. 193.

An essential thinker does not choose his thought, he obeys the situation he is exposed to.

Unlike philosophy, "thought" implies a double understanding both of being (as entirely other than entities) and of the history of metaphysics (as the history of the ways of determining entities as such). Hence the proximity of Heideggerian thought to Hegelian philosophy, which both thinks Spirit as a power of negativity and thinks the successive forms of Spirit in their entire interconnection. Thinking is at the same time to be placed in the presence of the thing itself in order to say its being-present and to be able to relate this presence back to the tradition that passes it to us. Thinking is keeping the present open to its past, but also keeping it free for its future. "Thinking is not a conceptual grasping."[59] Thought is neither the self-movement of the concept, as in Hegel, nor self-perception, the immediate apperception of the faculties of the soul, as in Descartes. How far we are from the Cartesian definition (*Principes*, I, 9.): "By the word 'thought' I understand everything that arises in us in such a manner that we perceive it immediately of our own accord; for this reason not only understanding, willing, and imagining, but also feeling is the same thing here as thinking." Thought in its Heideggerian definition is neither apperception nor a "grasp," a *greifen* (which forms a *Begriff*) concerned with exteriority or interiority. Thought is detached from faculties, separated from the self-consciousness of an individual or a subject. Must we say that it is "universal," like the Hegelian concept? Not at all. Its finitude has to do with its epochal limit. Is not "thought" merely the fact that every word corresponds to a site to be "kept," to be "preserved" within the History of Being and from which this History can be seen?

Yet how can this "maintenance" (*Wahrnis*) of being in accordance with its historial dispensation constitute the action of thought? In what sense is this maintenance active? To which acts of thinking do those incessantly repeated images correspond in *The Origin of the Work of Art,* the *Letter on Humanism,*[60] and the *Beiträge:*[61] those images of man as a watchman or lookout, "guardian" (*Wächter*), "preserver" (*Bewahrender*), "shepherd" (*Hirt*) or even "messenger" (*Botengänger*),[62] the one who has to preserve

---

59. WhD, p. 128; tr., p. 211 (*"Das Denken ist kein Be-greifen"*).
60. E.g., Wm, p. 311 (tr., BW, p. 193): "The thinkers and poets are guardians [*Wächter*]."
61. E.g., GA 65, p. 240.
62. US, p. 136; tr., OWL, p. 40.

the news he has received before passing it on? To guard over being evidently cannot have the same meaning as to watch over some entity or other within the world. Being is invisible. Its preservation does not depend on the alertness of the "eyes of the soul." Rather it depends on acts of thought, which is thereby distinguished from the passivity of disclosedness or the pure light of the clearing.

Three kinds of act, closely blended and correlative, constitute "preservation." First, the *leap* (*Sprung*), that initial act through which thought at a single stroke joins the domain of being, where, nonetheless, it always already finds itself. Second, *commemoration* (*Andenken*) or the *step back* (*Schritt zurück*), whereby thought appropriates metaphysics in its unthought and sees beyond it. Finally, there is the act whereby thought inscribes its *saying* within language, which to a large extent always remains the language of metaphysics.

What is the "leap"? Why is a leap necessary? Is the leap really an *act*, a "voluntary" attitude of thought? Here we risk falling prey to the prejudice of subjectivity: the idea that thought must itself posit its object and take control of it by means of categories....We imagine that there is only one alternative: either thought is a conceptual *labor*, an operation of founding and objectivizing delimitation, or else it is a reflection, an image, an epiphenomenon. There may, however, be an activity of thought without there being objectivization, determination *in terms of* thought. Reflecting on the tradition of the word *noein* in the saying of Parmenides *(to auto esti noein te kai einai)*, Heidegger points out that the usual translation "to apprehend" or "to grasp" is ambiguous. *Noein* can mean a receptivity informed and transformed by conceptuality, in the way that the receptivity of sensibility in Kant is subjected to the spontaneity of the understanding. "However, it is precisely such passive acceptance which is not meant by *noein*."[63] *Noein* does not mean the opposite, either: grasping in the sense of taking, capturing, taking hold of. *Noein* is neither a passivity nor a taking in the sense of capture, but a "taking into custody" *(in die Acht nehmen)*. Thought as *noein* corresponds to a nondominating *logos*, a *logos* that is not rational calculation, but collecting, gathering, "letting be in a gathered manner."

The idea that all thought must initially be a willing, must initially posit being as object, is also based on a prejudice relating to action. It is believed that action must be creation, the producing of

---

63. WhD, p. 124; tr., p. 203.

results, that it must introduce something new and never seen before. However, it is impossible for action to be an absolute beginning, for it can merely be the continuation of that which is, an accomplishing. "We know action only as the production of an effect whose reality is judged according to its use. But the essence of action is accomplishing. Accomplishing means: unfolding something into the fullness of its essence, leading something forth into this, *producere*. What can be accomplished is therefore really only that which already is."[64] All action rests on that which is, but this does not prevent there being a leap between action and inaction.

In the same manner, there is a leap at the beginning of thought, in the sense that precisely thought is unable to begin of its own accord, yet nevertheless begins. Just as swimming demands that one throw oneself into the water, so thinking demands that one entrust oneself to the element that itself makes thought possible. Our access to this element is an act (which can only be sudden, without transition), a movement by which thinking *distances itself* from familiar entities without abandoning them, so as to bring itself before the enigma: that entities are. "The leap is always a departure, but is not an abandonment. On the contrary, the domain from which the leap distances us can be seen differently, from above, and only through this leap can it thus be seen. The leap of thinking does not leave that from which it departs behind it, but appropriates it in a more original manner."[65] The leap implies a sudden change of register or terrain, a way of seeing differently or from elsewhere, a new "focus," as we say in photography. It is a modification in our understanding of being that, from being latent, becomes explicit, becomes a question. This modification may be applied to entities in the world as well as to metaphysical propositions. Discovering the presence of things present, over and beyond everything we know about them, requires a leap. Likewise, passing from the principle of reason as the logical proposition: "no entity is without a cause that determines it to be what it is" to a statement concerning being: "nothing—no entity, i.e. being itself—is itself without-reason, is itself abyss," necessitates a leap. Whenever thinking passes from reflection on the principle of reason to meditating on the nonfoundational character of being, it does not abandon or repudiate the possibility of rationality but instead recoils, returns to this side of what is rational. The leap is a passage "on the

64. Wm, p. 311; tr., BW, p. 193.
65. SvG, p. 107.

spot" from entities to being. Such a passage does not allow for any transition, it can take place only in an *instant*, even if thought subsequently requires many words to clarify it.

By this leap thought attains or reattains at a single stroke, by an élan (*er-springt*, says Heidegger), its belonging to being. This élan of thought thereby anticipates its task, immediately attains the domain it must explore. "The leap traverses by its élan [*durchspringt*] the domain [*Bereich*] that extends between entities and being."[66] This 'between' (*Zwischen*), this distance that the leap covers is at once *imperceptible* on account of its minuteness, for nothing properly speaking separates entities from being (being is not in some separate place), and *immense*, for being takes its absence, withdraws into the massiveness of entities. Heidegger contrasts the suddenness of the leap with the slow passage (which Kant calls *deduction*) proceeding from the object back to its transcendental condition of possibility.

The simplicity of this "on the spot" leap contrasts with the complexity of representation. How do we make present for ourselves that entity which lies before us, for example a tree in bloom? Representational thought requires mediations such as judgment or a corporeal schema. The thinking of being is content to let the tree be where it is and say: *the tree presents itself to us*. Where is the leap here? There is a leap in the fact that we "return" from perception to being uncovered, to the self-giving of world that eliminates the primacy of perception. Presentation is not the affair of a subject and does not take place in our heads. It is to be found where the thing itself is. The leap therefore consists in rediscovering the original ground, in finding our footing again. "It is a strange, or even uncanny thing that we first have to leap in order to attain the very ground on which we find ourselves."[67] We shall understand that our standing face-to-face with things is not that of a subject before an object only if we actually return to the things themselves, and to do so we must throw ourselves out of that center which our subjectivity occupies as though it were self-evident. This is the leap that can be expressed in a straightforward question: "Is the Earth in our heads, or are we standing on the Earth?"[68]

That forgetting that prevents us from spontaneously placing ourselves in that position which always seems straightforwardly

---

66. SvG, p. 134.
67. WhD, p. 17; tr., p. 41.
68. Ibid., tr., p. 43.

"realist" to us is "uncanny," like the deadweight of a tradition of mistrust and uprooting. The leap first of all appears to be an inversion of metaphysics, if not indeed an aversion to it. The leap requires a liberation from representation, one that no reasoning can accomplish. Are we free to make the leap? Yes and no. "The leap remains a free possibility of thought."[69] It is *we* who make it. On our own initiative and of our own accord, though certainly not "at will." The leap reveals where the true "region in which the essence of freedom resides" is situated. We can surmise that this region is not man. For if we can attain it, it is because being allows us to by calling us to it. We are transported onto the terrain of being only by the "favor" (*Gunst*) of being. Just as entities could not appear before us without the light of being; just as there would be no leap, no possible thought, if being did not call us, did not draw us to itself.

And if being calls us, this is because it withdraws! Heidegger establishes a correlation between the *Entzug* or withdrawal of being, the *Zug* or draw of thought that is carried towards it, and the *Bezug*, our relation to being. "As a destinal withdrawing [*Entzug*], being is intrinsically and always already drawn [*Bezug*] to the essence of man."[70] There is thought, that is, a relation to unconcealment, only because being withdraws. We are propelled by the very movement of withdrawal. "That which withdraws from us draws us towards it precisely in this very movement."[71] Here again we see a docility of thought with regard to what being dictates to it. The fundamental relation will indeed be that which proceeds from being to man.

The leap, because it *returns* to its spot, because it leaves its place of departure only so as to better reappropriate it, is at the same time *remembrance* (*Andenken*). "The leap only remains a leap as remembrance [*als andenkender*]."[72] The second act that defines the essence of thought is Memory (*Gedächtnis*), the remembrance of the History of Being, of being as History. Why must the "step back"—the movement that goes back from metaphysics into its unthought essence, the ontological difference[73]—assume the instantaneous and immediate character of the "leap"? How can a remembrance come to be fixed in the instant? Undoubtedly this is meant to mark the fact that the History of Being is different from

---

69. SvG, p. 157.
70. Ibid.
71. WhD, p. 5; tr., p. 9.
72. SvG, p. 158.
73. Cf. ID, p. 40; tr., p. 50.

the logical-dialectical process of totalization, especially insofar as it offers a unique view of being in its being-present. The careful deduction of the epochs of being according to the guiding thread of the ever-increasing obfuscation of *aletheia* is less important than the contemporary concretion of this forgetting in the *Gestell*. *Gewesenes* (*essential having-been*) is *at present* gathered and can be held in a single look. The leap lets us *see* the totality of the past as one and the same destining of being:

> The history of Western thinking first shows itself and only shows itself as a destining of being [*Geschick des Seins*] if we look back [*zurückblicken*] *from out of the leap* [Heidegger's emphasis] on the whole of Western thinking and preserve it in remembrance as a destining of being that essentially has been [*das gewesene Geschick des Seins*]. At the same time, we can only prepare for the leap by speaking out of the History of Being which we have already experienced as a destining. The leap leaves its domain of departure and at the same time in remembrance [*andenkend*] attains this domain anew, so that that which has been can henceforth no longer be lost. The place that the leap leaps into, however, in anticipating, is not some realm of the present-at-hand which we can simply enter, but the domain of that which first comes to us as worthy of thought.[74]

What is surprising is that the power of retrospective, synoptic and panoramic vision, as well as an indelible (*unverlierbar*) conservation of the past (which seems hyper-Hegelian!), and finally a prospective vision should be jointly attributed to thinking as *Sprung* and to thinking as *Andenken*. For whatever is unified, acquired once and for all, and opens onto the future ought to be situated within being rather than within thought. The intervention of thought, however, is limited to taking note. It is not thought that gathers *Gewesenes*. Thinking acts, in its own way, by retaining a memory of this gathering. Why should it henceforth be unforgettable? Can History ever pass to "another commencement" unless the entire past of Being is in turn forgotten? Is not the faithfulness of *Andenken* still a form of *adequation* that must be overcome? Perhaps the translation of *Andenken* as "faithful thought" creates this impression. In any case, *Andenken* must not be taken as equivalent

---

74. SvG, pp. 150–151.

or even analogous to the Hegelian concept of *Erinnerung*. It has to do neither with an accumulative logic nor exclusively with a form of Memory. *An-denken* is taken in the modified sense of *Denken am Sein selbst*, thought that keeps itself alongside being itself. The word is identified with *An-dacht*, a term borrowed from the language of religious devotion and that designates the gathering of the soul in prayer or devoutness (thus the worship of the Holy Sacrament is called *Andacht*). *Andacht*, Heidegger says, means the "gathering of the soul" (*Gemüt*) alongside being. The Kantian word *Gemüt* appears in the elucidation of *Andenken*, provided by the course *What Is Called Thinking?* in terms of the words formed around the same root: *Gedanke, Dank, Gedächtnis*. The entire elucidation has an accent of *piety*. The soul in remembrance becomes obedient, without simply being submissive: it listens, in gathering, to what language says (*hörenden Andacht*). Thinking in remembrance is above all an act of gratitude, an action of grace. *Denken* is *Danken*. To think is to understand being as a gift, and to be grateful *to it*. "That to which we owe thanks we do not have of our own accord. It is given to us."[75] Yet although we can thank someone, how can we thank or experience gratitude for an anonymous dimension, even if it is the most original? Is there not a temptation here to "repatriate" on the ontological level a phenomenon belonging so intimately to religious faith?

All *Andenken* is memory (*Gedächtnis*)—yet not recollection— in the sense that thought re-*tains* [re-*tient*], persists, does not release its hold. To translate *Andenken* as "faithful thought," apart from the fact that it recalls the allegories of *la Carte du Tendre*[76] (faithful heart/ungrateful heart?), loses the initial sense of the word *memory*, especially the fact that it means the opposite of the forgetting of being. Translating it as "commemoration" gives too solemn and emphatic a meaning to the word. One must distinguish the equivalent we are proposing, *remembrance*, from the psychological concept of memory and recall (*Wiedergedächtnis*), though *Andenken* and *Gedächtnis* are the same activity of thought. *Remembrance*, or *memory*, Heidegger says, is originally "the soul as a whole"—which is the capacity to reside alongside...and keep to...—a wholeness of the soul that the metaphysics of subjectivity has restricted to the

---

75. WhD, p. 94; tr., p. 142.
76. Translator's note: Literally, "the map of the tender": an imaginary map of the Land of Love, from the seventeenth century novel *Clélie* by Madeleine de Scudéry.

faculty of recollection. To speak of recollection as a separate faculty would thus be to reduce the whole to the part.

> Initially, "memory" does not at all mean the faculty of recollection. The word names the soul as a whole in the sense of an intimate and constant gathering alongside that which constantly addresses itself to all thinking [*Sinnen*]. Memory [*Gedächtnis*] originally means *An-dacht*, a ceaseless and gathered remaining alongside..., and not merely alongside what is past, but in the same way alongside that which is present and that which may come.[77]

It is strange that Heidegger grants such a capacity for constancy, for constant presence, to "memory" in the broad sense. If thought is also essentially and continually recollection, how can it ever *forget* being? And yet human memory does not of its own accord possess any original power to gather and preserve.

> The gathering of remembrance is not founded on any human faculty such as the faculty of recollection or retention. All remembrance of what can be remembered itself already inhabits that gathering through which all that remains to be thought is protected and concealed in advance....Memory [*Gedächtnis*] as human remembrance [*Andenken*] of what is to be thought rests in the safeguarding [*Verwahrnis*] of that which is most thought-provoking. This is the essential ground of memory....Man does not create this safeguarding.[78]

Man can only "keep in memory," or indeed "keep" in general on the basis of this "safeguarding" that has always already been accomplished in being. Our keeping rests on something already kept. We can "keep in mind" only what being preserves for us. "Only the safeguarding frees and *gives* that which must be kept in thought..."[79] The human faculties therefore vanish, or at least their condition of possibility in man. For man finds himself stripped, if not of the "use" of his faculties, at least of any power over them. Yet what are "faculties" over which we have no power?

Thought, as a "placing in memory," insofar as it "keeps" to the

---

77. WhD, p. 92; tr., p. 140.
78. Ibid., p. 97; tr., p. 151.
79. Ibid.

unity of the three ekstases of temporality and not solely to the past, is not limited to a retrospective relation. It is also anticipation, a view on the future. *Denken ist andenkendes Vordenken.*[80] "Thinking is thinking ahead in remembrance." This foreseeing is different from a representation; it has nothing in common with a prophecy, with something construed by science fiction, or with a sociological, economic, or political futurology. Of what does this nonrepresentational view of the future consist? The future to come is not *constructed* at all, for what is at stake is something unthought that is yet to come because it still remains to be thought (*zu-denkende*). The future is unknowable in terms of its contents, but it is *prefigured* in its essential structure that we know via the History of Being. Thus we know that the epoch of the will to will is not going to disappear tomorrow, nor the day after tomorrow, but will be intensified in keeping with an accelerated planetary uniformization that the development of information Technology and cybernetics contribute to in particular. The future is coming towards us from the most distant past. The exigency—especially that of rationality—inscribed in the Greek commencement always summons us anew. And only *Andenken* can "foresee" such an ancient future.

Thought and Language

A third "act" of thought, not simply in addition to the "leap" and *Andenken* but simultaneous with them is the insertion of thought into language. "Only insofar as man speaks does he think, and not vice versa."[81] Thought is not an internal or *mute* unfolding of ideas. It is always thinking language, speaking thought. It must find its language, search for words. Here again there is an ambiguity between that part which concerns man and that which concerns being. For thought is inscribed straightaway within a particular language in which it traces its path. What autonomy can it have, given that "Language speaks, not man. Man speaks only insofar as he corresponds [*entspricht*] historially to language"?[82] Man, as thinking, does not manipulate words as instruments with the purpose of communicating some message, but always already "dwells" in language, "the house of being and shelter of the essence of man."

---

80. SvG, p. 159.
81. WhD, p. 51; tr., p. 16.
82. SvG, p. 161.

And yet Heidegger maintains that thought "acts": "Thought is attentive to the clearing of being whenever it inserts its saying into language....In this way thought is a doing [*Tun*]."[83] Thinking acts to the extent that it "brings being to language." What is meant by this famous expression *zur Sprache bringen*, which by definition is the very equivalent of thinking? "To bring to language thus means: to first raise to language that which remained unformulated, that which was never said, and to make appear, by a saying that shows, that which until then remained withdrawn."[84] This relatively late text (1958) would appear to take up once more the activism of *Introduction to Metaphysics* (1935): "The creator [*der Schaffende*] enters into the un-said, irrupts into the un-thought, forcibly brings about that which has not yet happened, and makes appear that which has yet to be seen..."[85] The act of *zur Sprache bringen*, however, is the very opposite of an activism—which in the 1935 text implied a conquering of unconcealing—the opposite of a struggle against withdrawal, of an extracting from latency, for since *The Origin of the Work of Art* (1936) all *schaffen* has been interpreted as a *schöpfen*, a drawing from the reserve of being. Raising the unsaid to saying is certainly the proper work of the thinker. Yet this can be accomplished only under the "dictate" of being; that is, on the condition of a thrust of being itself towards its coming to light. By his or her word, the thinker or poet helps being to appear, but does not *make* it appear, especially not by force. Everything depends on a listening, an awaiting (though not an awaiting of something already determined). This attentive listening from which language emerges demands silence, a restraint (*Verhaltenheit*), an awe (*Scheu*)— moods without which there is no integrity of saying—and it also demands a meticulous, skilled "labor" on language: a "frugality with words,"[86] a "care for the letter as such."[87] Being does not inscribe itself in the letter of its own accord. The word-to-word of truth is left to man. Only thinking-language, if it is "attentive to the fittingness of the saying of being,"[88] attains sufficient simplicity, "poverty," that is, renunciation of the effects of manipulating language, to somehow efface itself, become inapparent, to become the

---

83. Wm, p. 357; tr., BW, p. 239.
84. Hebel, p. 25.
85. EM, p. 123; tr., p. 161.
86. Wm, p. 360; tr., BW, p. 241.
87. Ibid.
88. Ibid., p. 359.

"language of being." Fittingness (*Schicklichkeit*) means the fitting, appropriate articulation of that which is destined (*geschickt*), sent or dispensed. "It is the fittingness of the saying of being as that of the destiny of truth that is the first law of thinking, not the rules of logic..."[89] Thinking operates by making itself more simple, more responsive, more translucid: "Thinking gathers language into a simple saying. Language is then the language of being, like the clouds are the clouds of the heavens."[90]

Heidegger has provided many examples of this simple saying or this language of being. Such language would attempt to have recourse not so much to new words as to a new syntax. *Being and Time* already foresaw this: "It is not only the words which are most often lacking for this task, but above all the 'grammar'."[91] For thought is indeed usually obliged to use the words of metaphysics, even if they are quasi-dead (the *corpus* of the tradition, ossified language...), to employ them as "sticks and crutches."[92] There are not so many new words even—indeed especially—in the "later Heidegger," as rather words *heard differently*: thus *Ereignis, Gestell, Geviert, Sage, Brauch,* and many other essential terms are words quite current in ordinary language. The aim of this attention to words is also to awaken an archaic, prelogical meaning in classical concepts, and thereby to turn them away from their unquestioned metaphysical employment that has become *selbstverständlich*, self-evident, and pseudo-transparent. Thus, *Satz* is not simply understood as *proposition*, but also as the leap (towards the "principle," towards being); *Notwendigkeit*, necessity, becomes the "turning [*die Wende*] of distress [*der Not*]."[93] *Bedingung*, condition, is that which procures or ensures a thing (*Ding*). This movement leads us back from pure logic to its lost concretion, by way of a quasi-Husserlian step. Likewise *Möglichkeit*, possibility, is linked back to the verb *mögen*, to like or desire. *Erörterung*, discussion, when we trace it back to its root *Ort*, becomes a "return to the site," a "situating." The *Weiser*, the sage, is someone who can point out (*weisen*) a path. It is wrong to judge these language games according to the norm of etymological and philological exactness. What is at stake is to

89. Ibid.
90. Ibid., p. 360; tr., BW, p. 242.
91. SZ, p. 39.
92. NII, p. 397; tr., NII, vol. Four, p. 250.
93. This deconstruction of the word is already found in *Thus Spake Zarathustra*. Cf. NI, p. 471; tr., NI vol. Two, p. 207.

rediscover hidden possibilities in language, to "remain open to the force and range of its saying."[94] The repeated, mechanical, and sedimented employment of words without returning to the experience of the thing they point towards has weakened, exhausted, and made excessively banal those original words that have precisely lost their "apophantic" capacity, their power to point out.

The loss of the "things themselves" comes from the loss of the words themselves. "No thing where the word is lacking."[95] Yet the word may fail even when present; it may simply lack apophantic *force*. Hence the constant return to a more simple, more "material" meaning, which entails a deconstruction of traditional logical meaning. Thus, *logos* is taken back to the "sensible" meaning of posing (*legen*) and collecting or gathering (*lesen*); *aletheia* is traced back to nonlatency, un-concealment; *phusis* to emerging into light (whose heart remains obscure and in reserve). A new and more straightforward understanding of the concepts of classical rationality sometimes arises from their simple transposition or from rewriting them: an understanding in which their "sensible" meaning resonates once more. Thus *Differenz* becomes *Unter-schied, Aus-trag*, which points to the active sense of separating or dividing (*scheiden*) and sustaining (*tragen*) two elements, one outside the other. Similarly, a straightforward splitting of the words *Gegen-stand* and *Ab-grund* points to the roots *stehen* and *Grund* that we ordinarily overlook. When *Wahrheit* is written *Wahr-heit*, what is restituted is the primitive act of uniting and guarding, *wahren*, in the sense of guarding (*hüten*) a flock. Writing *Be-stimmung* brings out the sense of mood, attunement, from the abstract signification of the word, which means "definition" or "destination." Writing *An-fang* lets us hear anew the act of capturing, of initially catching (*fangen*), taking-hold, within the abstract term meaning "commencement." *Bewegung* written as *Be-wëgung* converts the abstract banality of "movement" into the tracing of a path (*Weg*), though at the expense of what seems a very arbitrary etymology. Thus a new hearing of metaphysical concepts written differently restores their carnal and in some sense "performative" dimension. From this point of view, German has resources unavailable to the French language.

On the question of a new syntax, the accusation of "jargon"[96] is meaningless, for one could just as well accuse Plato of having

---

94. Wm, p. 469.
95. US, p. 163.
96. Cf. Adorno, *The Jargon of Authenticity* (Suhrkamp, 1964).

invented the substantive *ousia* when Greek language previously knew only the present participle of the verb *einai, ousa,* or say that Aristotle coined the nonexistent word *energeia,* or that Hegel ought to have chosen between the different accepted meanings of the term *Aufhebung!* And if "to jargon" means to repeat insistently the same concepts, then let one reread the *Critique of Practical Reason,* where *autonomy* and *heteronomy* reappear incessantly like two sides of the same coin. What a philistine platitude! The eternal resistance to philosophy on the part of common sense! It must be acknowledged that there does indeed exist a Heideggerian jargon, but it is that of poor translations. And it is not Sartre or Corbin who are responsible for this in France, but alas Beaufret himself, who has put a number of contradictory translations into circulation (for example, the translation of *Unverborgenheit* by *Ouvert sans retrait* [*Open without withdrawal*],[97] when un-concealment always entails withdrawal), and certain ultra-Beaufretians who have sometimes pushed archaizing preciosity or false simplicity to the point of comical silliness (let us recall among hundreds of unfortunate "cases" the terms *porriger* and *entonner* for words as simple as *reichen* and *stimmen*), and who, through their coquetry, have often made numerous contradictions, false meanings and nonsense. Their jargon is undoubtedly the reason why Heidegger has been rejected by a large part of university philosophy in France, and this reaction has been quite justified and sane. There would be little philosophical interest in speculating on the reasons for the isolationism of the post-Beaufretian clan. On the other hand, many translations need to be redone, starting of course with the confusing and baroque "bilingual" French translation of *Being and Time.*

To return to the Heideggerian syntax, it is quite contrary to the truth to affirm, as do some,[98] that Heidegger's only moves away from metaphysical discursivity are his use of tautology (for example, "time temporalizes") and analogy (for example, "being as clearing"). To begin with, one condemns a priori these stylistic turns, in the name of old prejudices that are both metaphysical and logical-grammatical. On the one hand, it is thought that sound logic tells

97. Cf. for example Heidegger, *Questions IV,* pp. 131–139: "l'état de n'être en nul retrait" ["the state of being in no withdrawal"] (!), or the *sans-retrait* ["without withdrawal"] (?).
98. L. Ferry and A. Renaut, in "Heidegger en question," *Archives de Philosophie* 4 (1978).

us that the circle is vicious. One ignores the circular, anticipatory structure of all understanding. On the other hand, analogy and image are confused in the idea of a proportional transposition of the intelligible into the realm of the sensible. Yet being does not first have an "abstract" meaning that then becomes concrete, for the word *is* has an indeterminate meaning—understood each time in a determinate manner—that cannot be reduced to a *concept.* Analogy exists only within the metaphysical thought of a hierarchization of levels of entities. Every entity, however, is directly a presence of being. Moreover, it is possible to "judge" Heideggerian tautology and analogy only by looking at what they deconstruct: in the first case, the authority and primacy of the subject over the verb; in the second case, the metaphysical difference itself. But there are other forms of syntax in addition to these two, such as the *chiasm* (for example, "the essence of truth is the truth of essence")—but one would have to analyze the change in the meaning of *Wesen* and *Wahrheit* in the two expressions, even though the systematic recurrence of this structure has been decisively shown with complete textual precision, as has been done by J.-F. Mattéi.[99] In addition, we find extended *parataxis* (concerning not the *juxtaposition of words* in a phrase, but the *juxtaposition of phrases* in certain texts, permitting the breaking of links of subordination and deductive structure in particular);[100] the different *emphasizing* of words in a proposition (for example, in the analysis of *Nichts ist ohne Grund,*[101] sometimes the *Nichts,* sometimes the *ist,* and sometimes the *ohne Grund* carries the meaning of the phrase). One ought to point out that an expression such as *die Sprache spricht*[102] is in fact not a tautology at all, but an attempt to *intensify* the role of the "verb," the phenomenon, and to diminish that of the subject, of substance. Nietzsche had already noted the purely grammatical, false substantialization of the subject that occurs when language forces us to say "lightning flashes": we wrongly isolate the lightning that cannot in fact be distinguished from the phenomenon of "flashing."[103] When one maintains, like Renaut and Ferry, that "a discourse can only be rational, i.e. syntactic,"[104] what one calls *rational* is straight-

---

99. See *La métaphysique à la limite* (P.U.F., 1983), pp. 49ff.
100. For example, in *Overcoming Metaphysics*, VA, pp. 67–95.
101. Translator's note: *"Nothing is without ground."*
102. Translator's note: *"Language speaks."*
103. *Genealogy of Morals*, I, Section 13.
104. "Heidegger en question," p. 632.

forward grammatical convention that is blindly accepted in all its opacity. A rather un-"critical" position for critics!

Thinking and Questioning

Irruption into being, the vigilance of remembrance, simple saying— are we not forgetting in this threefold definition that, as anyone who has read a little Heidegger will realize, the exercise of thought is primarily manifest as an unceasing questioning? From the first words of *Being and Time*: "The question of being has today been forgotten..."—to the famous concluding words of the essay on "The Question Concerning Technology"—"Questioning is the piety of thought"—it seems that *Denken* and *Fragen* test and determine one another. The term *piety* indicates the most *intimate* heart and essential resource of thinking: as long as questioning remains *safe*, thinking remains alive and has a future. But safe does not mean holy or sacred. This sudden religious turn of phrase perhaps translates a repressed nostalgia.

But what is questioning? From where do questions and the power of questioning come to us? *What Is Metaphysics?*, *What Is Called Thinking?*, *The Question of the Thing*, *On the Question of Being*, and so forth.

The origin of the question is twofold, and there are fundamentally only two questions for Heidegger. On the one hand, the metaphysical tradition asks: What are entities as such? This is the question of *ti esti*, that of "essence": the *Leitfrage*[105] or "guiding question" running throught the entire History of Being precisely as a guiding thread. On the other hand, the question comes from being itself: something glimpsed by *Being and Time* in saying that *Dasein* is that entity whose being is "in question" in its being, or that through it the meaning of being comes to be questioned. This first work of Heidegger's designated its proper task to be "the concrete working out of the question of the meaning of being": concrete, that is, in and through *Dasein*. This second question, the "fundamental question" or *Grundfrage*, What is being as such?, digs an abyss under all foundations, for being is not an essence, a reason or ground, and the return to being no longer permits us to reply to the question "why entities?" by way of a "solution"—it no longer permits any transcendental deduction. As opposed to the question that secures

---

105. Cf. GA 44, pp. 205–215.

an essence for itself, the *Grundfrage*, in opening the openness of the open, constantly suspends man and every entity and places them in question. This putting into question does not depend on any decision made by thought, for it is the result of both *Ereignis* and the completion of metaphysics. The activity of thought consists in working out the question, in interrogating the question, but it is unable to wholly determine it initially by posing it freely and deliberately, releasing and controlling it at will, or "keeping it at bay" so to speak, also in the sense that it might not pose it. The "primacy" and "necessity" of the question of being are so uncircumventable, so anterior to all logic and all will, that the question has always already posed itself, if only implicitly, whenever we begin to think and speak. It has posed itself in and through language, in the name of an understanding of being that is borne by language, in the name of the call and demand harbored in the little word *is*. Being is the prior positing of its question. This spontaneity of the *Grundfrage* attests the power of being over language. Being speaks and questions us *itself* through language, at least if we are adequately able to *listen* to it.

This is why it is not at all a matter of a recantation when, very late in his journey, Heidegger in *Unterwegs zur Sprache* (1959) seems radically to relativize the instance of questioning: "It is not questioning that is the true gesture of thinking, but—listening to the address of that which is to come into question."[106] In other words, we can be attentive only to the question or questions that pose themselves. Every true question in effect *poses itself* before we pose it. We merely have to awaken it. A "problem," on the other hand, is something we construct out of many pieces, mostly to protect ourselves from a true question behind a kind of shield (*problema* in Greek means armor, barrier, or rampart). "A problem is a question whose answer is left blank," as Leibniz put it. The kind of thinking that obeys the principle of reason, calculative thinking, also questions— but it procures in advance what are called "the given facts of the problem." Above all, it gives itself the limits of its questioning. For it knows in advance that it will find a cause, a sufficient reason, a raison d'être, because being equals reason. The kind of questioning belonging to meditative thinking, on the contrary, is not *Grund-legend*: it is not a questioning in the sense of an interrogation that posits and demands in advance a first reason and ultimate reasons. Heidegger here realizes the wish that Husserl was unable to realize

---

106. US, p. 175; tr., OWL, p. 71.

for lack of radicality: the complete absence of presuppositions. That thought should be pious, *fromm*,[107] we are told in *Unterwegs zur Sprache*, means that thought is "pliant [*fügsam*] to what thinking has to think," namely, language. This pliancy or obedience to the "things themselves" that are henceforth borne and presented by the words themselves, this "initiative" on the part of language, runs ahead of all questioning as the first moment of thought, a moment that cannot be the assuredness of whoever is interrogating or asking for an explanation. If it remains faithful to the helplessness and terror of our twilight—to which questioning can respond only inadequately, without ever being able to annul them—then no thought in our epoch can identify itself with questions and be satisfied with them or within them. The simple language-bearer of being, thought sees itself deprived of its questions.

To what extremity of destitution will the essence of man find itself reduced, if we now examine it in terms of the relation in which being holds it throughout its History and especially at its end?

---

107. Ibid. That translation which gives *preux* [valiant] for *fromm*, *prouesse* [feat] for *Frömmigkeit*, and two equivalents for *fügsam*, introduces a "heroic" nuance foreign to the text, while hiding the obvious relation of proximity and tension with respect to piety in the theological sense of the word.

Chapter 5

BEING'S RELATION TO MAN

"Man stands within the relation of being itself to him, man."[1] What is meant by this? Not only is man not enclosed within self-consciousness, nor even within the subject-object relation, but his ekstatic élan does not proceed to encounter being as a face-to-face. The human ekstase does not encounter being on its own path, so to speak. Being is not that which opens *before* man or proceeds *towards him*, for being repossesses man and encompasses him from head to toe. Being is just as much behind him, beside him, on all sides. A more ancient "region" (*Gegend*) than human space-time surrounds his "locality" (*Ortschaft*), without this topology having anything to do with a natural phenomenon. In other words, human transcendence and facticity are always already gathered, taken up and metamorphosed in and through the primary movement, which is that of being towards us.

Several consequences flow from this. (1) Our relation to being is *secondary*: it grafts itself onto the relation that proceeds from being. In all his steps, man responds, receives; he *administers* (Heidegger's image: man is the *Verwalter* [administrator][2] of freedom, as he puts it) domains of *possibilities* that are already accessible. (2) Man is *maintained* within the primary relation, whether he wants to be or not, whether he knows it or not. This "maintenance" or this "usage" (*Brauch*) that being makes of him determines a necessity: it "compels" man to being; being "provides itself [*begabt sich*] with this

---

1. NII, p. 358; tr., NII, vol. Four, p. 217.
2. GA 31, p. 134.

gift" which is man. (3) Thought, however, is not a transfer of this primary relation, for it is that through which man maintains himself in this relation, relates to it in interpreting entities as such, that is, in thinking them metaphysically ("Man maintains himself in the relation...insofar as man comports [*verhält*] himself as man with respect to entities as such," says the sentence in its entirety). The relation proceeding from being is not in itself complete or achieved unless man *thinks* it. Man thereby brings it to its fulfillment; such is the very definition of thought: "thought brings to its fulfillment [*vollbringt*] being's relation to the essence of man."[3]

The fact that our relation to being is immanent to the relation proceeding from being has, in a general way, the consequence of radically submitting thought, which the second relation amounts to, to the "power" of being. Man is able to think only because being disposes him to do so. "Being enables thinking."[4] In the expression *the thinking of being,* the genitive is both "subjective" (according to the metaphysics immanent to grammar!) in the sense that thinking is *vom Sein ereignet,* "an event of being," and "objective" in that it "listens to being" (*auf das Sein hört*).[5]

Thus all activity proceeds from being: being gives man the possibility (*Möglichkeit*) to be himself, and to do so it "desires" him (*Mögen*). Being frees man into the dimension of original freedom (*Freiheit*) that is the truth of his own disclosedness; it addresses itself to man, calls him (*Geheiss, Ruf*), claims or calls for him (*Anspruch*), makes "use" of him (*braucht ihn*), destines its sending to him (*Geschick*). All the most eminent "faculties," every form of *Vermögen* or capacity, everything that was once most proper to man, is attributed to being: in particular the *mögen* (desire, power) of *Möglichkeit,* the gift of *Freiheit,* the *heissen* of *Geheiss,* the *ansprechen* of *Anspruch,* the *brauchen* of *Brauch,* the *schicken* of *Geschick.*

Does not this attributing result from an obvious anthropomorphism? Is being not personified, reclothed with the remains of man; is it not animated with capacities that, apart from man, have hitherto only been bestowed upon God—love, desire, demand, will? In a word, do we not find being raised to a phantasmatic, supernatural, mythical Actor? Is it not mythological to describe being as using man to say itself; to present human saying as "bringing to lan-

3. Wm, p. 311; tr., BW, p. 193.
4. Ibid., p. 314; tr., BW, p. 196.
5. Ibid.

guage" a gathering of meaning, a *Logos* already accomplished in silence? How would such a schema be any different from a metaphysical representation, for example that of Spirit in Hegel, that effectively uses human beings and peoples as instruments with a view to realizing its rational teleology? Is not Heideggerian man the medium, the figurehead, but also in a much more worrying sense the toy or puppet of being, as this game is aimless? For despite the bold crossing-out of being in *On the Question of Being* (1955) and all the efforts to bring together, if not to identify, man and being in a "belonging together," it nonetheless remains the case that there is something proper to being that is absolutely distinct from what is proper to man. In effect there is no real reversibility—despite what Derrida seems to maintain ("Man is the proper of being...being is the proper of man"[6])—between the properties of man and those of being. As we have shown earlier,[7] there is a radical disproportion between, on the one side, the poverty and basic receptivity of man and, on the other side, the richness and inexhaustible, effusive capacity of being. Hence the fragility of the concept of "belonging together," which implies a reciprocity that so many analyses of the human situation will succeed in undermining.

To focus our question somewhat better: Would not the proper of being be the inverted image or mirror image of the traditional essence of man? Is not Heideggerian thought, by this fact, a straightforward inversion of metaphysics?

Let us not forget, to begin with, that in the eyes of common sense all philosophy represents "the inverted world" and that the truth of a fundamental thought cannot be measured by the norms of good sense, common sense, or everyday likelihood.

Two further reasons argue against there being a simple *reversal*. First, the explicit relation between Heidegger and metaphysics, especially Hegelian metaphysics, cannot be established in terms of a *turning back*. Hegelian philosophy had already removed man from its center in principle, and in one sense Heidegger pursues this movement. Instead, it is a matter of a relation of appropriation or *Verwindung*, by way of a return to a domain of truth prior to every metaphysical construction: the *unthought*. The difference between absolute Spirit and the particular forms of natural consciousness

---

6. *Marges de la philosophie* (Minuit, 1972), p. 160. Trans. A. Bass, *Margins of Philosophy* (University of Chicago, 1982), p. 133.
7. Cf. the section on "The False Symmetry of the Double Relation Between Man and Being," pp. 63ff.

must be rethought on the forgotten basis of the ontological difference. What distinguishes the Heideggerian thinking of man from the Hegelian conception that thinks in terms of metaphysical representations is the absence of all *finality*, whether rational or irrational, in being's relation to man. Being does not "want" to attain some result or other via man, unlike Spirit that, for example, uses the passions to further the rationality of the real. Being pursues no goal. The unfolding of being is "play";[8] that is, it is impossible to decipher any program in it, any raison d'être or any foundation. What escapes the human mind in this or that epoch is not recaptured or retained on the part of being, as though in a Subject that had absolute Knowledge for all eternity. *Being does not know its own withdrawal.* It is neither God, nor absolute Subject; it is not that entity *most in being*; it is not transparent to itself, nor present to itself. In Hegel, the being of entities knows itself entirely, whereas man must educate himself and only gradually discovers knowledge. From there, the relation between the being of entities and man assumes the form of a theological drama. In Heidegger, nonrepresentation is the impossibility of a *theology of totality*, or of a philosophical knowledge of totality. Being, even and especially when it comes to be totalized in Technology, is defined by the constitutive absence of any self-adequation. Withdrawal or latency does not come to be added to being, but is correlative to it.[9] In other words, that part of being which is concealed is not given, is not "in the clear," neither there nor anywhere else. Being means self-withdrawing from full presence. This lack, linked to the temporality of being and its historiality, cannot be filled, compensated or overcome. Withdrawal has no content, and yet it is not an absolute nothing. Being, in its reserve, does not yet contain that which will be. It makes possible without having any intrinsic, preformed possibilities.

The fact that being "speaks in accordance with a sending in each case" (*spricht je und je geschicklich*)[10] is not the result of some speculation or other, but constitutes an actual fact, something given by the History of Being. This fact cannot be deduced from a previous state, although it can be situated in a process that is essentially that of the epochal mutations in the essence of truth.

The second reason that speaks against a straightforward reversal is that Heidegger does not reverse the traditional essence

---

8. ID, p. 58; tr., p. 66.
9. SvG, p. 122.
10. ID, p. 41; tr., p. 51.

of man, as he *displaces* the question of essence in general. Any determination of essence demands a displacement that is a regression from the domain to be defined towards that which makes it possible. Essence is possibility, not in the Platonist sense of an ideal possibility or a logical, universally valid truth, nor in the Aristotelian sense of potentiality, but in the sense of an act of making-possible or a potentiality for being that sustains whatever is made possible. Just as the essence of mathematics cannot be reduced to a mathematical formula nor the essence of physics to a physical reality, so "the essence of man is nothing human."[11] To think the essence of something is not to bring it into full view, but to point out its limits and what exceeds it. The essence of everything maintains itself secretly behind it, at the rear. It is not in the nature of essence to be something evident. As with phenomena, essence needs to be explicitly made manifest. A regressive move is needed, then, towards what is hidden: it must be shown that the essence of man is thought, that the essence of thought is a relation to being, that the essence of this relation itself is being's relation to man—for none of this is obvious at all.

Nonetheless, the appearance of a reversal persists: being seems to have faculties, a strategy, a quasi-human comportment with respect to man, since it "desires" human thought, "gives" itself to it, "needs" it. What can be meant by a desire, a gift, or a need in a nonhuman, impersonal power? Once more, is it not a *Schwärmerei*, a mystical exaltation coupled with inconsistency, to say that being likes man, reveals itself or conceals itself from him, awaits something from him? For how could the nothing, that which is "entirely other than entities" "comport" itself or "relate" to us of its own accord? *We* have a relation to the nothing, but does the nothing have a relation to us? A doubt suddenly crosses our mind: might not being be a hypostasis of the contingency of the world? The idea of an activity of being that would "throw" us into the midst of entities, that would itself, as being, have a "hidden projection on time," seems to be our projecting into a Subject that which escapes us. Being possesses a powerful and coherent unity, whereas it may be that all our blind perspectives are nowhere unified, and that the nothing which begins beyond our limits has—as Malebranche said—"no properties." Any reading of Heidegger that would *exclude* such questions seems threatened by dogmatism. A further question

---

11. NII, p. 377; tr., NII, vol. Four, pp. 232–233 (*"Dieses Wesen ist nichts Menschliches"*).

raised by the description of being's relation to man as desire, gift, and need is whether we are dealing with an ontological transposition of the mystical schema of *dispossession*. It is not I who speaks, but God who speaks in me. It is not man who thinks, but being that makes him think. Heidegger would undoubtedly reply that being's relation to man is more "ancient" or more original than all mysticism and all philosophy. He might quote Heraclitus in testimony: "If it is not me, but the Logos you are listening to..." The question, however, must be posed.

The Possible, or the Relation of Shared Desire

Man, therefore, is not the bearer of "conditions of possibility." Even less is he the author of them. He does not keep hold of the possible, but receives it as the sphere and limit of his action and thought. Only that which is is possible. "Only that which already is can be accomplished."[12] This restriction ("only") points to the finitude of being itself. This does not mean that many things are possible, but not everything. It always means, among other things, that thought and human action further (or accomplish) whatever being (i.e. this or that *situation, world,* or particular *epoch*) makes possible; that is, that which discloses itself to us as possible within a given framework.

Yet although there is receptivity with regard to what is possible, man is not passive. For something to be *thinkable*, it must first be and give or present itself to us. The next thing that is necessary, however, is that we are turned towards it just as much as it is towards us. "It is only when we like [*mögen*] that which is to be thought in itself that we have the capacity [*vermögen*] to think."[13] In other words, it is necessary that our desire to think being respond to that movement which brings being towards us, towards that space of presence and clarity that we are. For Heidegger, this movement is none other than the originary desire to appear and to be thought. This, however, is where the thought of being seems to coincide with a mystical presupposition. Why mystical? Because the agreement between being and us does not lend itself to any transcendental exposition or deduction like the subject-object agreement. It is founded on a shared *philia* or *eros*, something that demands the indemonstrable coincidence of our capacity for "agree-

---

12. Wm, p. 311; tr., BW, p. 193.
13. WhD, p. 1; tr., p. 3.

ment" (i.e., our movement towards being) and of an "amorous" (*mögen*) élan of being towards us. This élan of being is equally a tranquil inclination (*Zuneigung*). Let us read the wonderful meditation on the possible and the capacity for thinking at the beginning of the essay *What Is Called Thinking?*

> Man can think insofar as he has the possibility [*Möglichkeit*] of doing so. This possibility alone, however, does not yet guarantee that we have the capacity [*vermögen*] to do so. For being capable of something means: our receiving something in accordance with its essence, and inherently guarding this reception. Yet that of which we are capable [*vermögen*] is always only that which we desire [*mögen*], that which we are fond of, in that we grant it admission. We only truly desire that which in each case desires us in advance [*zuvor*] of its own accord, indeed us in our essence, in that it inclines to this essence. By way of this inclination [*Zuneigung*], our essence is laid claim to [*in den Anspruch genommen*]. Inclination is address [*Zuspruch*]. The address addresses us with respect to our essence, calls us forth into our essence [*Wesen*], and thereby maintains us in this essence. To maintain [*Halten*] properly means to guard [*hüten*]. That which maintains us in our essence only maintains us, however, so long as we ourselves, of our own accord, retain that which maintains us. We retain it if we do not let it out of our memory. Memory is the gathering of thought.[14]

From this passage, which is both simple and complex due to the multiple connections it makes, we can see above all that the key to being's relation to man is the silent "address" (*Zuspruch* and *Anspruch*) that language makes to man. It is not a mystical idea that language speaks to us—this is perhaps the way in which Heideggerian phenomenology escapes being classified as mystical, a point we shall come back to—but the fact that there should be attached to this call *a desire for the essence of man on the part of being*, namely, thought, is what seems hard to justify by pure description. Heidegger postulates the *identity* of two modes of being's relation to man, or the identity of two moments (that of desire and the possible and that of thought-language) that characterize the text. This identity centers on the pivotal phrase: *"die Zuneigung ist Zuspruch."*

---

14. VA, p. 123.

On the Side of Being: The Call		On the Side of Man: Response
1. Möglichkeit		
mögen	⟶	*mögen*
Zuneigung		Vermögen
2. *Zuspruch*		denken——*Sprache*
Anspruch	⟶	behalten——hüten
halten		Gedächtnis

Two essential terms respond to one another each time *from the two sides* of this double relation: *mögen* and *sprechen*. Only desire and language are found on both sides; apart from these everything is different. For *Zuneigung* and *Anspruch* are totally different from *Vermögen* and *Gedächtnis*, which are purely human. The postulate, if we can say such a thing, is thus straightforward: *being and man share a desire that is fulfilled in language.* What Heidegger means is clear: the "condition of possibility" of thinking is not to be found in man, nor in some abstract generality, but in the aspiration of being that "holds" man in suspense through its own desire for him, i.e. for the "acceptance" (in the sense of *receiving* or *admitting: einlassen, zulassen*) of the presence of things themselves.

Yet what is the status of this originary desire? What is meant by its sharing, or its original agreement on both sides? Where does the harmoniously preestablished reciprocity of desire come from: "we desire only that which for its part desires us ourselves, that is, us in our being"?[15] Is not such reciprocity merely the metaphoric expression of the fact that every human faculty must be rooted in a possibility situated outside of it, and that all thought is articulated in the solicitation of a language? Can being desire us or love us? In what sense? Is not being's desire itself only a metaphor for the call or claim (*Anspruch*), for the source of the call? What does man desire when he receives, admits, lets something come to him to be thought? Does he not desire to know? Or is he mistaken about his desire to know, which might be a desire to love or rather to respond to love? Is this the profane repetition of a Christian *topos*: "We enter into truth only through charity"? We are faced with many questions here that are both necessary for the health of our critical spirit and yet insoluble! Is it love that makes things possible, or is it possibility that falls in love with whatever it makes possible?

---

15. WhD, p. 1; tr., p. 3.

Plunging into a vertiginous "below," Heideggerian thought echoes the *phusis kruptesthai philei*, just like Pascal ("the heart by nature loves universal being"[16]), but almost escapes our conceptual grasp. Heidegger himself, however, perhaps gives us a way of thematizing *mögen* through the concept of attunement (*Stimmung*): thought is always put in a position to think by a fundamental affective disposition, such as anxiety, terror, astonishment, self-evidence, and so on.[17] The shared character of the relation of *mögen* might be established on the basis of a mood in accordance with which man finds himself transported and first experiences the power of being that makes him exit from himself. Shared desire would then be the ordeal of *the attraction of being*, in which its "eroticism" is necessarily two-sided, as Heidegger's commentary on the *Phaedrus* shows: "As soon as man, in looking at being, lets himself be bound by being, he becomes transported beyond himself, so that he stretches, as it were, between himself and being and is outside himself. This being raised over beyond oneself and being attracted by being itself is *eros*. Only insofar as being is able to unfold 'erotic' power with respect to man is man able to think of being itself and to overcome the forgottenness of being."[18] Note that Heidegger speaks of "'erotic' power," rather than *its* erotic power. Love, which according to Dante's very Aristotelian expression "makes the sun and the stars move," unfolds "between" being and man.

One may, however, reply that, although every amorous relation is ekstatic, not every ekstatic relation is one of love. In its classical, Cartesian definition love presupposes a will: to love means, if not "to willingly meet,"[19] at least to wish for good, to desire the other as other. In his interpretation of Nietzschean *amor fati*, Heidegger gives the following definition of love: "that will which wills that the object loved be what it is in its essence."[20] Love is a doubling and a reaffirming of being. Yet can man love being? It seems not, to the extent that he cannot, in some distinct projection, posit being as an object. He could desire being only in the sense of an unending quest. There is, however, a "projection of being upon man" to the extent that being "endows itself" [*sich begabt*] with

16. *Pensées* §277.

17. On this point, see my essay "*Stimmung* et pensée," in *Heidegger et l'idée de la phénoménologie* (Kluwer Acad. Publishers, 1988).

18. NI, p. 226; tr., NI vol. One, p. 194.

19. *Traité des passions*, art. 79.

20. NI, p. 470; tr., NI, vol. Two, p. 207.

human thought.[21] The result is that the relation of *mögen* is not entirely shared, nor entirely harmonious. It can be reversed at any moment. On one side, being infinitely surpasses us: it is not we who give ourselves being, but being that gives us. On the other side, how do we know that being desires to be thought by us, unless because we in effect think so?

One of the main texts dealing with the connection between thought and the bestowing desire of being is to be found at the beginning of the *Letter on Humanism*:

> Thinking is—this means: being has in each case accepted its essence in accordance with its destiny. To accept a "thing" or a "person" in their essence means to love them [*sie lieben*], to desire them [*sie mögen*]. Thought more originally, this desire [*Mögen*] means: bestowing essence. Such desiring is the proper essence of capability [*Vermögen*] which is not only able to achieve this or that, but can let something "essentially prevail" ["*wesen*"] in its pro-venance [*Her-kunft*], i.e. be. It is "through" the ability of desire [*das Vermögen des Mögens*] that something is properly able to be. This capability is that which is properly "possible," that whose essence resides in desire. Out of this desire being is capable of thinking. It makes thinking possible. Being as desiring capability is that which is "possible" [*Mög-liches*]. Being as the element is the "quiet force" of desiring capability, i.e. of that which is possible.[22]

We are rendered capable of thought by that power that desires that we may be who we are. Rather than the "capability" or faculty (*Vermögen* is the term used by Kant, who speaks of *die Vernunft als Vermögen*) being originarily ours, all our faculties are not only referred to the desiring capability of being as their source, but are taken up into it. The essence of every human capability is relocated in the silent power, the "quiet force" (*stille Kraft*)[23] of being, which itself is capability (*Vermögen*) par excellence. Man finds himself dispossessed of his faculties. To the extent that he is not the seat of

---

21. See, for example, NII, p. 377; tr., NII, vol. Four, p. 233.
22. Wm, p. 314; tr., BW, p. 196.
23. The expression is placed in quotation marks because it is a quote from SZ, p. 394: "historical inquiry will disclose the quiet force of the possible all the more penetratingly, the more straightforwardly and concretely it understands having-been-in-the-world in terms of its possibility…"

power or the possible, he has no proper faculties and cannot make possible even his ownmost faculty, thought. The definition of love provided here—to take charge of, accept: *annehmen*, to accept in its essence, to bestow essence—signifies that being *makes* thought *be*. An amorous substitution! Is to act in our place in this way really to love us?! To love, in the strong sense in which Heidegger understands it here, no longer means wishing that someone or something should be, but to act in such a way that he, she, or it may be. This love or "creative" desire in truth leaves little room for the other. The connection between being and thought would not be identity, the famous Parmenidean tautology ("being equals thought"), but desire would instead open being to thought. There is, however, a fortunate ambiguity in *sein lassen*, which can mean both *to make be* and *to let be, to preserve*. This "respectful" sense of *mögen* and *Vermögen* appears at the end of the same paragraph: "to render something possible [*etwas vermögen*] here means to preserve it in its essence, to maintain it in its element." In other words, we can think, that is, "preserve" and retain being only because it preserves and retains us in the first instance, because being respects the space in which we are able to think it.

Faced with the superlative power of being, man comes across as a very weak partner, but at least one delivered from his solitude! This is certainly one of the surprising implications of the later Heidegger's position, which is the very opposite of a thought of dereliction. However, here one must not be too quick to decipher the nostalgic search for a consolatory presence destined to compensate for the flight of God. Being does not play the role of God. It loves us in its own way, but does not think of us. Whoever can do most—as we may rightly say here—cannot do what is least, unlike us. Is it true that being holds us, as it does not know that it does so? It is true, nevertheless. For we can be held even by a necessity that is ignorant of this fact and ignorant of us. But this is not the case with being, which is at once free *and* necessary. We shall analyze a little later what freedom and what necessity we are dealing with here.

The philosophy of *Dasein* situates our possibilities within the world, with the exception of our ownmost possibility, that of death. By situating them all in being, Heidegger decisively takes leave of any subjective making-possible, without falling back into factuality. We certainly do not produce what is essentially possible. Yet how can one show with complete assurance that these essential possibilities are focused in being, emanating from this unique source, so to speak? Yet what if it were not being that held them? "Who...could fail to presume that being itself enables what is possible?"[24] It is necessarily being that unifies, gathers, and makes possible. Why is a third way excluded from the outset: that of an erratic, multiple, and nonfocused making-possible?

Freedom as a Property Little Shared by Being

During the period of *Being and Time*, freedom is nothing other than the free disposition of one's ownmost possibility; namely, running ahead of this possibility. Freedom is to be found in the movement of self-appropriation and hierarchization of possibilities in terms of this essential possibility of the potentiality for death. Heidegger thinks in terms of possibilities that *Dasein* gives itself, in terms of transcendental "conditions of possibility." "In being ahead of oneself as being towards one's ownmost potentiality for being there lies the existential-ontological condition of the possibility of *being free for* authentic existentiell possibilities."[25] "Freedom for death" is a conquest of authenticity; that is, *Dasein*'s taking possession of its own possibilities at their source.

The essay *On the Essence of Ground* (1929) continues to present freedom as transcendental, as a "founding transcendence." However, unlike "freedom for death," this freedom escapes *Dasein*'s control. Although it grounds every ground or reason (*Grund*), it itself is *Abgrund*, an abyss. "Freedom is the abyss of *Dasein*." Finitude in its many forms, such as being invested in entities, their encroachment on *Dasein*, the uncontrollability of attunement, the facticity of our specific ipseity, temporalization springing forth in us of its own accord as an "original event" (*Urgeschehen*)—none of these phenomena are "within the power of this freedom itself."[26] Freedom does not emerge unscathed from this plunge into impotence (*Ohnmacht*). "The abyss that opens up in this foundational transcendence is, rather, that primordial movement [*Urbewegung*] that freedom accomplishes through us ourselves."[27] This "primordial movement" prefigures a nonhuman freedom that somehow uses "human freedom," whose power will contract in the extreme.

With the Turning, indeed, it seems that we are witnessing a

24. NII, p. 377; tr., NII, vol. Four, p. 232.
25. SZ, p. 193.
26. Wm, p. 172.
27. Ibid.

total *inversion* of subjectivism, anthropocentrism, and the movement of self-possibilization. All freedom is made possible in the first place by being. Unlike existentialism, the Heideggerian thesis proclaims that man is not the possibility of freedom, but the freedom of being is what makes man possible. What is this freedom that we do not have, but that permeates us or that we come to meet? In what sense can it still be called *human*? In a 1930 course[28] we find this apparent reversal formulated for the first time and with great vigor. "Human freedom henceforth no longer means freedom as a property of man, but the converse: *man as a possibility of freedom.* Human freedom is freedom insofar as it breaks through in man and takes him on itself, thereby making him possible."[29] Man is merely the "occasion" (*Gelegenheit*), as the text goes on to say, of an emergence of freedom that has its own proper reign. Freedom is not an entity of the world, nor a faculty of man, but *"by its essence more original than man."*[30] It is the possibility of entities as a whole becoming manifest. It is the possibility of any metaphysical truth. Freedom is thus on the way to being integrated into the essence of truth. Every anthropological approach is shattered.

On the Essence of Truth, a transitional text if there is one—for the first version was a lecture given shortly after the course just referred to (autumn 1930) and the text itself was published only in 1943—outlines this new interpretation of freedom. It is a matter of combating the "stubborn prejudice" that "freedom is a property of man." To do so, we must be capable of making a leap, "ready for a transformation [*Wandlung*] of thinking."[31]

Freedom is defined, initially in an ambiguous manner (because of the double meaning of *lassen*), as *sein lassen* and as an activity of man. "Freedom...lets each specific [*jeweilige*] entity be the entity that it is." *Lassen,* Heidegger remarks, does not mean to leave in the sense of "letting go." "Here the term is not thought of as omission or indifference, but as the opposite." Freedom therefore, as one might expect, implies an act of adhering. "Letting be means adhering [*sich einlassen*] to entities." Yet this act of adhering, the text informs us, is not concerned with a technical type of action operating on entities: "doing, guarding, maintaining, or planning."

---

28. *Vom Wesen der menschlichen Freiheit* (*On the Essence of Human Freedom*), GA 31.
29. Ibid., p. 135.
30. Ibid., p. 134.
31. *On the Essence of Truth,* Section 4. Wm, p. 185; tr., BW, p. 127.

It consists in placing oneself in the openness of the open, in *aletheia*. This term must be understood, Heidegger tells us, not only as *Unverborgenheit*, "unconcealment," but as *Entborgenheit*, "being uncovered," and *Entbergung*, "uncovering." In what, then, does *letting be* consist? It consists in two simultaneous but non-contradictory movements, for neither the one nor the other is a fusion: a recoil (*Zurücktreten*) in the face of entities as such, and an exposure (*Aussetzung*) to their being uncovered. Every comportment that is "exposed," that is, transposed (*versetzt*) into the open, is free. What does this mean? Freedom is the act through which *Dasein* surpasses every particular entity as well as the totality of entities. This surpassing is accomplished solely by its ek-sistence and ekstatic movement. This freedom, defined as *Dasein*'s being exposed to uncovering, would be *prior* to all traditional definitions of freedom: arbitrary freedom or whimsical choice, absence of constraint, being receptive to a demand or an ontic necessity. "Prior to all this (prior to 'negative' or 'positive' freedom), freedom is an adhering [*Eingelassenheit*] to the uncovering of entities as such. Being uncovered is itself preserved by this ek-sistent adhering, through which the openness of the open, i.e. the 'there', is what it is."[32]

Yet is not this definition one of a pure act of thinking? What can adhering to the uncovering of the whole mean for someone who acts? An action can take place only *within* a *determinate* situation and would be unable to view the totality or raise itself *above* it. The remainder of the text clearly shows that what Heidegger, strangely enough, calls freedom in reality designates the arrival on stage of metaphysical thought in its Greek origin (*phusis* is mentioned): "It is only where entities themselves are explicitly raised and preserved in their unconcealment, only where this preservation is understood in terms of questioning concerning entities as such, that History commences."[33] Explicitly introducing a difference between *man* (the particular historical human being) and *Da-sein* (written with a hyphen to indicate the ek-static site of unconcealment—and no longer the *Dasein* that is "always mine"), the text passes imperceptibly from "freedom," written in quotes, to truth. "It is not the arbitrary human being who disposes over freedom. Man does not 'possess' freedom like some property, but at most the situation is the opposite: freedom, *Da-sein* as ek-sistent and uncovering, possesses man, and does this so originally that it alone guarantees humanity a relation to

---

32. Wm, p. 186; tr., BW, p. 128.
33. Ibid., p. 187; tr., BW, p. 129.

entities as a whole and as such, a relation which founds and defines all History."[34] The two terms, *Da-sein*, taken in the broad sense of the clearing of being, and *freedom*, are identified and grasped as the foundations of History, opposed to "nature." We are already dealing with the History of Being, or that of metaphysics, because it is a question of "the history of the essential possibilities of a historial humanity." Heidegger indeed wants to indicate that the ontological condition of the exercise of any "empirical" freedom within a determinate epochal field is linked to the very emergence of this field, something not dependent on human decision. He has thus attained a new concept of freedom that *accords* with human letting be, but does not depend on it, nor indeed on any act of thought explicitly undertaken. We are already dealing with the freedom of being unfolding as truth, that is, the "uncovering of entities."

"Freedom thus understood, as the letting be of entities, accomplishes and fulfills the essence of truth taken as the uncovering of entities." Freedom, as the "essence of truth," henceforth has a paradoxical relation to human comportment. It is revealed by letting be, but certainly not produced by it. Letting be appears as a mediation between the originary essence of truth and the "empirical" freedom of human comportment. "All human comportment and taking a stance are exposed to the openness of truth." Thus the "fulfillment" (*Erfüllung*) of truth that was at issue previously—a term borrowed from Husserl, and whose meaning is modified, as we are evidently not dealing with the fulfillment of an intentionality by a "corporeal" (*leibhaft*) presence—means the manner in which the essence of truth, itself an uncovering, is in each case received and understood by a particular humanity. That it may be understood as exactitude, conformity, the adequation of a proposition or a judgment to a thing— such is the paradoxical consequence of the "freedom" of truth.

Yet the "errancy" that means that man can "insist" on and within entities, and conceive of truth merely as exactness of representation, is not some arbitrary deviation, but a necessary nontruth. In effect, man is capable of *not* letting truth be as uncovering. Yet this nontruth cannot be the result of the "simple inability or negligence of man." Nontruth, that is, a lack of accord with uncovering, is itself a necessary structure of truth—it is itself in harmony with that which shows itself, as "because all human comportment is open in its own way and regulates itself harmoniously [*sich einspielt*] with respect to that which it relates to, the fundamental com-

---

34. Ibid.

portment of letting be, freedom, must have been granted to it as that gift [*Mit-gift*] of the intrinsic directive for representation to conform to entities in each case."[35] In other words, freedom also "gives" the necessity of being mistaken about truth, of forgetting it. Not letting be is still a letting be, nonfreedom is still freedom. Covering over, even when covered over itself, is still "free."

Paradoxically, therefore, freedom is omnipresent. There is no nonfreedom, even in nontruth. Yet this absolute freedom is also an absolute necessity. "Those rare and simple decisions of History are born in accordance with the way in which the originary essence of truth unfolds." Certainly the fundamental choices in terms of which an epoch orders itself are simple and few. But are they still choices, decisions (*Entscheidungen*) *freely made by man*? They are necessary options of History. If "freedom" merges with the successive epochal configurations of truth, then we are not far from Hegel. Nowhere more than in this very difficult text has Heidegger been so close to absolute idealism. The complex description of errancy is situated entirely under the banner of necessity. Errancy is not a fault of man. (Is this a way of excusing "going astray and venturing too far in one's essential attitudes and decisions"?[36]) "Errancy dominates man."[37] It constitutes part of "the full essence of truth" that includes its counterpart, nonuncovering. *Dasein* is thereby submitted to the "distress of constraint" (*die Not der Nötigung*), because it can escape neither errancy, nor forgetting, which is itself forgotten. Where does human freedom remain? There is none any more. Freedom takes refuge in being, where it becomes diluted into an originary radicality. The freedom of being nonetheless determines human necessity. If man is indeed what he is in each epoch, this is so by virtue of a free destining of being. All freedom resides in being. And it is nowhere evident that it gives itself to man. It "gives" man, but as we shall see remains free for itself.

These reflections have taken us outside the framework of the essay *On the Essence of Truth*, which in part remains within the continuation of the problematic of *Being and Time*, to the extent that it is primarily a matter of freeing man for his ek-sistent essence. The opposition between the "in-sistent" attitude that regulates truth in terms of entities or the real and ek-sistence that is open to being in effect merely displaces the authentic-inauthentic

---

35. Ibid., p. 188; tr., BW, p. 129.
36. Ibid., p. 194; tr., BW, p. 136.
37. Ibid.

opposition in the direction of the nonindividual and nonsubjective. The difference between insistence and eksistence, which would be relayed via the opposition between calculative thinking and meditative thinking, seems—somewhat like the Nietzschean split between the Last Man and the Overman—to implement a distinction between two *types* of humanity, or to proceed via a distinction within the essence of man.

After the Turning, the motif of freedom is no longer at the center of analyses, but appears obliquely and persistently in Heidegger's meditation on the History of Being. The "truth of being" is often referred to as *das Freie*, the "free dimension" or "free realm" to which metaphysical truth is traced back. Thus the clearing of being is its free realm: *das Freie der Lichtung*.[38] Authentic freedom is now situated in the movement through which *aletheia* uncovers itself and progressively veils itself, only to find itself beyond its extreme obfuscation in *Ereignis*. The freedom of being is its coming into its own. Therefore *Ereignis*, as *Er-eignis* (appropriation), would be the true name of freedom: *Ereignis der Freiheit*. *Ereignis*, however, must not be understood as an "event" situated at the end of this History, like Hegel's absolute Knowledge. *Ereignis* is nonhistorial. It is just as much at the commencement as at the end. "What is radiant in the worthy *Ereignis* of the commencement [*Anfang*] is the *unique liberation* [*Befreiung*] as *Ereignis* of freedom."[39] At the commencement, which is distinguished from a purely factual, historial beginning (the commencement still endures at present), being frees itself in manifesting itself for the first and *unique* time. Thus "freedom" at present means the identity and unity of the History of Being. The sovereignty of the History of Being rejects any reflection on the individuality of thinkers as mere psychologizing. Thinkers are not free. The thought of the greatest among them is held captive by the projection of being upon their thought. "What is most proper to a thinker is not his possession, but the property of being."[40] The "projects" of thinkers merely "catch in flight" what being "throws" towards them. They betray their "captivity" (*Befängnis*), their complete dependency in respect of what being has assigned them as a task. Yet does not being *need* them? Certainly, "being needs the reflection of an illumination of its essence."[41] Thus man in his most

---

38. US, pp. 257–258; tr., OWL, pp. 126–127.
39. NII, p. 485.
40. Ibid.
41. Ibid., p. 482.

elevated form, the thinker, is merely a pale reflection! And yet this need betrays neither a dependency nor "the unease of a lack."[42] This is a strange speculation on being's relation to man that amounts to lending an attunement to being: the absence of unease! In itself being is "the pure absence of need," and yet "from time to time" (*zu Zeiten*) being takes leave of its solitude to address itself to man. "From time to time being needs human beings, and yet is never dependent on an existing [*seienden*] humanity!"

If freedom is integrally situated on the side of being that "releases man's relation to it," necessity is more heavily emphasized on the side of man and the side of thought. Remembrance of the commencement comes from "a necessity full of distress."[43] This necessity too, however, must be the reflection in thought of a necessity and even a distress of being. The History of Being is no different from the History of metaphysics, and the latter is designated "a necessary epoch of the History of Being."[44] Is there not some anthropomorphism in suggesting in this way that being assumes its destiny, namely its alienation in metaphysics, as an alienation from which it suffers, but from which it will recover? "Where the danger grows..." But is not being "responsible" for its own obfuscation, as it is being that "abdicates" (*entlässt sich*) in entities, "refuses the clearing of the commencing of the commencement," "withdraws its worthiness into the concealment that is itself concealed"?[45] Being would suffer from the abasement to which it consents by a mysterious and unfathomable necessity. *Semetipsum exinanivit* (Paul, Philippians, 2:7), a proximity to negative theology rather than anthropomorphism. Is there a link, as in theology, between the free abasement of being and its love for man? If such a link exists, it is in any case not explicit.

Necessity, or the "Maintaining" of Man by Being

Heideggerian thought is more a thought of necessity than of freedom. "Becoming free means binding oneself [*sich binden*] to that which truly lights, that which permeates everything in freeing it, namely 'light'," we read in the first commentary on the cave alle-

---

42. Ibid.
43. Ibid., p. 486.
44. Ibid., p. 481.
45. Ibid., p. 486.

gory.[46] Man accedes to freedom only if he agrees to let himself be bound to the secret clarity of being. Perhaps it is necessary for man to be constrained in this way, for him to be freed by force and, like the prisoner in Plato, drawn up to the sun. Without going so far as to adopt the Platonic path of deliverance, Heidegger emphasizes that truth is "greater" than man, and that man is obliged to submit himself to it. Necessity, even in being, is stronger than freedom.

Yet what is this necessity? Evidently it is neither of a logical order, nor of a physical or mechanical nature. It is the result of a constraint or distress, of a *Not* that is intrinsic to being's very relation to man. "All necessity, according to its kind, comes from a constraint [*Not*]."[47] This constraint results from the fact that being's power of giving is stronger than man's power to receive. "This constraint is not an insufficiency, nor a privation, but the excess [Übermass] of a gift [*Schenkung*] which is undoubtedly heavier to bear than any loss."[48] Heidegger is here taking over the Hölderlinian idea that happiness is more difficult to bear than misfortune. The "constraint," however, is primarily that of being itself, for man receives this gift, is "used" (*gebraucht*) by being only because being "needs him" (*braucht ihn*) in order to appear. In a certain way, the "distress" of being is greater than that of man. The word *Brauch* designates both the need of being and the way in which its relation to man responds to this need by "using" man. "Man keeps himself 'in this relation' means the same thing as: man, as man, is essentially '*im Brauch*', 'maintained'."[49] This translation of *Brauch* as "maintenance" will be justified a little later. Let us say that we are kept or maintained to being. Being keeps us, but it also keeps to us because *we are necessary to it*. The call of being, its *Anspruch*, necessitates man in the double sense of a necessity that it arouses in man—to respond to it—and a necessity in being itself—the necessity of this response.

This dependency of being—in which it nonetheless retains all initiative—is strongly underlined from the 1935 *Introduction to Metaphysics* onward. The notion of *Brauch* will then be developed at greater length in *Holzwege* ("The Anaximander Fragment"), in *Nietzsche II*, in *What Is Called Thinking?* and in the last essay of *Unterwegs zur Sprache*. Man is indeed constrained by the "neces-

---

46. GA 34, p. 60 (Course given in 1931–32).
47. GA 45, p. 150.
48. Ibid., p. 153.
49. US, p. 126; tr., OWL, p. 32.

sity of shattering" against the "superlative power" (*Übergewalt*) of being. "Yet if man is constrained to such a *Da-sein*, if he is thrown into the distress [*Not*] of such being, it is because the overwhelming [*das Überwältigende*] as such *needs* [*braucht*, emphasized in the text] the site of openness *for itself* [*für es*] in order to appear in prevailing. The essence of human being opens itself to us only when it is understood in terms of this distress necessitated by being itself."[50] This distress (*Not*) just referred to is somehow shared by man and by being. It is therefore not primarily for man that being gives itself to him, but *for itself*: the *für es* expresses a strange reflexivity of being, a strange "for itself." How can being relate to itself so as to experience something as a need? Do we not find ourselves in full-blown metaphysical speculation?

The word *Brauch* attempts to rediscover the original meaning of "necessary" conveyed by the words *chre* in Parmenides and *to chreon* in the Anaximander fragment. *Chre* is normally the Greek equivalent of "it is necessary" and refers to an extrinsic necessity. Heidegger, however, links *chre* to the root *cheir*, the hand, and derives *chreon* from the verb *chrao,* meaning to handle, to lend one's hand to, to put into "use" or proper handling. The words *it is necessary* in Parmenides' saying "It is necessary to say and to think that entities are" would express an internal necessity governing all presence. Being disposes over present entities, somehow "handles" the lapse of time of presence. *Brauch* would thus designate a more extensive link (*Beziehung*) than the relation of being to man: it would be the link of presence to things present. "*Brauch* names the manner in which being itself unfolds as the link [*Beziehung*] to present entities, a link that concerns and main-tains the present as present."[51] *Brauch*, particularly in the Anaximander fragment, is concerned with the transitory character of presence and indicates the movement of being that "uses" presence in assigning it a limit in each case. Being's maintaining for its part consists in allocating to the present its part of presence, i.e. in delimiting the present. That the *apeiron*, the unlimited, is limited "in accordance with *to chreon*" does not mean that it is subjected to the abstract and universal necessity of nature, but that it receives a limit (*peras*) by way of its own movement. Thus Heidegger not only identifies the *apeiron*, as *arche* or

---

50. EM, p. 124; tr., p. 163. The *für es* reappears in a late text we have already cited: *Das Ereignis ereignet den Menschen in den Brauch für es selbst* (US, p. 261; tr., OWL, p. 130).
51. Hw, p. 339.

principle, with this obscure necessity of *chreon* understood as *Brauch*, but identifies these two terms with the profound rigor of being that destines entities to presence, at the risk of them "hardening into mere persistence" (*in das blosse Beharren*).[52] Being disposes both over presence subject to *dike* (translated as *Fug*, "the harmonious accord" among themselves of times present) and over that which cedes to *adikia* (*Unfug*, "discordance"). *Brauch*, Heidegger says, belongs to the essence of being (*das Wesende im Sein*) as time. The fact that entities are unwilling to give up their transitory stay, that they rise up against their limits in a blindness one could call *tragic* (though the word is not used here), would therefore equally flow from *Brauch*. Yet is there not something excessive or inconsistent about this interpretation of Anaximander? How can this "stance," which is close to in-sistence, and this resistance towards the restricted and limited character of presence, this forgetting of the fact that present time must give way, belong to *entities as such*? Only man can be blind towards his limits. That this blindness should be a "destiny" of being—perhaps; yet to ontologize this tragic error, in seeking to account for the terms *dike* and *adikia*, would entail effacing the difference between man and entities. Indeed, nowhere else in Heidegger's thought do we find either an example or a justification of such a leveling. Being does not "treat" man as just any other entity. An indifference of being with respect to man is quite unthinkable.

Such a leveling, indeed, would precisely contradict the essence of *Brauch* that, as both *Holzwege* and *What Is Called Thinking?* show, consists in maintaining every entity in its proper essence. *Brauch* is not a usage that uses and abuses, or consumes what is "utilized," as does empirical usage. "Proper maintenance first brings what is maintained into its essence and keeps it there....Maintenance means: letting something accede to its essence, preserving it in its essence."[53] In this sense, *Brauch* does not mean constraint or blind necessity, but "benign strictness" that retains every entity in what is proper to it and calls man to thought, to what is proper to him.

Does not being, in "maintaining" man and addressing a truth to him that man hears or understands inadequately, resemble a Providence—Stoic or Christian—that also "needs" man, that man understands badly, and that without man would have no one's hand to hold? Is not human errancy inscribed in a kind of "plan" from the

---

52. Ibid., p. 340.
53. WhD, p. 114; tr., p. 187.

outset, because it responds to the withdrawal (itself necessary) of being? The analogy does exist, but could not be pushed very far. For being has not created the world, and its truth admits of no absolute or ultimate revelation, of no apocalypse. In all probability, being does not conceive of its own necessity and does not know its own abyss. Consequently, the superiority of man, in the manner of the Pascalian reed, would be that man at least knows all this! Heidegger *never* draws this consequence. How can one fail to be astonished that being should be so powerful and so weak? Can we still believe in being? And yet, if we do not believe in it, how could we listen to it in contemplation, *An-dacht,* how could we be "grateful" to it, that is, think? There is no thought without faith. But what is meant by faith of thought? Trusting in the gifts of being, in its "benevolence"? Yet why does it withdraw? Where does the evil come from? If man is not responsible for errancy, because the withdrawal of being makes it possible, and if "the essence of evil [*des Bösen*] does not consist in the mere corruption of human action,"[54] is not being the source of evil? Here we see the traditional Stoic, Leibnizian question of *theodicy*—of justifying the "principle" in regard to this eternal accusation—bounce back in a strange manner. Because being is not a ground, it can easily be excused, but is it not that which maintains us in what we are, think and do, thus playing a part in this and inspiring it? Is it not thought of as origin? Must it not therefore at least "allow" evil?

The Limit of the Requisitioning of Man: The Absence of Distress

Being needs [*braucht*] accommodation. It takes the latter, in necessitating it [*be-nötigend*], under its requisition [*in seinen Anspruch*].

Being is necessitating in a twofold, though unified sense: it is that which is un-remitting and that which maintains [das Brauchende] in relation to its accommodation as the prevailing of that essence to which man belongs as the one who is maintained [der Gebrauchte]. This double necessitating is, and is called, distress [*Not*]. In the advent of the absence of its unconcealment, being itself is distress.[55]

---

54. Wm, p. 355; tr., BW, p. 237.
55. NII, pp. 390–391; tr., NII, vol. Four, p. 244.

This passage is taken from quite a long text by Heidegger, one that we must in fact call "speculative" and that concerns "the essence of being": the chapter of *Nietzsche II* entitled "Nihilism as Determined by the History of Being."[56] "Speculative," because Heidegger's meditation here bears on the role of being in the history of metaphysics understood as "nihilist" thought (in which being itself comes to nothing). The meditation at once locates itself "intuitively" at the heart of being to grasp its proper movement. Being "abandons" entities, veils itself, withdraws, hides itself from thought, yet it enters into a distress (which can become extreme) to the extent that its call or challenge (*Zumutung*) is no longer heard and no longer can be heard. This distress of being comes from the fact that it distances itself from man and no longer has the force to claim him.

In other words, the withdrawal of being is no longer thought, nor is its presence, which, nevertheless, continues to "promise" itself (*versprechen*) through its lack. Or to put it another way, being on the one side is the unchangeable, "unremitting" play of uncovering and withdrawal, and on the other side—because every gift comes from it, because it "maintains" everything—it is also its own absence that becomes History in the shape of metaphysics. Being itself engenders nihilism that, although initially hidden, ends up by triumphing in the technologization of the world. Distress means that the nonexperiencing of being affects being, makes it suffer, ruins it to the extent that being "needs" to be contemplated, to be sheltered by man. Is it not paradoxical that being suffers in this way on account of a situation that it itself has made possible? For it does suffer, unless we consider distress as beneficial or an advantage. We cannot avoid the question, How can it be that being "consents [*zulässt*] to the extreme absence of itself and thereby favors the onslaught of that which is merely actual—the much-vaunted 'realities'"?[57] Does not Heidegger constantly and explicitly emphasize that "the History of metaphysics is the History of being itself"?[58] And does he not emphasize this in the sense that being not only "allows" or gives its "permission" (*Zulassung*), but "provokes" (*veranlasst*) the double forgetting that such metaphysics entails? "The modern metaphysics of subjectivity is permitted by being itself which, in the absence of its truth, provokes the omission [*Auslassung*] of this absence."[59] Being produces

56. Ibid., pp. 335–398; tr., pp. 197–250.
57. Ibid., p. 376; tr., p. 231.
58. Ibid., p. 379; tr., p. 234, and elsewhere.
59. Ibid., p. 379; tr., pp. 234–235.

an abandonment of itself that it can then no longer overcome. Why does it plunge man, and itself, into distress? Why does it refuse itself, why does it absent itself?

All these questions, Heidegger would say, cannot be asked, because they are metaphysical. They seek a raison d'être for being. We are not allowed to ask why being hides itself, absents itself, or why being's relation to the essence of man has taken "the shape of withdrawal" (*in der Gestalt des Entzugs*).[60] We can only take note of it. There is no answer. The only answer is, "That's the way things are, this is *the enigma of being*." Heidegger takes care to repeat the word *Rätsel* several times to dispel any temptation to *explain* the enigma of withdrawal.

Yet does Heidegger himself not fall into an explanatory and teleological schema in this text by revealing straightaway "the secret of being" (*Geheimnis des Seins*)? For although the enigma of withdrawal is impenetrable, its secret is manifest. Withdrawal is manifestly call, challenge. Withdrawal draws thought towards being. The call, the challenging need that being experiences in the human essence, harbors a hidden "promise" (*Versprechen*). The simple, elementary secret that the call and withdrawal contain is that being itself withholds itself and *promises itself* to man. Not the promise of an ultimate or future plenitude of presence, but the promise of a *tie*: in claiming man, in requisitioning him, being *endows itself* (*begabt sich*) with man and thus could not cease to hold and maintain him. It promises *itself* that it will remain unfailingly attached to this human essence that it preserves.

A rather tautological promise, because being makes it to itself and keeps it secret! (Is it free not to make it?) Would this promise exist without the common relation of *Versprechen* and *Anspruch* to the verb *sprechen*? A rather fragile promise, because there is no assurance that it can be kept to the end!

Man is indeed unremittingly maintained in his essence by the paradoxical choice of being: "being determines that its omission occurs in human thought."[61] (Was it free to choose a different "shelter"? Could it have claimed an entity other than man?) But as forgetting increases, so this privileged site comes to be threatened. In the epoch of Technology, being and man slide imperceptibly from distress to the absence of distress.

---

60. Ibid., p. 397; tr., p. 249.
61. Ibid., p. 367; tr., p. 225.

The unremitting maintaining proceeds so far in the absence of its unconcealment that the site that shelters it, the essence of man, comes to be deserted, man to be threatened by the destruction of his essence, and being itself endangered in the maintaining of this site. Proceeding to this degree of absence, being bestows on itself the danger that the distress which it prevails as, in necessitating, never historially becomes the distress that it is for man. At the extreme, the distress of being becomes the distress of the absence of distress.[62]

In this extreme, excessive progression of itself—in which, however, being neither strays nor "risks itself" (*s'aventure*, as Klossowski's translation mistakenly puts it)—being remains perfectly in possession of itself, because it "bestows on itself the danger" that this new distress might no longer be able to be thought. Why could it no longer be thought? Because the reign of calculative thinking prevents it. This would be the sign of a "single-track" thinking, insensitive to all pain and all distress, cut off from all attunement and thus cut off from being. Yet then man would have lost his essence, which consists in being able to bring to language the destiny that being sends him. Man would be not biologically, but ontologically dead, because he would no longer be open to being.
Yet where does this threat of death come from, if not from being itself? And because it is being that is threatening itself, that by itself "gives itself" (*begabt sich*) this danger, is it truly a danger? There is truly a danger only if being can be threatened with disappearance. If man no longer responded to it with thought, being's relation to man would melt, and by the same token being would be annihilated, for it "needs" man. Yet for this to happen, man would have to lose his essence. Can he lose his essence? For him to be stripped of his essence, it would be necessary for him no longer to think at all; that is, it would mean that it would have to be impossible for either the metaphysical question of the being of entities or the question of being itself as different from every entity to arise. It would be necessary for man *no longer to be able* to pose anything other than technical and practical problems. In that case, with the unilateral and absolute reign of "calculative thinking," we would truly see the death of the human essence. It would be dead if it were congealed forever in technological rationality. "Man would

---

62. Ibid., p. 391; tr., p. 245.

have denied and rejected what is most proper to him, namely that he is a thinking being."[63] However, as long as man knows he is mortal, this hypothesis seems rather implausible. Supposing that man were to become incapable of intellectually escaping from *Gestell* and that he were to consider himself as a machine or computer, would not such an attitude still continue to conform to the epochal destining of being? Moreover, language is so heavily impregnated with metaphysical conceptuality that the most complete ignorance of the great thinkers would not abolish, but rather facilitate the resurgence of a metaphysics that would seem natural. Thus the idea that being itself, by the excess of its withdrawal, gives rise to "the danger of the annihilation of the essence of man"[64] seems to be doubly improbable.

As for the "absence of distress," is it not one of the forms of technical thinking? There is no problem that cannot be resolved. On the whole, we have what is real firmly in our grasp. The absence of distress even has its attunement, which is the feeling of the extreme secureness of every operation we can mount. And via this feeling, the world is perceived as a network of operations that can be mounted. The absence of distress is therefore not the absence of thought. There is an impoverished thinking, but it is by no means empty.

The absence of distress forgets every enigma, all possible withdrawal. It is the concealment of concealment. What can man do to struggle against it, since it is capable of indirectly threatening being itself? Quite simply, he can experience the absence of distress as a distress, as the distress of being in our epoch. But being able to experience errancy as such will not rid us of it. However profound this turnaround in our experience may be, it can merely *prepare* a possible Turning: only being can accomplish it, for the complete turnaround of historial time, the passage to a new commencement, is not in our power.

The relation between being and man thus finds itself unbalanced once more. Despite the absence of distress, another name for errancy—which being cannot know directly and which remains the work of man, marking his extreme alienation—being does not cease to claim man, to unremittingly necessitate him. Being has need of man and an unremitting care for him. Man for his part is spontaneously forgetful, for he can "in-sist" in errancy, become enclosed in

---

63. Gel., p. 25; tr., p. 56.
64. NII, p. 394, tr., NII, vol. Four, p. 247.

it, that is, close himself off from the possible experience of forgetting. He turns away from being in many ways, whereas being constantly turns towards him, signals to him, though in a veiled manner. There is a repeated blindness on the part of man, but also a lack of attention, a frivolousness or lack of respect (*Missachtung*). There is a fidelity, perseverance, and persistence on the part of being, even and especially in its enigmatic withdrawal, the obscure source of evil.

The Role of Man: "The Freedom of Sacrifice" Alone Can Overcome "the Misfortune of Reflection"

What remains *as proper* to man? Because he neither thinks nor acts by way of his own initiative, because he is likely to depart from his essence to the point of no longer even thinking, is he not left with a merely "negative" role? To paraphrase Hölderlin, is he able only to "find help in errancy and distress"?

If the origin of all forgetting is the concealment of being, it is nevertheless man who forgets and who, in forgetting this forgetting, falls into errancy. Man alone errs. Being does not err. Man errs, on the one hand, because he gives way to the forgetting of his forgetting and becomes imprisoned in it and, on the other hand, because he is "tempted," "seduced" (*verführt*) by entities. In Heidegger's itinerary, "falling," "insistence," "frenzied calculation" are the forms sucessively assumed by this temptation to believe only in what is real, to trust only what can be measured, to deny what cannot be calculated. But the entity that primarily seduces man is himself. To reduce every entity to its own measure, it must first straightforwardly be established as a particular entity in the world: a *sub-jectum*, a "real" basis by which the degree of reality pertaining to everything can be referred to and measured. In *Being and Time* the ontological self-abasement of *Dasein* hides its ekstatic dimension: *Dasein* is impelled to regard its possibilities in terms of properties similar to those of every subsistent entity, of every entity that is present at hand. In *On the Essence of Truth*, ek-sistence degenerates into "insistence," meaning that form of errancy through which "*Dasein* holds fast to what is offered by entities as though they were open in and of themselves."[65] The most readily accessible entity to which *Dasein* holds on, attaches itself, and clings is the human

---

65. Wm, p. 193; tr., BW, p. 135.

entity as *subject*. Subjectivity, the ego, that which is for-itself, is the result of *insistence* in finding an entity that will always be available for the purpose of *measuring* entities. Man borrows from worldly entities an idea of measure, that of the *res*, and transfers it onto himself "without stopping to consider the very thing that grounds such taking of a measure." The essence of insistence is the self-positing of man as measure—as the *res*—of all reality. "Man takes himself exclusively, *as subject*, to be the measure of every entity."[66]

Yet errancy in general is not some some misadventure that man could spare himself if he were careful. Rather it constitutes part of the very uncovering of truth that, to become epochal, must forget and ignore the fact that it is merely one epoch among other possible ones. "Without errancy, there would be no relation of destiny to destiny; there would be no History."[67] Errancy, therefore, is the opposite of an error, because it means correspondence to the withdrawal of being, a withdrawal through which being keeps itself in reserve for another possible History. Yet it can become an evil, a source of aberration in "insistence" to the extent that this correspondence can cease to be accessible to thought.

It is here that man can rediscover his own initiative. It is within his power, in the midst of his inevitable, epochal errancy, not to "insist," "*not* to let himself err," that is, *not* to let himself be fascinated only by the ontic formations of his epoch, but on the contrary to "experience *errancy itself*."[68] This experiencing of *errancy itself* does not mean being liberated from it, but escaping nihilism, which is complete forgetting in the absence of distress, and thus returning to the attunement of distress. To know that one errs does not do away with errancy. As in Hegel, no one can leap outside his or her time. Experiencing errancy does not lead to a floating detachment or relativism, but to the attitude of *Gelassenheit*, of letting-be, or of active releasement with regard to the epoch, that is, with regard to Technology. *Gelassenheit* is undoubtedly the greatest amount of "freedom" that Heidegger recognizes in man.

A limited freedom, by no means original, as being holds and deals out all the cards and as the essence of Technology escapes our will. Yet it is freedom all the same, because there is a remove or distancing from the world, something that depends entirely on us. Certainly, we cannot escape from the world as governed by Technol-

---

66. Ibid. (emphasis added).
67. Hw, p. 311.
68. Wm, p. 195; tr., BW, p. 136.

ogy. Nor can we simply renounce the use of technological objects on which our life depends. We are obliged to say "yes" to them. And yet, Heidegger assures us, we can and must also say "no" to them, by not regulating our thought in accordance with the logic implicit in them. We could "prevent them from exclusively claiming us, and thereby distorting and confusing our essence, letting it become desolate," prevent them from attaining "that which most properly and intimately concerns us."[69] We would thus be free not to be blindly subject to the epoch, free to see to it that its errancy does not corrupt us or reach us...in what? In our intimate essence? Does this mean in our "heart of hearts"? How could a being-in-the-world discover what is proper to it outside the world? Would this not be a vain and quasi-stoic "freedom of thought," the dream of an acosmic purity? For Heidegger, there is no freedom outside of world. But does not freedom, despite everything, presuppose a form of interiority, if only the ability to distance ourselves from established reality? And to whom can such an ability belong, if not to some form of individuality? We shall encounter this problem again later on. In opposing calculative humanity subservient to *Gestell* and man as freely meditative, is Heidegger not opposing the 'One', planetary man in general, to an individual capable of thought? Yet why does he refuse to this new human being, abstractly named *the mortal*, the trait of *individuality*? Undoubtedly for fear of reinstating subjectivity. And yet, a "yes," and a fortiori a "no," are unthinkable unless they belong to *someone* who affirms them and who confirms his or her existence by this affirmation.

One question remains, however: "Does overcoming subjectivity inevitably mean renouncing individualization?"

Whatever the case, for Heidegger the free part of man could not possibly reside in a "heart of hearts." Distancing oneself from the world still has to do with a relation to the world. It is impossible to take any distance without the support of an affective disposition. Attunement, however, is not a purely inner feeling, but a way in which all things "stand out"; that is, take shape and offer themselves. There is a fundamental and "universal" mood in all presence that excludes the idea of a freedom that would be cut off.

Whatever the part played by individuality, the latter is never devoid of attunement; that is, it is always inserted into the totality of world. Perhaps here we can locate a thin margin of freedom. For nothing belongs more to man than the free use of his dispositions.

---

69. Gel., pp. 22–23; tr., p. 54.

Inhumanity, by contrast, would be a lack of sensitivity, increasing in the epoch of Technology, towards every attunement. Pain, joy and worry teach us that things in the world cannot be reduced to being defined "in themselves," to an objective definition, and that they remain borne by being, suspended in the realm of the possible, for their meaning can change suddenly and utterly. Yet man does not passively undergo these dispositions. He can welcome them or close himself off from them, let them vanish or meet them with indifference and "ill humor" (*Verstimmung*, i.e. a distortion of attunement or *Stimmung*). Likewise, he can flee anxiety—at the expense of "anxiety in the face of anxiety"—or be open to it, let it lead him to a free decision. "Readiness for anxiety means saying 'yes' to the capacity to respond to the supreme requisition that reaches only the essence of man."[70] The ability to sustain "essential anxiety" demands a "clear courage," a "bravery," and even a paradoxical "coldbloodedness" or "equanimity" (*Gleichmut*). "Bravery recognizes in the abyss of terror the scarcely-entered space of being."[71]

These "moral" qualities of thought, which are eminently human (would that which is most proper to man therefore be the *heroic* capacity to bravely sustain anxiety?), are enrooted and gathered in that freedom which Heidegger calls *the freedom of sacrifice* (*die Freiheit des Opfers*). What freedom is this? What sacrifice? We shall have to return to this in another context. Thought must be capable of "sacrificing" all entities, capable of leaving everything, of absolutely losing hold of any form of reality. We are reminded of Schelling demanding that whoever wishes to enter philosophy must abandon every entity: "Here one must abandon the finite; everything that remains an entity must here disappear right down to its last point of anchorage; here we must abandon everything—not only wife and child, as people say, but simply everything that is, even *God*, for God too is merely an entity from this point of view."[72] Heidegger writes, more soberly: "Sacrifice is a taking leave [*Abschied*] of entities in a step which preserves the favor of being."[73] *Favor* (*Gunst*, from *gönnen*, to "freely grant") emphasizes the gift in what is exceptional, incommensurable, generous, overabundant, and *gracious* about it. The context thus evokes a quasi-religious relation to being, for thought considers entities as a gift that it sacrificially

---

70. Wm, p. 305.
71. Ibid.
72. Schelling, *Sämmtliche Werke* (ed. Cotta), vol. IX, p. 217.
73. Wm, p. 308.

returns to being to thank it and repay it for what it has received in overabundance from being. The "freedom of sacrifice" implies a divesting of not only entities, but human projects. "Sacrifice tolerates no calculation."[74] Man wants nothing and seeks nothing except in the pure renunciation of every specific goal, the sole welcoming of the gift, the singular, silent hearing of the voice of being. For from the silence of anxiety will be born that infrequent, vigilant speaking, economical with its words, in which being will say itself. Therefore a human freedom can exist, but only when the effacement of every practical or theoretical relation to entities will have extracted it from all subjectivity. The "sacrifice" arises, as the text says, from "the abyss of freedom" when it comes to meet the abyss of being.

Yet is not this strange freedom born of the quasi-disappearance of man? For man himself is an entity. Must he abandon himself? "The thinking of being seeks no support among entities."[75] Such asceticism arouses perplexity. For there to be thought, must there not be a thinker, a human being, an entity? Moreover, does being have a meaning independent of its relation to entities in general or independent of the ontological difference? And if we suppress entities, what remains but an undifferentiated abyss?

Once again, the role of man shrinks to the extreme. In addition, has it ever really been a question of man? Most of the fundamental attunements—at least those that are analyzed at length (with the exception of boredom), such as astonishment, anxiety, and terror—are ones that start *thought* rolling. Does man exist for Heidegger apart from as thinker and, of course, as poet? "Being, in its benevolence, has appropriated itself to the essence of man *in thinking,* so that man in his relation to being might assume guardianship over being."[76] If, as the entire tradition maintains, the essence of man is not only thinking, but the thinking *of being,* then those human beings who do not think being—to put it schematically, the nonphilosophers—would strictly speaking not be "free," would not be human beings. Whence the merely implicit, yet dangerous idea that the "functionaries of Technology," the slaves of *Gestell,* those who calculate and plan, the administrators and decision makers, exclude themselves from humanity. A fortiori, whoever is not a thinker or poet would not be *essentially* human! This indefensible

74. Ibid.
75. Ibid., p. 309.
76. Ibid., p. 307 (emphasis added).

consequence seems to be linked less to the refusal of metaphysical anthropology and subjectivism than to the refusal of individuality. "The thinker names being, the poet sings the holy." But ordinary human beings speak only of their own situation. And yet their humanity is defined by this. The human being is not an abstract species, "the mortal," defined both by his or her power to relate to death as death, and thus to being, and by his or her relation to language. Rather *he or she is someone whose word is unique.* There is a nonbiological singularity of one's own word, linked to one's own finitude. Why does the later Heidegger, implicitly denying the "mineness" of *Dasein,* pass over in silence the *specificity* of our relation to death; for example, in *The Thing* (1950) and *Unterwegs zur Sprache* (1959)? After all, death is not only "the shelter of being" in relation to nothing, but the shelter *of my being.* Language does not exist independent of a particular speaking. There is no human being without *ipseity,* without *selfhood* (*Selbstsein*), or without the possibility of turning back towards oneself or returning to oneself.

Heidegger does not deny this, yet whereas in *Being and Time* selfhood means mineness (*Dasein's* appropriating its ownmost possibilities), after the Turning we find the return to oneself maintained, but in a radically *nonsubjective* sense. How can we conceive of an *ipseity* that no longer takes the form of representational consciousness at all and that no longer leads back to an individual 'I'? How is it possible to reject the 'I', whether substantial or formal, to deconstruct both the subject and representation, and to paradoxically maintain "reflection" as the *essence of man*? What would a nonsubjective, nonindividual reflection be, one that would nonetheless bear the trace of *ipseity* yet not be the self-reflexivity of the absolute?

"Perhaps reflection belongs to the essence of man. Perhaps the *misfortune of reflection* does not lie in its bending back [*Rückbiegung*] as such, but in that which it turns back towards and to which the essence of man is inclined [*geneigt*]."[77] There is an ill-fated, unfortunate *leaning* (the word *Neigung* is implicit) of man in favor of the 'I' and the individual. There is a turning away towards egocentrism and individualism. But the return, the turning back, is not intrinsically ill-fated; quite the contrary: "Perhaps the essence of man is precisely an intrinsic re-flection, an original turning-towards [*Zukehr*] that is a re-turn [*Rück-kehr*], but one that entails the turning away and that which is turned away taking over and

---

77. GA 55, p. 209.

gaining the upper hand."[78] Reflection as the self-positing of the subject would merely be an *Abart der Reflexion*, a "derivative of reflection." We can make out what reflection turns away from in turning towards the 'I'. In fact the original possibility of reflection does not stem from the subject, but from *Dasein's* being included in the *there*, or man's being included in being. Selfhood presupposes a "reign of the proper" (*Eigen-tum*), an "appropriation" (*Eignung*). The latter is a dimension of both non-self-coincidence and liaison, an attachment to being. Man does not originally belong to himself, but belongs to the clearing within which alone he can find himself, identify himself. Man can detach himself for himself only because he is "placed in freedom," cast into the ek-stase of the open. This is why "returning" to ourselves, that is, to our initial state, is returning to being.

Our most intimate and most constant ground would thus be being and not ourselves! Being would be our nonindividual interiority. More intimate than my own most intimate, and yet not mine. A strange interiority that expels us from our own 'I'. A strange form of reflexion that introverts us only so as to better extrovert us and detach us from our 'I'. Where the 'I' was, being will arrive. For being only oneself, recognizing oneself only as subject, is the modern mark of blindness and of closedness towards being. Following the *Beiträge* (GA 65) of 1936–38, Heidegger broke with two essential features of *Dasein*: the purely formal character of mineness and self-appropriation as resoluteness. From then on, the 'I' is *always* considered ontic and substantial: "the merely self-same remains empty and can only be filled with what is present at hand [*Vorhandenen*]," and "the movement towards oneself, the *Zu-sich*, does not have the character of decision."[79] We do not have to decide for ourselves, for being claims us, holds us within the constraints of its requisition. "Coming-to-oneself is precisely never the isolated representation of an 'I', but a taking over our belonging to the truth of being, a leap into the *there*."[80] The "proper reign" (*Eigentum*) replaces *Eigentlichkeit*, except that *Eigentum* is concerned with a nonindividual realm of belonging: to be oneself is to be human; to be human is to be the property of being. I am no longer myself, I am merely my belonging to being. True "reflection" would be the free sacrifice of the *ego*.

---

78. Ibid.
79. GA 65, p. 320.
80. Ibid.

Yet *who* accomplishes this sacrifice? Is there not necessarily *someone* who must follow for himself or herself this path from the 'I' to being? This step of de-individualization, which is perhaps that of every philosopher rather than every human being, would bear merely the name of *reflection* unless it were something proper to an individual capable of saying 'I', even and especially if only to understand his or her non-self-coincidence.

Chapter 6

HISTORIAL FIGURES OF HUMAN BEING

There is no autonomous history of humanity. The history of the essence of man is strictly subordinate to the History of metaphysical truth. "Truth in each case demands a humanity through which it may be structured, grounded, communicated and thereby preserved....In this way, a particular humanity in each case takes on itself the decision concerning the manner in which it is to be in the midst of the truth of entities."[1] Man is claimed by being "in each case," in each of the metaphysical "epochs" in which being addresses itself and withholds itself in an *épochè*. Man does not decide in the first instance, but "takes on himself the decision," a decision to do with epochality itself. Man does not choose which essence of metaphysical truth or which definition of entities as such is to reign and constitute an epoch, or is to be assigned to him so that he may sustain or "ground" it, that is, justify it. Man is not master of his own essence, for this essence, as Heidegger shows, is necessarily inscribed within the more extensive essence of metaphysics. All metaphysics states *what* entities are as such and as a whole (their *essentia*), *the fact that* they are or the way in which they are (their *existentia*); provides an interpretation of the essence of truth; and finally, points to the History of that truth. The question "What is man?" always comes after these four primary features have been established.[2] A particular humanity "in each case" finds itself committed to the task of preserving truth. *What* this humanity *is* can be

---

1. NII, p. 257; tr., NII, vol. Three, p. 187.
2. Ibid., p. 258; tr., NII, vol. Three, p. 187.

metaphysically determined only if the being of entities has already been settled. The question of the essence of man is therefore the final feature that comes to be added to metaphysics to complete it, as the Kantian inquiry shows. Furthermore, at the heart of metaphysics, in onto-theology, it is not necessary that man appear, or in any case that he be defined as having a priority. He remains a corollary. Thus, precisely when, through the self-certainty of subjectivity, man places himself at the center of entities to take the measure of every entity, he submits to truth conceived as certainty. It is the self-certainty of knowledge—itself derived, Heidegger thinks, from the Christian self-certainty of salvation—that fashions a particular type of humanity and primarily requires that man be what he is; that is, capable of knowing clearly and self-evidently. It is not man who creates certainty, but certainty that creates man. The essence of man, however, does not change along with each transformation in the essence of truth. Thus, the human subject remains when certainty makes room for Leibniz's principle of reason or when the will to power succeeds the will to know. It seems that there are major epochal segments within which the idea of man remains stable.

Thus, despite the differences separating pre-Platonic man, fifth century man, and Alexandrian man, Greek man would seem to present a unitary essence in the form of his relation to *aletheia* as self-disclosure and to *phusis* as totality. Heidegger shows, for example, that the sophist Protagoras can define his *sophia*, which is restricted to man, only by limiting a larger *sophia* which was an understanding of the totality: he claims that this former understanding is inaccessible, yet uses it as a point of reference. To say that an essence of man corresponds to each epoch of truth is not to invoke a general, abstract truth, but to show that, throughout the secondary transformations, a primordial relation to the essence of truth is maintained that is determinative for this or that epoch. This indicates the importance of *aletheia* for the Greeks and indeed indirectly for all subsequent epochs.

There would, therefore, be only four historial figures of human being, corresponding to four epochs of the History of Being: the Greek, the medieval (or Christianity), the modern, and the planetary.[3] Heidegger describes Greek man and planetary man in much

3. Hw, p. 310; the "Hesperian" (*das Abend-ländische*) referred to by Heidegger in this context is nothing other than the thoughtful repetition of the planetary, or of the closure of History (its "eschato-logy," its coming to a last epoch).

more detail than medieval man (of whom he speaks infrequently) and, paradoxically, than man of modern times. Paradoxically, for the modern epoch of man as subject is the epoch of the "insurrection of freedom in man" and anthropocentrism par excellence.[4] Yet rightly so, for Greek man serves as a model or point of reference for Western man. As for planetary man, undoubtedly destined to have a long future, he is not the heir of the entire past, but draws his extraordinary power from an incredible narrowing of truth.

Following the epoch of the Greeks, *aletheia* is in fact reduced to the light of the *eidos*. In the Middle Ages, the self-productive, "physical" spontaneity of *energeia* is reduced to *actualitas*, that is, to causality: the active, the "setting itself to work," is replaced by the passivity of that which has been effected or caused, especially by the First Cause, the pure act. In Descartes the *subjectum*, which used to designate every substance, comes to be defined as the self-certainty of the subject. During this time, the *logos*, originally the gathering of *aletheia*, the understanding of the whole, becomes limited to the indicative statement, then to the demonstrative proposition, and finally becomes *ratio*, account rendered or calculation. The subject itself becomes reduced to the will as its essence. This will, conceived as will to knowledge, will to love, will to power, is identified with the being of entities. Finally, with the "will to will," the essence of Technology, all the metaphysical principles—and especially the principle of reason—are placed in the service of the efficacity of production for the sake of production. Their truth-character becomes effaced: they are understood as "self-evident" (*selbstverständlich*). The whole of reality is produced and producible. Nature is considered as a fund (*Bestand*), as a reserve of energy that can be infinitely exploited, transformed, and commuted. With *Bestand* the difference between subject and object disappears in favor of a stock of interchangeable resources. Planetary man, however, although already fully absorbed in universal exploitation, is not yet entirely functionalized: he is not yet detached from his former subjectivity. Before sinking "into the leveling-out of organized uniformity,"[5] the human subject has a last burst of light: the luxury of anthropological quest, the enhancement of "lived experience" (*Erlebnis*) exploited by commerce and art and testified to by the media.

This pessimistic vision does not exclude the possibility that another human being, that of *Ereignis*, "the mortal," will escape

---

4. See Hw, pp. 98–103; tr., QT, pp. 145–153.
5. Ibid., p. 103; tr., QT, p. 152.

imprisonment by *Gestell*. Yet *where*, in what world might this human being exist? How would he relate to the one world governed by con-sumption? Would he be a "marginal figure" like the Nietzschean Overman? Would he be outside of History? For Heidegger, the essence of man is intrinsically determined by epochality. For him there is no nonhistorial or transhistorial human essence. And yet just as the essence of being persists through its History, must there not necessarily be a human essence that does not change? The simplicity of the mortal, inhabiting the earth with others, exposed to the heavens, belongs neither to the dawn nor to the dusk; it is of all time, ageless; it is at once archaic and of an extreme, immemorial youth. Must we not ultimately counter a Hegelian and Heideggerian excess by rehabilitating the nonhistorial?

Greek Man

All the particular features of Greek man stem from his primary experience of *aletheia* as a presence that unfolds of its own accord, disclosing itself in the movement of all beings coming to light in *phusis*. That *aletheia* initially corresponds to *phusis* signifies both that the presence of that which is "true," that is, uncovered, does not manifest itself primarily in man, and that this presence is inhabited by a withdrawal, a veiling that cannot be overcome. The Greeks feel presence as a perilous gift that is never full, as a separation, a struggle between light and dark that cannot be appeased. From Plato onward, philosophy would apply itself to reducing the degree of shade, to drawing truth onto the side of pure visibility, the side of the Idea. It would have averted the inaccessibility of withdrawal by reducing it to the controllable obscurity of the unformed and material. To what extent is this premetaphysical experience of *aletheia*, if not a construction, at least a reconstitution after the event? Heidegger acknowledges that *aletheia* is not thought as such by the Greeks, that it is not thematized. Yet it does appear if one knows how to listen to the Greek language with a Greek ear, for it governs the original meaning of words: thus, the withdrawal proper to *aletheia* is understood in *phusis*, in the emergence that shelters itself in its own reserve; it is understood in *techne*, in that knowledge which can set entities into the work by respecting the reserve of *phusis*; it is understood in *logos*, that gathering and uncovering which language has always already accomplished in silence; it is understood in *dike*, the latent jointure; and in *polis*, the invisible "pole" of being-together. This premetaphysical experience can also be read in the first poets and tragedians (Homer and Sophocles), as well as in the pre-Platonics (Anaximander, Heraclitus, and Parmenides). Despite the transformations and covering over which it undergoes, *aletheia* determines not only Greek man, but all the successive figures of Western man up to planetary man. For the forgetting or obfuscation of withdrawal will thrust man increasingly to the front of the stage. The Greek "commencement," the *Anfang*, richer than a simple beginning, asserts its hold on us to the end, and does so via the link between the History of metaphysical truth and the progressive dissolution of *aletheia*.

What constitutes the specifically Greek relation of man to being and being to man? What is the human essence that this relation gives rise to?

"Greek man *is* as the one who apprehends entities [*der Vernehmer des Seienden*]."[6] The verb *vernehmen*, which translates the Greek *noein*, designates an apprehending, a listening, a comprehensive grasp that contrasts with the act of representation. Greek man does not compare the entities before him; above all, he does not relate them back to himself in the first instance. Entities as a whole understood as *phusis*—that is, as that which freely spreads out and opens itself of its own accord—address themselves to man. Man does not inquire about his 'I', his subjectivity, to seek the conditions of possibility of entities as such. The form of *reflection* is not predominant for the Greeks. "For the Greeks, things appear. For Kant, things appear to me."[7] This is why there is a certain immediacy corresponding to the presence of phenomena in and of themselves. "The Greeks are that humanity which lived immediately in the openness of phenomena—through the explicit ek-static capacity to let the word be addressed to them by the phenomena..."[8] We can hear the German *ansprechen* here: letting oneself be interrogated and claimed by the phenomena, obeying one's own coherence or conflictual unity. "Saving the phenomena," one might say—before Plato comes to understand this as the movement of tracing them back to their intelligible essence—leaving them their own *logos*, that is, their own proper unity, their immanent "gathering." Such immediacy, maintained thanks to the attunement of astonishment, means that the passage from entities to being, the amazed discovery of the

6. Ibid., p. 84; tr., QT, p. 131.
7. VS, p. 67.
8. Ibid., p. 68.

presence of entities, does not depend on an interiorization on the part of man, nor on man's gaze upon entities. "Rather it is man who is looked on by entities, by whatever opens itself to the measure of the presence gathered around him. Looked on by entities, comprehended, contained and thus borne in and through the openness of entities, caught up in the cycle of their contrasts and bearing the mark of their dissension: this is the essence of man during the great epoch of the Greeks."[9] This "great epoch" is evidently that which Nietzsche calls *the tragic era of the Greeks*: the Presocratic epoch.

But what is meant by this bold expression: man is "looked on by entities"? Heidegger elucidates this, as we shall see, in his courses on Parmenides (GA 54) and Heraclitus (GA 55). Man finds himself carried to *Vernehmen*, to apprehending, by this "look" proceeding from being that is none other than its very lighting, the *Lichtung* without which we could not see. Furthermore, the human *logos* merely responds to the *Logos* of being, which has always already enveloped everything in its own unity. Paradoxically, the surpassing of anthropocentrism ends up endowing "being" with quasi-human faculties: the look (*Blick, An-blick*), which translates the Greek *thea* and the capacity for *Versammlung*, the power of gathering that is supposed to be the primary meaning of the nonhuman *logos*.

How do we know that for Greek man being is that which looks and originally gathers? Certainly we find in Fragment 50 of Heraclitus and in many other fragments (such as Fragment 45) the distinction between "me" (the word of a *sophos*) and the *logos* of things themselves. Yet it is hard to avoid the feeling that Heidegger's thought makes "projections" in these interpretations, and that Greek man is *Dasein*, being-in-the-world rethought in terms of the relation that maintains it in being.

A further paradox, perhaps more apparent than real, concerns the fact that, although the Greeks experienced *aletheia*, they did not explicitly formulate this. "The Greeks...*belong* to *aletheia*"[10] and yet, even in Parmenides, "the essence of *aletheia* remains veiled."[11] How is such a discrepancy possible? Must not their relation to *aletheia* have been brought to language? Despite their *thaumazein*, their marvel in the face of presence, the Greeks experienced the sense of *lethe*, of concealment that this presence entails.

---

9. Hw, pp. 83–84; tr., QT, p. 131.
10. VS, p. 68.
11. VA, p. 252.

Their experience of *aletheia*, as that which is inaccessible in what is manifest, is effectively translated in a nonconceptual and indirect way via language itself. Particularly in the use of the verb *lanthanein*, to be hidden, and its derivative *lethe*, forgetting. We say, "I have forgotten." In Greek, however, the middle voice of the verb *lanthanomai* means "something escapes me, remains hidden from me," or, as Heidegger translates it, "I remain hidden from myself." The Greeks notice the fact that something escapes our memory or our perceptual attention as a feature of all entities (including myself) insofar as they are turned towards appearance and can withdraw from this appearance. The basis of the Greek attitude implies that concealment, covering over, or withdrawal—in the same way as manifest presence—does not originally depend on an act of a subject. A withdrawal occurs. Man notices it. He does not attribute the cause to himself. The phenomena that we associate with the interiority of the subject and ground in it are referred to the law of presence. Those phenomena, including myself, are in the world. This is why the Greeks revere above all else that "awe" (*aidos, Scheu*), that attunement which allows man to respect whatever hides and withholds itself within the proximity of things present and their givenness. Heidegger quotes an episode from the *Odyssey* in which the tears of Ulysses escape the view of the Phaeacians not because Ulysses is hiding himself or his tears, although he is indeed veiling his head, but: *elanthane dakrua leibon*, "he remained hidden while shedding tears." The shame or modesty of Ulysses itself remains invisible, escapes possible witnessing. "For Greek experience, there reigns a concealment around the crying man which removes him from the view of others."[12] Such concealment belongs not only to this presence of Ulysses that is marked by a show of modesty, but belongs to every presence.

Greek man experiences his relation to this presence, at once powerful and fragile, luminous and concealed, as something astonishing or perilous. This is why he is torn between modesty or a sense of restraint and the temptation towards what the tradition conceives as "excess" (the hubris of the tragedians), and what Heidegger, in the *Introduction to Metaphysics*, interprets as confrontation with the enigmatic *limits* of presence. Greek man is "tragic" to begin with—though Heidegger uses the term only rarely and with restraint, even in his reading of Nietzsche—because his place in the world is grievously threatened and contested. He is tragic because he is destined

12. Ibid., p. 255.

to confront forces superior to his, yet that are at the same time his own forces. He perceives the limits of all things, including his own limits, as having to be discovered, torn from concealment and conquered at the expense of a struggle with and against the almighty power of that *phusis* that sustains him in being. His initial destiny is to rupture with being. Man, required by the Delphic *gnoti sauton* to seek his place, is located not in some essence that has already been determined, but at the limit of his emergence from *phusis*, his separation from other entities, and his standing before the gods. What is ultimately tragic lies in the fact that man is necessarily shattered in the movement whereby he conquers his essence. The originally Greek essence of man is to exit from himself, to "risk" his limitations, and to founder before the almighty power of being. Post-Platonic man is preoccupied primarily with his soul. Pre-Platonic man contests the space of his works within *phusis*, those works into which he builds, sculpts and inscribes his essential brokenness.

This definition of man by way of a finitude broken by a noninternal rupture—by his conflicting encounter with natural forces, other human beings, the gods—characterizes both Greek man and the transition from *Dasein* to man. *Dasein* would encounter its limit, death, essentially within itself, whereas man encounters his limits outside of himself. The difference between Greek man and man as "maintained" in being (To what epoch does this second figure of man belong? Might we, on Heidegger's own account, be dealing with a nonhistorial human being?) is that, whereas the first— Greek man—is engaged in a tragic struggle to conquer his essence, the second receives his essence with gratitude and serenity. Yet neither really has any interiority. Man as such is *exteriority*! Yet does not the total absence of interiority, of individuation, risk dooming Heideggerian man to abstraction or inhumanity?

We find this exteriority of finitude marvelously described in Heidegger's famous commentary on the first chorus of Sophocles' *Antigone*.

Polla ta deina kouden anthropou deinoteron pelei. Heidegger translates: "There is much that is uncanny, but nothing that surpasses man in uncanniness."[13] The whole reading rests on the translation of *deinon*—normally rendered as "wondrous"—by *unheimlich*, which the English *uncanny* renders somewhat imperfectly. The *unheimlich* is that which makes us depart from the *heimlich*, the familiar and habitual, our being 'at home'. Man is *the*

---

13. EM, p. 112; tr., p. 146.

most uncanny being, but not the most powerful, as one might think at first. For the chorus, especially in Heidegger's translation, seems to say that there is nothing "beyond" man. This *über*, however, does not exist in the Greek text. Man is "more uncanny" than other entities only because he is confronted with the power of *deinon*. *Deinon*, as the power of entities as a whole that both sustains man and is tragically opposed to him, is a power that surpasses every limit—a properly sublime power—an *overwhelmimg power*. (Note that the Greek text does not contain *as such* either of the two words that the commentary rests on and repeats; namely, *deinon*—there is only the plural *deina*—and *deinotaton*; only the comparative is used, and not the superlative to designate man.)

The overwhelming dominates man, permeates him. Hence the ambiguity of man. In one sense he responds to *deinon*, corresponds to it, even when he undertakes to fight against it. To being, tragic man opposes a force, a power, and "faculties" that he does not have, but that he draws from that power which both sustains him and involves his entering into dissension with the established order of entities. The entire activism and voluntarism of man who can raze and subjugate the earth, capture and tame wild animals, invent sciences, arts and techniques, institute political life—the whole deployment of human power and cunning (described by Heidegger with quasi-Nietzschean, or in any case Promethean overtones: "In his desire for the unheard of, he casts all help aside"[14])—this entire power of man is only a *response to the overwhelming* that somehow "provokes" man to irrupt into the unexplored, venture into the impossible, and risk his ultimately inevitable annihilation. The initiative of being commands him. "It is being itself that tears man away and throws him onto this path..., compelling him towards being so that he may set being into the work."[15] The motif of *Brauch* appears here in the *Introduction to Metaphysics* for the first time. Man is held to the "necessity of shattering."[16] He finds himself "thrown into the constraint [*Not*] of such being, because the overwhelming as such *needs* the site of openness for itself in order to appear in its prevailing [*Walten*]."[17]

This constraint, however, is not a violence. The reign of *phusis*, which man must control and tame and which overwhelms him

14. Ibid., p. 125; tr., p. 163.
15. Ibid.
16. Ibid., p. 124.
17. Ibid.

(*überwältigen*), as well as the reign of those powers that prevail through (*durchwalten*) him—language, understanding, and attunement—demand a power or force (*Gewalt*) from man in turn, rather than a violence, so that he in turn can dominate them. The translation of *Gewalt* by *violence* is quite misleading in this respect. It gives the impression that being's relation to man, and man's response, are marked not by necessity, but by "acts of force" and violent moments. No control can result from violence. No violence can exert itself with perfect continuity and remain violent. The activities that Heidegger lists under the term *Gewalttätigkeit* ("activity of power")—poetry, thought, the founding of states—cannot be thought as acts of force, because they consist in harmonizing and *taming* the overwhelming via art, knowledge, the *logos*, *nomos*, and the "technical." All that the Greeks call *techne*, the capacity to set truth into a work, cannot be the result of a "doing violence." Certainly, as the commentary shows, knowledge and the work of art, because they shatter the habitual and familiar, belong to *deinon*, to the uncanny. But the uncanny that confronts the overwhelming is not the violent one; it is man himself. As a cultural being, man could not have violence as his essence. The Heideggerian superlative *deinotaton* merely indicates the movement through which Greek man succeeds in dominating the overwhelming *for a while*, before being inevitably exposed to the nothing. What is most uncanny about Greek tragic man is that, however supreme his victory, "he can never master the overwhelming,"[18] but encounters death whose excess surpasses any inscription he can make of it in his works. This ultimate "risk" does not mean that "violence" is present at every moment for him. On the contrary, because *deinon* is identified with the words *logos* and especially *dike* (translated as *Fug, ordered jointure*), no violent disjunction can be inscribed in the essence of being. The overwhelming "maintains" man; that is, orders and enjoins him to adjust. This is how—in a nonmoral way, yet as we have seen earlier, in accordance with the temporal limitation of presence—Heidegger interprets *dike* in Anaximander as "jointure."

Yet does one find this *deinon*, this overwhelming power of being, in Sophocles himself? Again, the "concept" of *deinon* is at most merely latent, for the manifest content of the text is a straightforward enumeration of human activities. Certainly man is doomed to Hades, to death. The famous *pantoporos aporos, ep'ouden erchetai*, however, is surely overtranslated by "he comes to the noth-

---

18. Ibid., p. 123; tr., p. 161.

ing" (*kommt er zum Nichts*). It is more likely that the common wisdom of the chorus states that when man fails to find his way (*aporos*), he "achieves nothing"! Apart from Parmenides, the nothing as *ouden* is rarely to be found to mean a route that cannot be taken. It is rather unlikely that Sophocles would have thought of the nothing as the face of being! The notion of the overwhelming seems foreign to the text of the chorus, which Heidegger always makes extreme demands on. Thus *me kalon*, the nonbeautiful or displeasing, is translated as *Unseiende*, which would refer back to the Platonic *me on*. Does the link between the nothing and death on the one hand, and the powers or gifts of being, on the other, belong to Greek man, but *on the level of the unthought*? Undoubtedly, but this boils down to admitting that "Greek man" is not only what he has been, but also what he is today *for us*. The inquiry into Greek man is an inquiry into modern Western man. Even if Sophocles did not think the Heideggerian concept of *deinon*, he revealed a *formidable* audacity and risk belonging to the spirit of human activity. Modern man would not only have forgotten "being," that is, the fact that he does not give himself his own powers, and would not merely have forgotten his inability to master the overwhelming, but would have lost the ability to be astonished at himself and fear his own power. He would, then, have to learn from Greek man the fear of the power belonging to *phusis* and *techne*, as well as a *tragic* awareness of his own limits—two of the things missing in contemporary man.

Yet had not the sophist Protagoras already destroyed this sense of the tragic and broken the link with *aletheia* by proclaiming: "Of all things, man is the measure, of those that are, the fact that they are, and of those that are not, the fact that they are not"? On two occasions,[19] Heidegger attempted to show that man according to Protagoras belongs to the same essence of man as do the tragedians and Heraclitus. We are too quick and indeed wrong to understand the human measure in terms of the modern Cartesian or Kantian primacy of subjectivity that claim that the human subject is the condition for every object. Such a conception is unthinkable for the *sophia* of the Sophists, which remains in the realm of the *sophon* of Heraclitus, that is, still thinks being in terms of *phusis* and *aletheia*, presence absencing. What is at issue is indeed entities that are and are not, that come into or fail to come into presence. But the sophist Protagoras meant to limit to man any

19. Hw, pp. 95ff. (tr., QT, pp. 143ff.) and NII, pp. 135ff. (tr., NII, vol. Four, pp. 91ff.).

relation to *phusis*. He maintains that man can *know* nothing of a nonhuman *phusis* or of the gods. Measure, Heidegger states, has the sense of control and moderation, delimitation and *restriction of aletheia*. Even if, according to Plato in the *Theaetetus*, Protagoras refers truth to man as *ego*, this *ego* is not that of Descartes. The ipseity of man is not yet the egoity of the subject. Man does not posit *phusis* before him to ask it to submit entirely to the jurisdiction of his subjectivity. Entities as a whole are *confined* to the "world," says Heidegger. "For the Greeks, the ego is the name for man who submits to this restriction and who in himself is *himself*."[20] *Panton chrematon metron estin anthropos*—this is not a statement concerning beings as such and as a whole, but man is measure of *panton chrematon*, of all items of use (*chrema* comes from *chrestai*, "to use"), of all entities "to hand," of the entire *Zuhandenheit* that constitutes world.

Nonetheless, this interpretation hides the fact that, although the link with *aletheia* perhaps still exists, sophistry undoubtedly broke the link attaching man to pre-Socratic *phusis* or totality, and probably did so in favor of a "world" restricted in turn to the "affairs" of the city. Why is Heidegger so keen to safeguard the unity and identity of the essence of pre-Platonic Greek man? Must we not presume that that epoch was able to permit several types of humanity? Although we can understand why the subject in the transcendental sense, as the counterpart of objectivity, must be absent and why we must speak of Greek man in terms of being-in-the-world, it is less comprehensible why Greek man should be deprived of individuality and why in general this man should be man.

Commenting in the Heraclitus course on Fragment 101 ("I myself have sought myself"), Heidegger concludes: "The sentence can only mean: I have sought the site of the essence of man."[21] It cannot be concerned with a self-analysis in the individual sense. And this is so, he states, because Heraclitus in Fragment 50 asks us not to listen to him himself, "not me" (*ouk emou*), "but the Logos" according to which *hen panta*: *all things are One*. Yet the two demands are not mutually exclusive or contradictory. Heraclitus could have affirmed a *Logos* of being without denying his own individuality. The reason Heidegger tries to maintain the coherence of an originally Greek human essence has to do with the logic of the History of Being. If there were an original diversity among Greek

20. NII, p. 138; tr., NII, vol. Four, p. 94.
21. GA 55, p. 325.

humanity, then the Platonic "catastrophe," the arrival of both the subjugation of *aletheia* by *homoiosis*, that is, adequation, and the premise of an interiority of the soul would merely be one transition among others. The fact that *aletheia* should be incompatible with the self-centered perspective of subjectivity is self-evident, but that it should exclude individuality makes man, according to Heidegger, into a being strangely deprived of that trait which remained essential to *Dasein* in *Being and Time*: mineness. Both Greek man and man open to *Ereignis*, before and after the reign of subjectivity, would not be able or would not want to say 'I'. What is the significance of such an *essential* deindividualizing of man? Is it necessary? Is it even thinkable?

Just as he restitutes the Greek sense of measure and immeasure to *aletheia* and *phusis*, Heidegger reinterprets the well-known Hellenic primacy of vision in terms of the disclosure of being and its light. Being does not belong to the visible, it is not part of the visible. It is the inapparent that lets us see. Heidegger's analysis of the Greek look at once introduces the contrary of an anthropology. For the Greeks, the human look would be the response to another look that was always anterior and somehow anticipatory. The analysis rests entirely on the translation and interpretation of the verb *theao*. The medial reflexive form of this verb (the only one in use) means to look or contemplate, and gives us the word *theatron*. But *theao* in itself, *as root*, would mean to offer a view, present oneself, appear (but where is the textual evidence that would confirm this?). And this permits a reversal from the very outset of the interpretation: "To look, including the human look, means, when originally experienced, not to grasp something, but to show oneself—and only in relation to this is a look that grasps possible."[22] *Theao* would thus point back to an original look, a look providing aspects and views into which the human look could dip. The look is that which makes the essence shine. Plato, in thinking being as "view" (*idea*) and "outer aspect" (*eidos*), would, at the end of Hellenism, have echoed a more ancient tradition. The *theaon*, the look (*Blick*), looking, that which looks (*das Blickende*), would be "the fundamental mode of appearing."

It is difficult to prevent a certain doubt from arising here. To appear is not to look. To say that being looks at us, not in the figurative sense, but in the proper sense, that is, "sees us," seems like a pure anthropomorphism, reinforced by importing a very prevalent theological claim, namely; that "God looks at us." In what respect

---

22. GA 54, p. 152.

does the fact of showing oneself, offering a view, or presenting various aspects and forms imply an *activity* of seeing on the part of whatever offers a view of itself? The fact that the light of being makes vision possible does not mean that it itself must have the possibility of seeing. That which is most capable (appearing) is not necessarily capable of the lesser possibility of the human look. The Greek look would imply both being seen by being, and the divine essence of being as primarily "visionary": the divinity of that which originally makes us see and itself sees. This is why we find in the Greeks an identity of being and god or the divine (an identity that Heidegger himself does not accept, because for him the holy appears in being, and god in the dimension of the holy). On account of its "visionary" capacity, being would endow itself with a divine "personality." Heidegger bases this interpretation on a threefold philological link (but is it philologically defensible?) between

- *theao* and *daio*, seeing and "making a sign," from which we get *daimon*;

- *theaon* and *theion*, the view and the divine;

- *théa* and *theà*, the look and divinity, literally, the "goddess" (two words that differ only in the way they are accented).

The *daimon* is that power emanating from the divine, which makes a sign, reveals, initiates, instructs, all *in an instant*. The *daimonion* designates the sign of the heavens, the flash of the unheard-of that suddenly shows itself: *both being and the divine*. Heidegger translates *daimon* by *Ungeheuer*, the enormous, the inhabitual, the unheard-of that looms in the habitual and familiar. The *theion* is the look of being, the *daimon* its call. The Greek gods would be the mediators and witnesses of the light and the call, those who accompany and harmonize the dangerous passage from the familiar to the unheard-of. They would be those invoked by human beings, those to whom they pray to help them sustain the dazzling view of that which looks at humans in looking of its own accord. "Because the *theion* and the *daimonion* [the divine aspect] are that which cast a look into unconcealment, because they are the unheard-of as it presents itself in the realm of the habitual, the *mythos*...is the sole appropriate manner of relating to being in its appearing."[23] Yet in that case, how is it possible that precisely the "mythical" figures of the Greek gods

---

23. Ibid., pp. 165–166.

seem "anthropomorphic" to us, if it is true that "the gods are being itself casting its look into entities"?[24] It is because we stick too closely to the external form of mythology and try to make out its letter and spirit from this. The *mythos* is discursive language that translates the converse, inhabitual relation *of being to man*. The *mythos* names being in terms of itself and not in terms of man; the fact that it grasps being by way of human images is scarcely important. Mythology would be closer to *aletheia* than any thought has ever been. It would in any case express the fact that the essence of man is not only *zoon logon echon*, but *zoon mython echon*, that is, the one who names the relation of being to himself by naming the gods. He would be the first of these only because he is the second. The *logos* would be rooted in the *mythos*. Greek man would therefore name the gods "in accordance with the essence of *aletheia*" (*gemäss dem Wesen der aletheia*), so as to be able to say the truth in terms of itself. As for Schelling, Greek mythology for Heidegger would be the primary revelation of truth. Conversely, the later atheism of the West would be the sign of the almost complete forgetting of *aletheia*. Nevertheless, one may ask whether the Heideggerian interpretation of the gods as figures of the authentic relation of being to man is not itself too humanist, too incredulous, too "logical," too belated, too extrareligious.

Let us note that the definition of man as "the one who is looked at" (*der Angeblickte*)[25] is valid not only for Greek man. It returns at the other extremity of the History of Being to characterize the human being of *Ereignis*; that is, man as capable of apperceiving the light of being in its extreme veiledness, in the essence of Technology. This human being, however, does not grasp this essence because he is particularly clairvoyant, but because he is *grasped, struck* by the "lightning flash of being" that has emerged from the transformation of *Gestell* itself. "Human beings are those who are looked on [*die Erblickten*] in this insight [*im Einblick*]."[26] The "insight," strangely, comes from *Ereignis* understood as *Er-aügnis*,[27] "caught sight of." "The verb *ereignen* comes from *er-aügnen*, meaning: to catch sight of, to call to oneself in looking, to ap-propriate."[28] What is proper to man is to be a look that is looked at, the bearer of the look, to be

---

24. Ibid., p. 164.
25. Ibid., p. 160.
26. TK, p. 45; tr., QT, p. 47.
27. Ibid., p. 44; tr., QT, p. 45.
28. ID, pp. 24–25. (Translator's note: The English translation of *Identity and Difference* omits this sentence.)

caught sight of, illuminated by the original, nonhuman looking (*Blicken*). Being uses someone illuminated—tactfully—without, as in Plato, completely extracting him from his fundamental obscurity, but preserving in man the obscure role that being equally preserves for its part. "In the look and as look, the essence enters its proper illumination....Yet looking at the same time preserves [*wahrt*], in illumination, the concealed obscurity of its provenance as that which is un-lighted."[29] What is this "concealed obscurity," this un-lighted origin in man? What is un-lighted in being is withdrawal; the un-lighted of man is perhaps the forgetting of being, but is it not also the Earth, "nature"? Another dissymmetry, another question. Can man be exclusively and to the core this being of the look, this extrovert he has been since the Greeks and that he remains until the thought of *Ereignis*?

But let us return to the Greeks. There is a look in Greek man only because he *"has the logos"*. "Man, and he alone, is that entity who, because he has the word, casts his look into the open and sees the open in the sense of *alethes*."[30] To see entities is to be able to name them. The animal cannot see; it keeps watch and looks out for prey. The originally Greek opposition between the animal and man has to do only with the *logos*. In effect, the *zoe* of the *zoon* designates emergence, "rising" (*Aufgang*), unclosing, the thrust of *phusis* towards the light, an emergence that man shares with the animal. The root *za*, like the root *phu*, expresses the luminous. But man is that being who is not a prisoner of *phusis*, the one who emerges from emergence by naming his relation to it thanks to the *logos*; or rather, man is situated *within* the *logos*, which is much more than language as the ability to speak. The unthought in the Greek definition of man would be that "the *logos* has man" and not the reverse. As the course on Heraclitus (GA 55) shows with an extraordinary scope and rigor, the *logos* is originally not at all a faculty of man and especially not reason, nor is it the statement, proposition, or proportion, as it will become later; it cannot be reduced to language, but is that which unifies beings, bringing them together and to their proper identity: "the original *Ver-sammlung*."[31] The *logos* is perhaps language as not yet spoken: language that has always already gathered and uncovered things. The Greeks, Heidegger notes, never said that man was the being capable of moving its tongue, *anthropos*

---

29. TK, p. 43; tr., QT, p. 45.
30. GA 54, p. 231.
31. GA 55, p. 295.

zoon glossan echon, but the one who has the *logos*, that is, the very space of *aletheia*, the space in which was inscribed both the Greek *ethos* and the *polis* with its institutions, games, and festivals... Greek man, he states, is also *anthropos ethos echon*. Heraclitus distinguishes between a purely human *logos* and the original *logos* that makes it possible and that would be being itself. Is this distinction in fact perceived by Greek man? Is he aware that all his activities occur on the basis of an original *logos*—set down in his tongue, his *ethos*, the *polis*—a *logos* to which he spontaneously submits, and wisely so, to escape the hubris of separation. Is it for all the Greeks or only for Heraclitus that *logos*, *aletheia*, *phusis*, and the One, are the Same (*das Selbe*)? Is there not a certain ambiguity in the idea of this original and immanent Greek wisdom? Are all the Greeks *sophoi*, or still related to the original *sophia*, if only to refuse it? Does not Heidegger take up in another form the Hegelian idea of the "beautiful totality" of the Greeks as immediate spirit? By no means. Certainly the Greeks *do not know* what the primary meaning of the *logos* is, or rather, they do not *think* about it, but they do have a preconceptual understanding of it. Their "practical" adherence to being, which does not exclude questioning—quite the contrary—constitutes their rootedness, whereas our distanciation, our theoretical desire for clarification constitutes our uprootedness.

Likewise for the *polis*. "Who says that the Greeks...were in the clear about the essence of the *polis*?"[32] For them, this essence is both immediate and in dispute, "obvious" and worthy of question. As is shown even by a text as late as the *Republic* (which is the Roman name for what has become the *res publica*, the reification of the *Politeia*), the question of the essence of the *polis* has nothing to to with what we today call political science. The *polis* is neither the State, nor public affairs. The *polis* is the place of *aletheia*, the ever-conflicting *site* of unconcealment, the place in which all essential relations are decided: the relations between the citizens in the assembly, the relation between master and slave, between just and unjust, between men and gods. Temples, festivals, and games; men of war, governors, poets, and thinkers all receive their truth from the *polis*. Heidegger connects the word *polis* with *polos*, the pole. "*Polis* is *polos*, the pole, the place [*Ort*] around which everything that appears to the Greeks as entities turns in a peculiar way."[33] Neither simply a town or city, nor an atopical State, the *polis* would

32. GA 53, p. 99.
33. GA 54, p. 132.

be the "essential site" (*Wesensstätte*) of Greek man, the space in which he comes into his own, attains his history. The proof that Greek man did not lose being until a later epoch, the proof that he remains within the orbit of *aletheia*, is given by the fact that he fears being ostracized just as much as he fears death. He could not be tranquilly "apolitical." The greatest threat that can weigh on him is to be "excluded from this site," *apolis*, as the *Antigone* chorus says, for this would mean his being cast out from the place of his essence. This is why the Aristotelian *zoon politikon* can be a definition of Greek man as a whole and not merely of one human activity. "Man is that being who is capable of belonging to the *polis*."[34] Man's belonging to the *polis* and his belonging to being as *aletheia* and *phusis* are one and the same dimension.

In a manner reminiscent of Hegel, Heidegger—without mention of a "beautiful totality"—often insists on the fact that all the elements of Greek existence are harmoniously interconnected and linked to the *polis* as the *site*[35] in which truth appears. Within the *polis* art, *techne*, and man's relations to the gods in works, cults, theatrical liturgies, and sacrifices take on meaning and find their place. For Greek man, *techne* refers back to the *theion*, and both refer back to a totality. There are in fact no works of art that can be separated and given over solely to subjective pleasure. *Techne* implies much more than a *savoir faire* or even an art in the sense of a specialized artistic practice such as painting or music. It entails a view of entities as such and as a whole: the Greeks understand "art" as an extension of *phusis* and as corresponding to it. There can be a *savoir faire* only if there is *savoir*, knowledge in the broadest sense of an understanding of being. Similarly, the Greek relation to the *theion* is not so much, as people often say, an awareness of the "limits" between men and gods, but is primarily inscribed in an understanding of being.

For Heidegger, the proximity of the gods in the Greeks, their presence alongside men, does not have to do with any magical or "mythical" anthropomorphism in the pejorative sense. It is not even "religious" in essence, for *religio* is the Roman invention of a *tie*: not so much one of union between men and gods, as of obligation to certain scrupulously observed rituals. Commenting on Heraclitus' saying *einai kar kai entautha theous*, "here too the gods are present"— spoken to some visitors as an invitation to approach him when they

34. GA 53, p. 102.
35. GA 54, p. 133 and GA 55, pp. 11–12.

had found him heating himself by a humble baker's oven—Heidegger shows what this banal, everyday site means symbolically. To be near the oven is to be close to the hearth, that is, to the source of heat and light, thus—near to the gods! For, we recall, the gods or *theoi* in Heidegger's reading are those who, although remaining invisible, illuminate everything with their simple "look" (*thea*). The "look" of the gods would be the way in which Greek man understands the light of being that gives rise to the e-normous (*Ungeheuer*) amid the everyday and the normal (*Geheuer*): the unheard-of is nothing other than the emergence of entities as a whole, *phusis* grasped in its hearth. This is why men and gods can belong equally to *phusis*, which has nothing to do with nature in the modern sense. And this is why the Greeks call the gods "living beings" (*zoa*) and the *kosmos* a "great living being": the gods are not "animals," but the most shining, clearest, "truest" part of *phusis* (the prefix *za* would likewise indicate force, intensity: *zatheon* means "*very* divine"). The gods are "those who present themselves within the ordinary [*Geheuer*] as the extraordinary [*Ungeheuer*]."[36] Presence *as such*, glimpsed in its abrupt, unheard-of lightning flash—such would be the meaning of *divine* presence! If concern for the presence of the gods is so fundamental and determinative for the meaning of the *polis*, it is because the gods are the very being of every entity.

"The Greek's relation to the gods is a *knowing*, and not a 'belief' in the sense of some voluntary adherence on the basis of authoritative revelation. We are as yet unable to measure the primordial way in which the Greeks were knowers [*die Wissenden*]."[37] This Greek mythology that we take to be naive and regard condescendingly would implicitly embrace a true phenomenological knowledge of being. Thus Heidegger gives an ontological interpretation of the three attributes of Artemis, the goddess of Ephesus: the lyre, the bow, and the flaming torch. The lyre is the harmony of entities as a whole, the poetic play of *phusis*. *Phusis* is the bearer of life, but also of death. The bow expresses both the tension of opposites and the work of death. The flaming torch is both bearer of light and—when inverted and extinguished—of dark. This is why Artemis is the war goddess: this war would signify the struggle between the manifest and the latent, and the struggle of life and death would be only their outer image. But have not the goddess

36. GA 55, p. 9.
37. Ibid., p. 15.

and the myth suddenly become too transparent? Is not Heidegger unfairly translating Greek man's relation to the gods into philosophical thought that remained unformulated? Is it not unlikely that the divine light was experienced as the light of being, even as the unthought? The theologizing of being, which goes hand in hand with an ontologizing of the divine, identifies the man-god relation with man's relation to being, and paradoxically effaces a difference between being and the divine that is maintained elsewhere in Heidegger's thinking.

For Greek man, prior to the great metaphysical scissions, nothing human has become separated out, and no relation can be separated out. *Phusis, logos, polis, techne, theion*—each express relations to the unity and totality of being as *aletheia*, as well as the reciprocal relations. Man in the great Greek commencement finds himself included *within* the "overall Relation," but does not explicitly think about this. Perhaps, though Heidegger does not say this, it is because he is radically enveloped, absorbed and transfixed by *phusis, logos, polis, techne,* and *theion,* that he does not need to think them.

Is postmetaphysical man capable of rediscovering this overall inclusion? He will be able to aim towards this only by dispossessing and decentering himself. This would be one way of *mastering* in a voluntarist manner what the first Greeks found self-evident. To rediscover the unthought Greek definition of man, it would be necessary, paradoxically, to *reverse* this definition, which has degenerated down through the line of metaphysical sedimentations. Therefore Heidegger reverses the formula *anthropos : zoon logon echon,* which has come to read, "man, the animal who has reason," to give the following: *phusis : logos anthropon echon,*[38] "being, as emergence and gathering, holding man." Does not this formula, in addition to stating the unthought of the Greek definition, provide us with the *true* essence of Western man, an essence always missed and forgotten? Does not Heidegger thereby suggest that there is a true, *transhistorial* essence of man; namely, that entity endowed with the gift of collecting the gifts of being, or that entity to whom the gift is given? Yet is it a question of *willing* that which, for the Greeks, was "natural" spontaneity? Of "willing not to will"?[39] Is not Greek man in his immediacy lost forever? To avoid this accusation of nostalgia, Heidegger would displace the postmetaphysical into

---

38. EM, p. 134.
39. Gel., p. 30; tr., p. 59.

the remote dawning of "another commencement." Yet the "other commencement," capable of launching "another History," would undoubtedly not have taken place without a *forgetting of man* similar to what in the Greek epoch was the *forgetting of being*, whose gradual entrenchment is the continuous thread of our History.

At the extremity of this History, what has become of man? Does not "planetary man" present the inverted image of Greek man, every bit as wanting in the face of technological domination as Greek man was in the face of *phusis*, but *without knowing it*? Is man then condemned to oscillate perpetually between the illusion of his power and the tragic knowledge of his impotence? Heideggerian thought seems to be aimed towards at least rendering this impotence lucid, acceptable, and serene, if not happy.

Planetary Man

Why this name rather than others? In our epoch in which names wear out quicker than ever before, man in fact receives several names: "man of the atomic age," "the beast of labor" (*arbeitendes Tier*), "the functionary of Technology"...So why "planetary"? Unlike the fixed position or regular path taken by a star, what properly pertains to a planet is to *wander* (*planè* means a "wandering path"). After describing the increasing indifference and uniformity of the technically organized universe, Heidegger concludes: "The earth appears as the non-world [*Unwelt*] of errancy. From the point of view of the History of Being, it is the wandering star."[40] "Planetary" entails technological errancy on a world scale or simply its expansion to the level of the planet. For in order for things to happen on a truly world scale, it would be necessary for there still to be a world to share among us; and yet all the distinctions that sustain a world—those between things and objects, near and far, private and public, war and peace—are tending to be increasingly effaced today. What in fact remains of world is materials, including man, uniformly delivered over to technological power, wear and tear, and consumption.

Yet *who* is planetary man? We *ourselves*, it seems. For because we can still say "we," we recognize that we have scarcely crossed the threshold of the epoch. *Wir Subjekten*, Husserl would say. We remain subjects. Heidegger shows the continuity and strict enchainment

---

40. VA, p. 93.

linking technological man to man as subject. At a certain point of objectification, the meaning of what has been objectified undergoes a qualitative change: what has been calculated and manipulated becomes the "incalculable," the "immense," something beyond our grasp and without measure. At a certain point of development, the process of objectification envelops both the person objectifying and whatever is objectified, leveling them and making them equal. And this point has already been attained. The whole of the technical process is now beyond our grasp, beyond our control, yet the subject that was once central and measuring still remains standing and visible: the conqueror conquered by his conquest. He continues to emerge for some time before being leveled; that is, if not uniformly absorbed into the "fund," then at least made accountable in the general stockpile of *Bestand. Provisionally,* he is a subject utilized, exploited, both consumer and consumed. This is why we actually do not know who will be planetary man tomorrow when man will no longer take the shape of a subject at all. For the moment he remains the subject. He remains an aggravated, overstimulated subject: the one who wanted to become master and possessor of nature has become "the willing one of the will to will"; that is, the one who blindly obeys whatever Technology projects upon him. "In the planetary imperialism of technically organized man, man's subjectivism reaches its highest point, where he will enter into the leveling-out of organized uniformity so as to settle there for good; for this uniformity is the surest instrument of complete, because technical, domination over the earth."[41]

The description given of him points to the fact that planetary man has already entered this leveling-out and uniformity and is not exactly a subject any more. "At its highest point," subjectivity folds back on itself, becomes fixed and congealed, given over exclusively to its labor of production and self-production. "Metaphysical man, the *animal rationale,* is set in place [*fest-gestellt*; i.e. firmly established] as a beast of labor."[42] Man labors "like a beast";[43] that is, he works blindly for an end that he has not posited and that is nothing other than *Machenschaft,* production for the sake of production, or "productity," if we may risk this barbarism. For although he is activist, voluntarist, and decision-maker, man is subjected to the condition of

41. Hw, pp. 102–103; tr., QT, p. 152.
42. VA, p. 68.
43. Translator's note: The French *bêtement* (from *bête,* beast) commonly means "stupidly."

worker. To be man in our epoch means to be a worker, whether manual or intellectual; that is, to manufacture, produce, transform, consume, *and nothing else*. As Heidegger emphatically puts it: "man is constrained *to be nothing but* labor."[44] Yet why is all human activity constituted as labor? Because labor means corresponding metaphysically to the essence of Technology as the will to will, that is, the will to produce for the sake of producing (for to will is to posit being as an object). By reducing himself to the status of worker, man takes on and interiorizes the essence of Technology. Yet in so doing he *no longer* makes the association between "labor and pain," as did an entire generation sanctioned by Hegel's well-known formulation—a tradition taken up again by Jünger and that Heidegger vindicates in a certain way by bringing together *algos* [pain] and *logos*.[45] Without man knowing his relationship to the will to will, in labor he finds his metaphysical identity fair, adequate and satisfactory. "He wills *himself* as the one who is freely willing in the will to will...so that he can be sure of the illusion."[46] He is unaware that the aim of the will to will is "the nothingness of the nothing." He is proud to work. He does not feel pain, reaching out as he does towards his "goal," which is to work for the sake of working. The dominion of the will closes off man's access to his own pain. Whenever he happens to experience it, he encounters it as a mere foreign obstacle, "i.e. *passively*, like an object for action, and therefore as belonging within the same essential realm of action, the realm of the will to will."[47] The essence of work and the question of work have eluded man, just as all that is metaphysically determined by the will to will has become unquestionable, "self-evident" (*selbstverständlich*). Planetary man no longer has any *schole*; and this is perhaps why the essence of the school appears equally problematic for him.

Is the technical beast still a subject? Barely, for it no longer reflects, but "works" *instinctively*. "Animal drives and human *ratio* become identical." In technicized man the capacity to calculate, regulate, and organize "the using up of entities" imposes itself with the assuredness of an instinct, with the irrepressible and somnambulant force of an *élan vital*. Technical reason becomes instinctive, and all elementary forces are put in service of its calculating will. In fact, because there is no longer anything in man apart from the will,

44. VA, p. 69 (emphasis added).
45. Wm, p. 398; tr., QB, p. 71.
46. VA, pp. 68–69.
47. Ibid., p. 95.

this will can absorb drives, and technological rationality can inter-change them. In this way Technology would force the essence of man to become closed in on itself, identifying traditional opposites in a deadly manner. For what could be more sinister, more remote from the spontaneity of *phusis*, than a *calculating drive*? This mon-strosity would be prepared and prefigured by the secret rationalism of the will to power that bends all drives to the sole logic of its own unceasing self-intensification. A paradoxical interpretation of Niet-zsche's unthought, since the *artistic* will to provide the drives with a rule and a law becomes a prefiguring of the *technical* will.

In the first texts he devotes to the subject of Technology (*Beiträge, Vorträge und Aufsätze*), Heidegger's pessimism is undoubt-edly too complete and insufficiently nuanced. He utters an outright condemnation without any recourse to the entire epoch. Later, in *Gelassenheit*, he concedes that man must coexist with Technology, say a simultaneous 'yes' and 'no' to it, and that in any case it would be absurd to want to reject it "as being the work of the devil."[48] In "Over-coming Metaphysics," however, he announces—in the fatal and apoc-alyptic tone of a prophecy, and as a necessity—that humanity will be able to escape this impasse only via destruction: "being as will must be broken, the world collapse, and the Earth be driven to devasta-tion."[49] And he concludes: "The beast of labor is abandoned to the whirlwind of his fabrications, so that it may tear itself apart and annihilate itself in the nihilative nothing."[50] Is this cruel end likely, in which man seems to be punished for his blindness through self-annihilation? Is not being itself the source of all self-destructive des-tiny, if we are dealing here with the destruction of *all mankind*? Yet we know that being will be reborn unscathed from this trial, because it bears the promise of "another commencement." It seems, therefore, that Heidegger was tempted to think the ultimate failure of Technol-ogy as a purifying, a selection that, in eliminating planetary man, would leave another type of human being remaining. This other type of human being appears to be the one who would not be forgetful of our epochal situation, the thinker or poet, the human being who would experience errancy as such, who has recognized both the essence of Technology and its danger. Or is it that human being who would be forgetful in a more healthy manner, more deliberately turned away from the past and finally capable of "leaving meta-

---

48. Gel., p. 22; tr., p. 53.
49. VA, p. 69.
50. Ibid.

physics to itself,"[51] thus capable of maintaining himself *outside of History*: "the mortal"? Yet how could any humanity whatsoever survive a possible general disintegration of the epoch? A catastrophic ending to Technology would probably annihilate mankind as a whole. The idea that the "beast of labor" will inevitably self-destruct seems to be a *negative utopia*. Is it not more likely that both man and his labor will be transformed?

The nihilistic traits of contemporary man are outlined in *Introduction to Metaphysics* (1935) in the figure of "normalized man," leading a gregarious existence marked by the contraction of the planet (each global event is simultaneously broadcast and communicated at every moment; local times disappear).[52] The first detailed description of contemporary man is provided in the *Beiträge* of 1936–38. It is striking on account of its severity. Man is divided between "calculation" (*Berechnung*) and "lived experience" (*Erlebnis*), or between *Machenschaft* and *Erlebnis,* which constitute the titles of several sections (Sections 66–68). These two complementary aspects evidently correspond to the simultaneous exacerbation of the rational and the vital. Both studied action and self-indulgent passion, insipid and made acceptable by sentiment, are simultaneously exalted. The systematic development of calculative behavior goes hand in hand with "sentimental" fervor pertaining to the "dullest sentimentality," Heidegger comments. For *calculation* does not refer to the practice of mathematical knowledge, though this is indispensable to Technology, but to a "fundamental law" of human comportment, a new rule valid for every kind of action and not limited to technical activities. "Calculation is understood here as a *fundamental law of comportment,* not as the mere reflection or even cleverness of a particular action, which belong to every human activity."[53] Calculation ultimately becomes an attitude. The maxim of calculation consists in recognizing as real only foreseen, organized, and planned action. All spontaneous change, which would be linked to an intrinsic growth of things, is rejected and excluded in advance. Calculation inserts all events into manufacturing programs, formulas or operating sequences of which we can be certain because we have constructed them. Henceforth man applies to *all* phenomena the procedures of production, or rather of *Machenschaft,* of the universal realm of "productity": he makes them into

---

51. SD, p. 25.
52. EM, p. 28ff.
53. GA 65, p. 121.

preestablished assemblies. How is it possible for lived experience to escape the universal grid of programming? It indeed seems that "the hunt for lived experiences"[54] serves as a "supplement for the soul" of the human being belonging to *Machenschaft*. Yet how is this possible? Does not *Erlebnis* appear to be the opposite of "production"? In truth, the two have a "common root,"[55] which is none other than representation, the fact of relating back to oneself or producing out of oneself and before oneself either this calculated operation or else this expression of life. *Erlebnis* is conceived as a state with which the subject affects itself, one that it gives itself or "manufactures," as in the Sartrean theory of the emotions. By the same token, it closes itself off from attunement, from every affective disposition it cannot regulate or submit itself to as it pleases.

This insensitivity to attunements characterizes man in the technical age. Having only a subjective experience of anxiety, he cannot trace this experience to being. To protect himself from a more essential anxiety, out of anxiety in the face of anxiety or to flee boredom, he takes refuge in indifference or in the "absence of distress," in any case in the absence of questioning. For one consequence of the calculating attitude would be the impossibility of any genuine question, as everything seems to be accessible and at our disposal and as nothing can be thought as being fundamentally inaccessible or withdrawn. There are of course innumerable problems, but they can all be resolved. Heidegger states the following "optimist" slogan of technical thinking: "Nothing is insoluble, and solving things is merely a matter of an amount of time, space and force."[56] *Erlebnis*, although it itself is made problematic, vulgarized, and uniformized, nevertheless shows that in his beginnings, planetary man draws his strength from this subjectivity that is already on the decline. Later on, planetary man might be deprived of all interiority, which cannot fail to be worrying.

This is all the more worrying because the gregarious slave of *Gestell* would be enigmatically close to the man of *Ereignis*, likewise situated beyond subjectivity.

Two further features linked to *quantity* mark out technical mankind: *rapidity* and the *reign of the masses*. Rapidity (*Schnelligkeit*)—the fleeting and expeditious character of all his activities, the incessant busyness of organized man—rests on the quantitative

---

54. Ibid., p. 124.
55. Ibid., p. 129.
56. Ibid., p. 123.

increase in mechanical speed (*Geschwindigkeit*), on the accelera-
tion that scientific and technical progress makes possible in all
domains of human activity. The conquest of speed—speed of movement, of communication of information, of production, and so on—
induces an "attitude of rapidity" in man. Somewhat like "curiosity"
in *Being and Time*, rapidity includes the mobility and volatile character of interests, the accelerated succession of activities, the
search for novelty at any price, "a craving for the sur-prising [*dem
Über-raschenden*]," as the text says.[57] Anything that might endure
seems boring from the outset and is avoided. One loses oneself in
actuality and is eager to forget the past. One is incapable of putting
up with the slowness of anything that matures of its own accord,
and one forces it to mature more quickly. One hates silence and
patience. Heidegger thus retranslates the somewhat unhistorial
inauthenticity of the 'One' into the context of Technology.

The case is similar concerning the spread of the masses. The
reign of the masses constitutes part of the "gigantic" (*das Riesen-
hafte*), that is, part of "that through which the quantitative
becomes a quality proper."[58] We must not understand this reign
only as a social, demographic, or political phenomenon, even
though collectivism or Americanism may be the most striking man-
ifestations of it. The spreading of the masses implies a logical
transformation of the subject, foreshadowing its effacement. The
citizen of former times has now been suppressed and "recruited into
the We" that, via the intermediary of the means of mass information, normalizes and standardizes every possibility of economic or
political decision. Before disappearing, the subject finds itself elevated to the *totality*—of the people, of the nation, of the continent,
of the planet—and melted into wholes within which "man" exists
only as material to be exploited and manipulated for the sole ends
of conserving and nurturing such wholes.

Henceforth installed across the planet, whose innermost
recess is instantaneously accessible and where the conditions of
existence are rapidly tending towards uniformity, does man still
dwell *anywhere*? "The *where* of his dwelling...appears to be annihilated."[59] Dwelling means incarnation in the site of a relation specific to the world as a whole. To dwell means to be, and being means
dwelling. For this reason, the forgetting of being is also the forget-

57. Ibid., p. 121.
58. Hw, p. 88; tr., QT, p. 135.
59. NII, p. 395; tr., NII, vol. Four, p. 248.

ting of dwelling. Inserted into the vast planetary network of long-distance communications, moving increasingly often and rapidly, man is tending to lose his ties with a familiar place where his being is gathered and on which it depends: a place of birth or place of his choosing. It is not planetary expansion, however, that threatens or destroys the familiar place, but the converse: it is "homelessness" (*Heimatlosigkeit*) or the absence of any "at home" that arouses the need to occupy and exploit the planet, and subsequently cosmic space. "The half-conceded, half-denied homelessness of man with respect to his *essence* is compensated for by the organized conquest of the earth as planet and the expansion into cosmic space."[60] *Heimatlosigkeit* thus has a double meaning: it is the failure of existence and works to be rooted in a particular earth (the products of culture are becoming standardized and are being "universalized" more and more in the bad sense); and, more profoundly, it means a loss of man's familiarity with himself. Not that man could escape from *Unheimlichkeit*, from an estrangement in respect of his own essence, or still ground himself on himself, be his own fatherland in some way. The point is rather that subjectivity no longer affords him any support or stable foundation. He sees himself forced to flee from the void of his metaphysical identity by a purely quantitative increase of power, particularly over space. It matters little that the space he has conquered is immense; he must produce and dominate more and more of it, for such space is indifferent, insignificant and empty. All "reflection"—understood as a returning to oneself, and a fortiori as a return to being—that might lead man back to a new essence is impossible, because he is unable to put the technological universe as such into question, nor can he question his own situation in it. Such would be that incapacity of modern man to return to himself, his misfortune of being irremediably conditioned by his own world, which Hegel and Marx thought dialectically and somewhat optimistically in the concept of alienation. For unlike metaphysically alienated man, man as technically alienated cannot escape his alienation by "raising his consciousness": this is forbidden him. Errancy constitutes a more radical imprisonment than any alienation.

Excluded from every site of his own, cut off from his essence, planetary man in his forward movement of flight is likewise increasingly deprived of any relation with a nature outside him that would not be technically organized and exploited. If he seems

60. Ibid.

so desperate to seek contact with the natural elements (such as sun and water), if he fabricates "natural products" for himself, it is because the "natural nature of human dwelling" and the "technically controllable nature of science...are moving away from one another at an increasingly insane speed."[61] Yet what is "natural nature"? Can man simply immerse himself in it while rejecting Technology? Not at all. It is henceforth impossible for man to reject Technology. Nor is it a matter of immersing oneself in a so-called more natural nature. *Natural nature* is in fact defined in two ways: *directly*, in a straightforward yet disconcerting way, it means the seasons, the rise and setting of the sun, the night, the day, the gentleness and excesses of climate, and indeed the earth that "sustains and abides, bears fruit and nourishes,"[62] and protects the living creatures entrusted to it—in a word, the two dimensions of earth and heavens; *indirectly*, it means nature in a nonimmediate way, the "opening up and withdrawal of every entity in its presence-absence,"[63] unconcealment in the broadest sense in its folding back on itself, "what the ancient Greek thinkers formerly called *phusis*," adds Heidegger. Natural nature is therefore that which modern man can no longer think, or that which he rejects, yet which he is essentially part of. To what hollow extent does planetary man still know that his body belongs to the Earth, and that the Earth is bound to the cosmos? He no longer makes a distinction between day and night, between the near and the far, because for him everything is near or approachable, everything can be assimilated or acted on. He sees no natural phenomenon as a limit. For Heidegger, it is not so much a matter of "living according to nature" or, as one says, respecting natural equilibriums and limits, as of looking after and sparing that which hides itself of its own accord and not pursuing it to make it present itself and submit to force. What we call the protection of nature or the environment would therefore have to be based primarily on a respect for the concealment of being, of the Earth, and of world, which is what Technology radically refuses.

At first sight at least, rather paradoxically, it seems that some human beings can resist the technological fever and remain apart from the frenzy of "productity." Those Heidegger calls "the mortals" are presumed capable of *dwelling* in the strong sense; that is, of respecting Earth and world, welcoming and preserving their con-

---

61. Hebel, p. 23.
62. VA, p. 170; tr., PLT, p. 178.
63. Hebel, p. 22.

cealment, letting be the near as near and the distant as distant, acknowledging the holy, "being capable of death as death"...[64] Yet how can they coexist with planetary mankind? How can that which they consider to be the "world"—that is, the singular and multiple, secret and manifest belonging together of Earth and Heavens, Gods and themselves as Mortals—be reconciled with the "epoch," which is entirely foreign to this understanding? "The mortals are human beings."[65] And beyond that? Where are they situated within the epoch? Is the epoch, then, not totally determinative and encompassing? The mortals are manifestly the human beings of *Ereignis*, yet also necessarily—by their epochal situation—the human beings of *Gestell*. Can the human being of errancy and the human being likely to be "saved," that is, led back to his or her true essence, be *the same human being*? Heidegger hardly sheds any light on this: if it is true that the epoch has a double face, a "Janus head,"[66] can man have the same duality or ambivalence and retain one single essence? We are left to conjecture on this point.

The fundamental hypothesis we are trying to defend—sometimes against the letter of the Heideggerian text—is that there is a *nonhistorial essence of man*. For Heidegger, man is intrinsically historial,[67] intrinsically limited, defined and determined by the epochs of the History of Being. Yet is it conceivable that man understood as "the mortal," not linked to any historial or historical tradition, could appear *only* in the epoch of Technology and "simultaneously" with it? Must he not necessarily have existed *before* the History that emerged from the Greek commencement, in particular in other civilizations beyond the limits of that History, and perhaps, in an underlying or marginal manner, *even within* that History?

In any case, the emergence of this quasi-immemorial human figure alongside planetary man raises the question of whether today there are actually one or two essences of man. Sometimes Heidegger contrasts the two types, represented by the calculating type (the worker, "seeker," or consumer) and the mortal. The mortal necessarily bears the traits of thinker or poet, for in addition to his capacity to "dwell" on the Earth, he has sufficient "vigilance" and attentiveness to words to return from objects to things, from repre-

---

64. VA, p. 144 and p. 171.
65. Ibid.
66. See the "Seminar on *Time and Being*," SD, p. 57.
67. After the Turning, the phrases *historial man* and *historial essence* are constantly repeated. See, for example, GA 51, pp. 85 and 90.

sentational calculation to thinking that is attentive to the language of being. On other occasions, Heidegger envisages a new type of human being who would be situated halfway between these two, a human endowed with an extraordinary sense of balance, because he would lean "*with equal force* towards the technically administered universe and towards the world conceived as the house of a more original dwelling."[68] Referring to the Alemannic poet Hebel who celebrated "the Friend of the house," Heidegger symbolically names him the Friend. Yet the Friend is lacking. "We are missing the Friend who could restore the measurable and technical character of nature to the open secret of something natural in nature newly experienced."[69] Even as a possibility, such a synthesis is surprising. If the world is "administered technically," how can man find a "place" there or "dwell" in the presence of nonobjectified things? How can we "restore" (*zurückbergen*), that is, immerse into *phusis* via thought—as though it were a pool of rejuvenation—the nuclear installations, the agricultural industry, and the highways? Who would have the titanic ambition or the naïveté to conceive of this fantastic bringing together of opposites? Certainly not the thinker, for he knows that Technology will pursue its unstoppable movement of the forgetting of being and the destruction of the Earth. *Who*, then, would this strange friend be? Some engineer who is also an ecologist? No, for ecology remains an intrinsically technological project entailing the planning of nature. The Friend, says Heidegger, would be the poet.

"The poetic essence of human dwelling has need of the poet who, in a more profound and very broad sense, is the Friend: the friend of the house of the world."[70] The poet alone is capable of being the Friend, because he "brings to language" human dwelling, makes the Earth and world "habitable" by showing them *as* Earth and world, and does so despite the domination of Technology. In spite of the withdrawal of the holy in this "night of the world" that is Technology and in the brutal clarity of an artificial lighting permanently illuminated, the poet can make "the trace of the holy" appear.[71] He does so precisely by pointing out this effacement of what is intact, by showing that which hides itself, by remaining

68. Hebel, p. 24.
69. Ibid.
70. Ibid., p. 25.
71. Hw, p. 294.

faithful to *Unheimlichkeit* and to the *Heimatlosigkeit* of modernity. To do this, he merely has to lay bare the distress as such. Yet is he still able to connect to one another these two worlds that are moving apart at an increasingly insane speed? How is he able to preserve or repair the unity of the torn essence of man? He seems unable to. As long as there is poetry, language will not be reduced to a purely instrumental function, nor will it become eroded into the jargon imposed by data processing, computerization, or cybernetics. Yet no poet can now conciliate, let alone reconcile, the two faces of nature and the double face of man. We are living in this rift. Is not the planetary identity of the essence of man now only a dream or an abstraction? The aspiration for the immemorial and the pressure of modernity are diverging in a definitive, implacable, and frightening manner. What hides the utopia of a reconciliation between these two worlds is an effective split in the essence of man, one from which we are all suffering, even the most calculating among us. The well-known *Gelassenheit* that entails saying both *yes and no* to Technology well illustrates the depth of this split. For no one can say yes and no *simultaneously!* As planetary, therefore, we are alternating, cyclical, periodic human beings. Our errancy is a constant coming and going. We pass through phases of enthusiasm for Technology that leave us dissatisfied and through phases of rejecting it that we then come to regret. Everything leads us to believe that the law of this alternation, as well as its rhythm and contents, do not rest on our free decision, but on this call that, although making itself heard within Technology itself, is nevertheless the call of being.

The Historiality and Nonhistoriality of Man

To what extent is man historial? Heidegger maintains that man is entirely and exclusively historial. And this is so because every phenomenon is contained within an epoch of being; that is, determined through and through by a particular figure of the essence of truth.

And yet this claim is questionable. Historial man begins with the Greeks. In a radical leap, he thus passes from the nonhistorial to the historial. What are we to make of his previous nonhistoriality? It cannot be absolutely nothing, for it must constitute the basis of a transformation. Yet Heidegger says nothing about it, and has nothing to say about it, for truth is its very presupposition. Would not the uninterrupted reign of the historial, however, be a forgetting?

The event of the Greek commencement is connected to the pronouncement of the relation between being and thinking in the words of Parmenides' poem. "What is accomplished in this saying is nothing less than the knowing entering-into-appearance of man *as historial man* (preserver of being)."[72] This event is the "knowing appearance [*wissende Erscheinung*] of man as *being historial.*"[73] Man becomes historial when he distinguishes and separates himself from being, at the birth of metaphysics that always entails a doctrine of the beingness of man. Yet to say that man becomes historial is implicitly to admit that he was not always so. Does this change entirely efface the preexisting situation? Does it leave nothing remaining of previous human beings or prehistorial man?

Throughout the transformations in the essence of truth—from *aletheia* to *homoiosis*, from adequation to certainty, from certainty to the will to knowledge, and from the will to knowledge to the will to truth—what persists, in connecting the transformations with one another, is the progressive withdrawal of *aletheia*. In addition to some new element, every transformation requires something that persists. And thus prehistorial man, even if covered over, would not disappear entirely. But how and where are we to conceive of him? It seems that every definition we could give of him would remain purely negative. Indeed it can easily be shown that every attribute of man is epochal; that once these attributes are removed, we would have no concept by which to characterize man; and that the idea of "human nature" is of no help at all, as it already presupposes the metaphysical antithesis of history versus nature, one that is entirely intrahistorial. Furthermore, the nonhistorial is surely not to be sought in some original "nature" prior to all history (for we have no knowledge of this), but rather in the realm of the possible limits of History within each of its epochs. The nonhistorial would be the trace of something prehistorial or immemorial that has disappeared forever. It would merely appear *indirectly* via History. It would somehow be the flip side of History, but not its opposite, for through History it would be made present in the world or worlds.

Yet through which worldly phenomena can History manifest limits and reveal a field that resists it and that it cannot entirely stamp with its imprint? And what does this entail for the essence of man?

Every worldly phenomenon possesses both an epochal aspect

---

72. EM, p. 108; tr., p. 141.
73. Ibid.

and a nonhistorial aspect. Thus *dwelling*—in the ontic sense of a domicile, a residence in the town, in the country, or somewhere between, and also in the sense of that place to which we withdraw, where we sleep, where we receive our mail—presents these two aspects. It is inserted into History to the extent that each epoch has its own kinds of houses or apartments, domestic customs, conceptions, and manner of residence. Dwelling instantiates an essential mode of the nonhistorial, however, to the extent that despite the whole variety of cultural forms of dwelling, something immemorial persists: the *shelter*. Sheltering oneself cannot be reduced to protection against bad weather, but establishes an intimacy around a "hearth." The hearth, despite what we might think, is not simply a worn-out metaphor. The term expresses well the necessity for every human being to establish a place of peace, rest, warmth, and stillness, a center or *focal* point of familiarity from which he or she can go from an inside to an outside, from a private to a public realm. Inside and outside, private and public have in turn both historial *and* nonhistorial features. There is nothing purely or "absolutely" nonhistorial. Is it not the immemorial character of the hearth that founds dwelling? Yet dwelling, taken more or less in its imposing modern sense, is what reveals the hearth. To the degree that Heidegger, when commenting on Hölderlin, writes that "being is the hearth,"[74] he himself acknowledges the nonhistorial aspect of being. For someone who elsewhere refuses to admit this nonhistorial dimension, the description given of the "world" as the "play of the fourfold"—Earth and Heavens, Mortals and Gods—has little sense. For Heidegger here invokes an immemorial whole that does not concern any precise epoch. This immemorial whole can or must be inserted—though this seems quite difficult nowadays!—into a historial world conceived as the entirety of options open to a particular culture together with its language, its institutions, its Technology, its ethical rules, its sacred and profane; yet it can never be identified with, or coincide with any epoch or with any particular History. The division into Earth and Heavens, Mortals and Gods is prior to the primordial Greek oppositions such as being and thinking or being and appearance and prior to every definition of man or to the appearance of this or that god.

Yet the nonhistorial dimension does not refer only to the archaic. It belongs to an everydayness that is no longer pejorative as it was in Heidegger's early philosophy. The everyday gesture of

---

74. GA 55, p. 140.

pouring water or wine from a "pitcher" (*Krug*)—just as, one might add, the repetitive nature of the need to drink—escapes historial worldliness. Unlike the tool in *Being and Time*, the pitcher, whether made by an artisan or in a factory, does not refer to the totality of an instrumental context, but rather shines forth into a confined and much more narrowly circumscribed world. The microcosm around the pitcher corresponds to a "locality" of the world. This small world differs from every "universal" and thus historial instrumental relation. The "minuscule" (*gering*) gathering of Earth and world is the thing itself, not the human gesture that operates it. With respect to the gesture, there is nothing instrumental about it, because it does not seek to transform anything. This noninstrumental aspect can be valid only in this place or that—for this or that entity, Heidegger might also have said—and not indifferently at any point of worldly space whatsoever. Both local enrootedness and noninstrumental relationality belong to the nonhistorial dimension. A train or airplane pertains to the historial world, but when, sitting in a train or on a plane, I serve myself or a friend a drink, the microcosm opened up by this gesture in part escapes the planetary universe. For trains and airplanes reach into the distance. The proximity belonging to drinking or eating, on the other hand, constitutes a break with the space-time captured by Technology, even though Technology is grafted onto such activities. One cannot say the same for the activity of reading (even, indeed especially, of reading the Presocratics), as it is entirely stamped by my belonging to this particular epoch of being....

Generally speaking, the nonhistorial is always linked to the Earth. Man is not pure ek-sistence and pure historiality; he is not only an ekstatic openness towards being, but is a living being bound to life on earth. The Earth as "living nature" in the sense of a spontaneous emergence of forces and forms, a continuous flow returning to itself, resting in itself, and never becoming entirely exterior: this Earth is the limit of History. How might we think more precisely the terrestrial and nonhistorial in man that enables him to escape from absolute historiality? A passage from the *Beiträge* unambiguously points the way, even though Heidegger's work in general barely develops the following themes: "life" and body (*Leib*), reproduction (*Zeugung*) and sex (*Geschlecht*), and lineage (*Stamm*)—*the Earth,* to use their essential name.[75] The human body, as a living body endowed with ipseity, with "propri-

75. GA 65, p. 399.

ety," is incontestably immersed into the nonhistorial, yet opens onto the historial. It is immersed in the nonhistorial because our sensory or motor possibilities are as ancient as life; it opens onto the historial because both our acquired habits in respect of particular actions and our "spontaneous" gestures are fashioned by cultural models. The Heideggerian analysis of the sense-organs tends to forget completely the nonhistorial, however, and to insist exclusively on the historial determination of the sensible while rejecting the idea of something purely sensible as being metaphysical. His analysis first underlines the nonprimacy of perception: for us to be able to perceive anything at all, the epochal unconcealment of world must already be given. We can perceive only that which is already uncovered and accessible in an openness. Second, as is shown in *Being and Time*, we do not hear bare sounds or sound waves, but always a sound in the world relating to this or that object, for example the sound of a motorbike. It is the whole human being who hears a fugue by Bach and not just his or her ears. Undoubtedly. Finally, if the Greeks were able to "see Apollo in the statue of a young man,"[76] and the medievals an angel in a similar statue, it is because their epoch, their language, their myths, their culture, and their thought had taught them what they were about to perceive. And yet we do not have to fall into biologism or some obscure naturalism to maintain, as does Merleau-Ponty, that the most general laws of perception, like a background structure, do not vary from one epoch of History to the next. Everything points towards a continuity of the nonhistorial body prior to, during, and after the era of subjectivity. The paintings of antiquity and the stained-glass windows of cathedrals prove to us that the Greeks and medievals saw the sky as blue and the forests as green. The fact that their language and epochality may *immediately and in advance* have attributed meanings to the sky and forests other than those that we ascribe to these phenomena by no means excludes a simultaneous and fundamental nonhistoriality: quite the contrary.

Like Earth and world, the historial and the nonhistorial are narrowly interlaced, interwoven, and interdependent in such a way that it would be futile and illusory to claim that one could describe the nonhistorial essence of man in isolation, as if it were some pure nature. We can merely glimpse it indirectly through epochal determinations. There is no pure nature, yet nor is there any pure History. There is only the world as enrooted and founded upon an

---

76. SvG, p. 88.

Earth. Thus, when Heidegger shows that the *fundamental* attunement changes with each epoch (astonishment for the Greeks, terror for us[77]), he is implicitly acknowledging that the fact of finding oneself disposed and experiencing corporeal being-in-the-world according to constantly changing moods belongs to every human being in every epoch. Must there not have been a transhistorial dimension in Greek astonishment for this still to have some meaning for us? The doctrine of transformations of truth and the History of Being have distanced Heidegger from the deep nonhistoriality of *Dasein*. Ever since man has been man he has had language and tools. Differences between languages and equipmental contexts matter immensely. Yet although inscribing themselves on each occasion within cultural spheres that are strictly delimited in space and time, language and equipmentality (which are transhistorial rather than nonhistorial) by their very constancy come close to nonhistoriality, or what Merleau-Ponty does not hesitate to call the *quasi-eternity* of embodied being-in-the-world.

The radical historiality of truth, gravely lacking in Husserl, will remain one of the decisive insights of Heideggerian thought. It is not a matter of renouncing this achievement so as to fall into some natural immediacy, stupor, or silent bliss. The nonhistorial cannot be understood as a "state of nature" or a site of rest and withdrawal, sheltered from the convulsions of history. We can gain access to it only through History, just as we can gain access to the Earth only through world.

Making a distinction between the historiality and the nonhistoriality of man does not introduce a new scission or a new dualism to be added to the traditional dualisms of soul and body, freedom and nature. For these two dimensions are inseparable and indissociable, like the two sides of a coin, hot and cold, day and night. In a like manner to Earth and the world, they form a struggle, yet their conflict sustains and silently inhabits not only the work of art, but every work of man and indeed his whole existence. There is a tendency for History to want to reduce and dominate the nonhistorial, just as there is a tendency for the nonhistorial to dissolve historial determinations. And yet each of these two dimensions rests on the other. Manifestation has need of the nonmanifest, the "phusical" has need of the "phantic" at the peril of losing the luminous distantiation of phenomenality. "The Earth cannot renounce the openness of world if it itself is to appear as Earth, under the free sway of its

77. GA 45, p. 197.

self-closing. The world, in turn, cannot detach itself from the Earth and hover above it [*entschweben*] if, as the prevailing expanse and trajectory of every essential destiny, it is to found itself on something decisive."[78] Technology undoubtedly represents the danger of an exclusive preponderance of the historial. It is more in this sense that it threatens to destroy the Earth than through an ecological catastrophe. By showing that the Earth is only one particular instance of the *Verbergung* and withdrawal of being, by reducing *phusis* to *aletheia*, Heidegger himself seems to be contributing to the forgetting of the Earth. Yet his description of the Earth's resistance to unlimited objectification points to what we call a *possible nonhistorial*[79] that extends from natural, nonobjectifiable presence to ethics and culture.

The physicochemical analysis of a block of stone, for example, leaves its reserve of opacity and heaviness, its intrinsic consistency, unexplained and intact. The stone will show itself *as Earth* only if it remains intact and is not unconcealed from the point of view of objectivity, if it *also* offers itself in its simple solidness. Likewise, the unique mixture of sounds and meaning, of Earth and world, that constitutes a poem cannot be paraphrased or "translated" into prose without destroying both the "terrestrial" integrity of language and the work as a manifestation of this earth of words. Similarly, there is a terrestrial, nonepochal essence of man that resists every formalization. It never appears in isolation, outside of the phenomena of culture. But it is undoubtedly predominant in embodied being-in-the-world, in attunement, in the incorporation of a site we inhabit, in a relation of love, in meeting and mixing with others, in our access to works of art, and in the commerce of everyday affairs. Without it the world would be deprived of consistency. To really unfold the entire breadth of this dimension, we would require extensive phenomenological analyses, a new *Being and Time*!

The nonhistorial essence of man is not a subsisting essence that would amount to his embodiment, his lived moods, or his private life. It shows through the surface of *all* the phenomena of an epoch and can be read only via them. Thus the "rights of man" as a historially determined achievement (proceeding from the universalist rationality of the Enlightenment and still remaining within this universalist horizon) have meaning only relative to the

78. Hw, p. 38; tr., PLT, p. 49.
79. See *Le Chant de la Terre* (L'Herne, 1987), pp. 198f.

fragility and suffering of man, the latter belonging to his nonhistorial essence. Likewise, the historial ways of determining the balance between sickness and health—ways connected in particular to the advance of contemporary medical Technology, as well as to the modern way of life—still point to the nonhistorial phenomenon of man in sickness and health. Or again, the contemporary specificity of the idea of woman (the equality of her rights and place in society) does not prevent us from discerning an extrahistorial essence of the feminine. Similarly, as we have seen, the details of modern dwelling allow the nonhistorial essence of dwelling and the "hearth" to show through. We could say the same about clothing and food. The nonhistorial, as phenomenon, does not pertain to the immediacy of what is straightforwardly given, but demands the task of description and explicit demonstration. This is all the more so when we are dealing with the religious and the political, where it is most profoundly concealed.

This is why we must obviously distinguish this nonhistorial essence from what one might call "the bad nonhistorial," which is based on the blind refusal of the historiality of being and leads to the complete forgetting of all tradition. This bad nonhistorial is particularly rife in the epoch of Technology. It can very easily be reconciled with the greater-than-ever development of historicizing research. Technology effectively regards every event as a product, as something fabricated within the actual present. It uproots and decontextualizes. It is equally unaware of secret maturation and of that which is entirely other than the epoch. The technical world withdraws from the meaning of its destiny, that is, from the meaning of its provenance, as long as it forgets the Earth. "The will to will ossifies everything into an absence of destiny. The result is that which is nonhistorial [das Ungeschichtliche]. It is characterized by the dominance of historical science [Historie]."[80] The nihilism of productivity needs a forgetting of the tradition, for it is necessary for man to forbid himself to take any distance with respect to the epoch. The mass of historical knowledge, just like the hypertrophic development of journalism and the media, gets in the way of the possibility of our becoming aware of major and fundamental epochal differences. "The increasing flight from the historical tradition is for its part a sign of the claim under which our epoch stands. Sometimes it even seems as though this flight from History will eliminate the final barriers still preventing an unrestricted and

80. VA, p. 76.

complete technologizing of the world and of man. The disappearance of our ability to make historial distinctions goes hand in hand with this flight from History."[81] The bad nonhistorial thus acts *against* the Earth as a power to decontextualize, delocalize, uproot. Its alliance with historicism shows the extent to which History *on its own* is not sufficient to provide man with his roots.

What is sometimes rashly termed Heidegger's *antihumanism* is basically a radical rupture with the anthropocentrism that has been dominant since the dawn of modern times. Man does not produce himself. He does not create being. He does not hold the ultimate condition of possibility of his own faculties. He controls neither the provenance nor the secret necessity of the structures of the world. He can merely administer them. Only rarely and obscurely does he perceive the possibility of the Earth, which is embraced in art.

With *Dasein* and its "ekstatic temporality," Heidegger believed he could grasp and articulate the ungraspable essence of man. He pushed the movement of self-enabling and self-determination attempted in the metaphysics of subjectivity to their extreme limit, at which point this ultimate possibility of originary temporality escapes the "subject." The reversal undertaken from the perspective of this limit recognizes being as that which alone is possible: being "enables" man, "enables" thought. If something about this reversal is exorbitant—in the proper sense of the word—and excessive, it is not because man finds himself belittled. The acknowledgment of human limits is not a plea in favor of the inhuman or barbarism. Nothing is more human for man than to situate himself at his true height and in his true place. Nor is it the reminder of the excessive and enigmatic character of the human essence. What is proper to man is to be. Yet being—as that which is entirely other than entities or nonentities, as the very emergence of truth—cannot be possessed or appropriated. Man's proper "site" escapes him. He is definitively *un-heimlich*, "a stranger in his own essence," deprived of any ontological "at-homeness." He is inhabited by the nonhuman, which does not mean the inhuman, as has sometimes been written! Heidegger reminds man of the *essential* dispossession of himself. This is what he calls the *poverty* of *homo humanus*, as opposed to the richness of the subject who rationally administers his animal drives. If there is a Heideggerian excess, it is not his demonstration that the human subject (even when enlarged to the

---

81. SvG, p. 138.

level of the unconscious or the social) is not its own measure. Subjectivity has not been, and undoubtedly will not be, the sole possible figure of man.

The first of Heidegger's excesses is his attempt to suppress not only the metaphysical subject, but also *ipseity* as such in the shape of individuality. Already during the period of *Being and Time* there was something of a contradiction in positing "mineness" as an originary existential while declaring the individual to be merely "ontic."[82] At the end of the Preface to the *Phenomenology*, Hegel merely asked that the individual "forget himself as much as possible," rather than that he disappear. The human being lacking interiority who is the "mortal" transpropriated to the *Geviert*, or the sayer who listens to language, cannot be the artist or poet, for although the latter are mediators, they are not straightforward *mediums*. And subjectivity, as self-affected embodiment or a return to oneself that does not necessarily take the form of self-certainty, indeed resists the transparency of an openness claimed to be neutral.

The second of Heidegger's excesses, the great illusion he sometimes communicates, in part thanks to an admirable talent for writing, is that being could have the *force* to manifest itself spontaneously, in and of its own accord; hence, the expressions *sich zeigen*, *Entbergung*...Yet this power of self-manifestation can belong only to *phusis* or to the Earth. Heidegger ontologizes *phusis*, shapes it to the mold of *aletheia*, only to better "physiologize" being. Because being is not a substantial foundation, however, but merely the "clearing" of which man is the "site" or "watchman," does it follow that being possesses its own power to appear? The clearing or "lighting" (*Lichtung*)—at least to sustain itself and find its limit— has need of what we must indeed call "the darkness of the forest" (as Roger Munier puts it), of what Heidegger himself calls "the thick of the forest" (*Dickung*[83]), without granting it any explicit ontological status in the specific text where he defines the *Lichtung* ("The End of Philosophy and the Task of Thinking"). This obscurity exterior to the clearing is the Earth that "sustains" that region of lesser density where the light plays. From where does the clearing draw its ability to uncover or un-conceal? It presents itself as an irruption of light on an obscure background that it never entirely leaves, or as an island in a sea that cannot be marked and in which all traces are effaced. But if we are not to consider the clearing

---

82. GA 26, p. 172.
83. SD, p. 72.

itself as a simple fact or some ontic given—for this is wholly excluded—we must ask ourselves whether the opening irruption of the openness and the simple maintaining of clarity do not demand a certain thrust, a certain productive *source*. To use the previous metaphors, it is the day that holds the limit of the night at a certain distance, the earth of the marine basin that holds the island out of the sea. Heidegger believes that the *Lichtung*, "the freedom of the open" is (to use a term of Goethe's) an *Urphänomen*, a radical origin. On this point he recalls the maxim of phenomenology already enunciated by Goethe and Hegel: "Let us go in search of nothing behind the phenomena..."[84] In other words, being is the alpha and omega. We must not ask where it comes from. It emerges from itself. A "phusical" spontaneity once again. All things, including space and time, are contained in the Clearing. It is not the light of day that gives birth to a clearing by separating part of the forest from darkness. It is the space *already* separated off, the abstraction already made from the forest that permits the light to play. "It is only possible for something to shine if the Open has *already* been granted. It is not the ray of light that *in the first instance* produces the Clearing, the Open; rather it merely traverses it while measuring it. It is the Open alone which can first make way for any giving or taking, in first granting all evidence the free realm in the midst of which it can reside and must move."[85] Thus the freedom of the Open conceived as a "state of presence" (*Anwesenheit*) precedes every "*natural* light," such as that of reason, vision, or the sun. Is it not a priori, as demonstrated by the terms *schon* (there must *already* be the Open) and *erst* (it is not light that *in the first instance* produces the Open), which we have emphasized? An a priori signifies a transcendental condition from which all temporal genesis is excluded and before which there is nothing. Has metaphysics really "forgotten the Clearing"? It would be better to say that it situated it, in one epoch, within the subject.

Yet as the Clearing itself precedes all time, what is the point of mentioning "the darkness of the forest" if this boils down to a frame of reference that has always already been removed and if it is not a "foundation" (certainly not one that is founding, fundamental or principal)? Is it not rather the case that this forest darkness—"hyletic" in the proper sense of the word, for *hule* means "wood"—must have been pierced, torn, cleaved, dispersed into fragments,

---

84. Ibid.
85. Ibid., p. 73.

and by some force, for the clearing to have occurred? If the clearing never "occurred," if it is not historial but eternal, then it falls back into facticity and becomes ontic once more. The Clearing must itself have *occurred*, it must be historial or transhistorial, being the condition of History rather than "within" History. Is not the Clearing therefore concomitant with the appearance of man himself, is it not linked to the uprooting that constitutes him as such? If we follow *Being and Time, Dasein* itself is the *Lichtung*!

The Clearing is at once very old and ever new, yet not without age. It is not *one* event, but the very arrival of History.

Yet the Clearing itself must have appeared on an Earth, rendering this Earth manifest for the first time. It is born of this dark Earth that carried it to the light of being and that continues to carry it, as it carries our flesh. *Die Erde ist die bauend, Tragende...* "The Earth is a building, sustaining Earth..."[86] This is why we dare to maintain, breaking with the genetic interdiction of phenomenology, that immemorial *phusis* is the origin of *phainesthai*, and not the converse. The original Earth precedes the world, even though it must always be rediscovered in experience.

---

86. VA, p. 170; tr., PLT, p. 178.

WORKS CITED

German Works by Heidegger

BZ *Der Begriff der Zeit* (Tübingen: Niemeyer, 1989).

ED *Aus der Erfahrung des Denkens* (Pfullingen: Neske, 1954).

EM *Einführung in die Metaphysik*, 5th edition (Tübingen: Niemeyer, 1987).

GA 20 Gesamtausgabe, vol. 20, *Prolegomena zur Geschichte des Zeitbegriffs* (Frankfurt: Klostermann, 1979).

GA 24 Gesamtausgabe, vol. 24, *Grundprobleme der Phänomenologie* (Frankfurt: Klostermann, 1976).

GA 26 Gesamtausgabe, vol. 26, *Metaphysische Anfangsgründe der Logik im Ausgang von Leibniz* (Frankfurt: Klostermann, 1978).

GA 29/30 Gesamtausgabe, vol. 29/30, *Die Grundbegriffe der Metaphysik* (Frankfurt: Klostermann, 1980).

GA 31 Gesamtausgabe, vol. 31, *Vom Wesen der menschlichen Freiheit* (Frankfurt: Klostermann, 1982).

GA 45 Gesamtausgabe, vol. 45, *Grundfragen der Philosophie* (Frankfurt: Klostermann, 1984).

GA 51 Gesamtausgabe, vol. 51, *Grundbegriffe* (Frankfurt: Klostermann, 1981).

GA 54 Gesamtausgabe, vol. 54, *Parmenides* (Frankfurt: Klostermann, 1981).

GA 55 Gesamtausgabe, vol. 55, *Heraklit* (Frankfurt: Klostermann, 1979).

GA 61 Gesamtausgabe, vol. 61, *Interpretationen zu Aristoteles* (Frankfurt: Klostermann, 1985).

GA 63 Gesamtausgabe, vol. 63, *Ontologie (Hermeneutik der Faktizität)* (Frankfurt: Klostermann, 1988).

GA 65 Gesamtausgabe, vol. 65, *Beiträge zur Philosophie* (Frankfurt: Klostermann, 1989).

Hebel *Hebel der Hausfreund*, 6th ed. (Pfullingen: Neske, 1991).

Hw *Holzwege*, 6th ed. (Frankfurt: Klostermann, 1957).

ID *Identität und Differenz*, 8th ed. (Pfullingen: Neske, 1986).

KPM *Kant und das Problem der Metaphysik*, 4th ed. (Frankfurt: Klostermann, 1973).

NI, II *Nietzsche*, vols. I and II (Pfullingen: Neske, 1961).

SD *Zur Sache des Denkens*, 2d ed. (Tübingen: Niemeyer, 1976).

SvG *Der Satz vom Grund*, 6th ed. (Pfullingen: Neske, 1986).

SZ *Sein und Zeit*, 15th ed. (Tübingen: Niemeyer, 1979).

TK *Die Technik und die Kehre*, 6th ed. (Pfullingen: Neske, 1985).

US *Unterwegs zur Sprache*, 6th ed. (Pfullingen: Neske, 1979).

VA *Vorträge und Aufsätze*, 5th ed. (Pfullingen: Neske, 1985).

VS *Vier Seminare* (Frankfurt: Klostermann, 1977).

WhD *Was heisst Denken?*, 4th ed. (Tübingen: Niemeyer, 1984).

WiM *Was ist Metaphysik?* 4th ed. (Frankfurt: Klostermann, 1943).

Wm *Wegmarken*, 2d ed. (Frankfurt: Klostermann, 1978).

W. Phil. *Was ist das—die Philosophie?* 7th ed. (Pfullingen: Neske, 1981).

Works Available in English

BW *Basic Writings*, ed. D. F. Krell (London: Harper and Row, 1978).

BZ *The Concept of Time*, bilingual edition; trans. W. McNeill (Oxford: Blackwell, 1992).

EM *An Introduction to Metaphysics*, trans. R. Manheim (New Haven, Conn.: Yale University Press, 1959).

GA 20 *History of the Concept of Time*, trans. T. Kisiel (Bloomington: Indiana University Press, 1985).

GA 24 *The Basic Problems of Phenomenology*, trans. A. Hofstadter (Bloomington: Indiana University Press, 1982).

GA 26 *The Metaphysical Foundations of Logic*, trans. M. Heim (Bloomington: Indiana University Press, 1984).

GA 29/30 *The Fundamental Concepts of Metaphysics*, trans. W. McNeill and N. Walker (Bloomington: Indiana University Press, forthcoming 1994–95).

GA 54 *Parmenides*, trans. A. Schuwer and R. Rojcewicz (Bloomington: Indiana University Press, 1992).

Gel *Discourse on Thinking*, trans. J. M. Anderson and E. H. Freund (New York: Harper and Row, 1969).

ID *Identity and Difference*, bilingual edition; trans. J. Stambaugh (New York: Harper and Row, 1974).

KPM *Kant and the Problem of Metaphysics*, trans. R. Taft (Bloomington: Indiana University Press, 1990).

NI *Nietzsche*, volumes One and Two (New York: Harper Collins, 1991).

NII *Nietzsche*, volumes Three and Four (New York: Harper Collins, 1991).

OWL *On the Way to Language*, trans. P. D. Hertz (New York: Harper and Row, 1982).

PLT *Poetry, Language, Thought*, trans. A. Hofstadter (New York: Harper and Row, 1971).

QB *The Question of Being*, bilingual edition; trans. W. Kluback and J. T. Wilde (London: Vision Press, 1974).

QT *The Question Concerning Technology and Other Essays*, trans. W. Lovitt (New York: Harper and Row, 1977).

SvG *The Principle of Reason*, trans. R. Lilly (Bloomington: Indiana University Press, 1991).

SZ *Being and Time*, trans. J. Macquarrie and E. Robinson (Oxford: Blackwell, 1987).

WhD *What Is Called Thinking*, trans. J. Glenn Gray (New York: Harper and Row, 1968).

Index